AGAIN AND AGAIN . . .

Hilton night manager Jose Miranda had begun his shift at 3 p.m. that day. His day had been routine until he heard his hand-held radio crackle with a message that there was trouble in the lobby. He jumped up from his seat in the Marina restaurant where he was doing his daily paperwork. Miranda's watch showed 8:45 p.m., running faster than the others.

By the time he reached the lobby he saw two people lying on the floor.

"My first thought was that somebody had a seizure," a not uncommon occurrence in a busy hotel. He quickly realized that it wasn't a medical emergency he was dealing with, but a fight. He bluffed, telling the assailants that the police had been called as his employees cleared the lobby.

He then went out the front doors, noticed Clara Harris being escorted to her car, and started walking down the sidewalk.

Moments later, he heard someone shout "Here she comes!" He was then almost hit by Clara's Mercedes, which he saw round the wall on the hotel's west side.

Running now, he reached the wall's end. When he made the turn, Miranda was devastated by what was happening. David Harris was lying on the ground, and Clara Harris was running over David's body, again and again . . .

OUT OF CONTROL

Steven Long

St. Martin's Paperbacks

OUT OF CONTROL

Copyright © 2004 by Steven Long.

Cover photograph of Clara Harris courtesy AP/Wide World Photos. Cover photograph of car courtesy of the author.

ISBN: 0-312-99027-8

Printed in the United States of America

St. Martin's Paperbacks edition / April 2004

10 9 8 7 6 5 4 3 2 1

To Vicki, my wife and best friend

ACKNOWLEDGMENTS

This book is my return to the world of serious journalism after a too long sojourn. There are many to thank. At the very top of the list is my wife Vicki who had the faith in me to endure the poverty that accompanies a comeback. Joining her are two journalists to whom I will be forever indebted, George Flynn, managing editor of the *Houston Press,* and freelancer writer Steve McVicker. After a five-year absence from writing even a single word, George encouraged me to take on a story. I didn't know if I still had it in me. What followed was a series of hard news articles in the *Houston Press* for which I am proud to this day. Without a recommendation from my able colleague Steve McVicker, my warm and productive relationship with the *New York Post* would not exist. It was my work for the *Post* that was the genesis for this book.

This work would not have been written without the encouragement of best selling true crime author Suzy Spencer. It would also not exist without the guy she told me to pitch the book to, Charlie Spicer of St. Martin's Press. Thanks to both of you.

Charlie had the wisdom to give me the editor of my dreams, Joe Cleemann. I am truly blessed.

It is tradition for writers to thank their agent. It is with special warmth, affection and friendship that I thank Jane Dystel for her faith in me since that day in February 1986, that I took a call from her on a pay phone in the Bexar County Courthouse in San Antonio where I was covering a murder trial that would become *Death Without Dignity*. The road that we have traveled together has been long now, and rocky, but I think that it is finally about to be paved.

Writing this book has been a joy, and there are many who made it so. Thank you to George Parnham, Mary, Winnie, especially Winnie, and all of the folks who make up Parnham and Associates. Special thanks also go to Suzy Ginzburg, the able publicist who has become such a dear friend.

Thank you also to Mia Magness and Dan Rizzo of the Harris County District Attorney's office. Thanks must go to Bobbi Bacha of Blue Moon Investigations who provided much needed insight into her world and the world of her clients. Greg Enos and Paul Nunu were extremely helpful, and I thank them. Thanks also to CBS' Jenna Jackson. Many thanks as well to Gina Treadgold of ABC.

Janet Warner, the able media liaison for the Harris County court system provided me with a good seat during the trial and always had a cheerful smile for the press.

Very special thanks to Debbie and Jim Shank, and Lindsey Harris, for posing for a photo immediately after the sentencing. You certainly didn't have to do it. Your kindness will always be remembered. May God bless you, Lindsey. I too lost a father when I was your age. I also thank John A. Davis, your attorney, for setting it up.

Thanks also to my daughters, Michelle and Monique, who have kept the e-mail flowing, encouraging me to keep writing.

Thank you to Roger Deeds for the years of instruction into the still mysterious world of cyberspace. I often think that I would have no career without your patient help.

Finally, my thanks goes out to my steadfast proofreader, Gailyn Smith, who, along with Vicki, has faithfully corrected my errors since I returned to writing, and did it again for this book. Also thanks to Brenda Greene, who has a great eye for typos.

And special thanks go to my oldest friend, U.S. District Judge Stephen Mathew Reasoner, who has read every word of the manuscript.

ONE

Three women got out of a late model car in front of South Park Funeral Home, dressed as if they were about to attend a Junior League luncheon. One was a beautiful blond with alabaster skin. Another was a statuesque brunette with striking Mediterranean or Mexican features. The third, tall and erect with unnaturally blond hair pulled back into a black bow, walked slowly between them. All three were dressed for success, their breeding evident in their bearing. The woman in the center was more tentative. The other two women were there for her, her closest associates, her employees, her friends. Clara Harris had come to see her husband David.

Her lawyer, George Parnham, had arranged a private viewing for her, the new widow. The viewing would be away from the rest of the family, and considering the circumstances, the decision was a prudent choice. Joining them later for the wake might be awkward—Clara Harris had killed her husband. For this wake, there would be just the four of them, the three women, and the man lying cold and dead, his corpse battered and broken by the wheels of a $40,000 luxury car that had been turned into a 4,000-pound killing machine.

This was Clara's time alone with him. It would be her only opportunity to tell him, "I'm sorry."

She had tried before, wailing, "David, look what you made me do," as he lay dying on hard asphalt warmed by the relentless Texas summer sun.

The two women took the arm of Clara Harris as the trio walked through the front door of the mortuary and were greeted by a representative of the funeral home. Slowly, tentatively at first, they were escorted to a small viewing room. On a stand outside was the name of Dr. David Harris in white plastic letters pressed on a black background. Clara Harris gripped her friends' hands, preparing to look at the now-lifeless body of the man she loved.

The three walked slowly to the expensive coffin sitting upon a catafalque, its lid raised. There, Clara looked down at the man she had killed just hours before. He did not look like the handsome young doctor she had married ten years ago on Valentine's Day next door to the Nassau Bay Hilton. Her murder weapon had done far too much damage to the body for even the most skillful mortician to mask with the oils, paper, wax, wire, and makeup that are the tools of the undertaker's trade.

"David," the murderess gasped, collapsing in uncontrollable sobs, cradled in the arms of her friends. The idyllic life the couple had shared was now over for Clara Harris. David's was not the only lifeless body in the room—Clara too had given up her charmed existence as a beauty queen, wife, mother, and doctor after succumbing to sudden passion the night before when she had been momentarily out of control.

The realization that Clara Harris intended to commit murder came home quickly to 16-year-old Lindsey Harris, sitting in the front seat next to her.

"I'm going to hit him," Lindsey later testified that

Clara had said as she aimed the Mercedes at her husband. "She said it like that was going to happen."

"No!" screamed Lindsey, who was spending the summer with her dentist father.

"She stepped on the accelerator and went straight for him," the high school senior remembers.

Lindsey looked into the eyes of her father as the Mercedes came barreling toward him.

"He was really scared because he was trying to get away and couldn't," she said.

David's hand reached for the front of the hood, leaving his last living fingerprints there as if by will alone he could stop the machine. The automobile struck him, sending him flying through the air as his daughter watched.

"Clara had no expression on her face," Lindsey said as the woman circled around and ran over him—some would claim as many as five times.

"I felt the bump," she said, knowing that the car was rolling over the body of her father. "I knew it was him and I said, 'You're killing him.'"

Lindsey was able to distinguish between the hard, unyielding bump of tires on the concrete curb of an esplanade separating the hotel parking lots, and the softer bump that the auto made as it rolled over soft tissue and brittle bone.

"The bump over the median was different from when she was going over my dad," she would later testify.

When the Mercedes rolled to a stop, Lindsey Harris opened the door so that she could help her dad.

But first Lindsey remembered "I went around and hit her."

Clara then ran to the body of her husband lying on the ground next to a curb. Lindsey remembered bitterly what she saw next.

"She kneeled down and said, 'I'm sorry, so sorry, I am so sorry. It was an accident," she recalled.

"She wasn't sorry, she had killed him!" Lindsey said.

Millie Harris walked the slow walk of a mother's grief as she entered the modern Christus St. John Hospital. She and her husband Gerald had taken a call from a woman named Gail. There was panic in her voice. The woman put the couple's granddaughter on the telephone, sobbing.

"There has been an accident, come quick," she was told by Lindsey Harris. As the call progressed, the elderly woman and her husband, tall, dignified Gerald Harris Sr. learned at that moment that their son was breathing his last breaths, breaths more like gasps, making the gurgling sound that he had made for the past thirty minutes struggling to take in air, fighting the blood that filled his lung.

The assault upon David came as a surprise, a shock, a nightmare in late July. There had been trouble between their son and his wife, but this sort of end to their marriage was totally unexpected. What had happened? There were so many unanswered questions as the two had rushed to the hospital. St. John's is one of two major medical facilities that serve the area around Clear Lake and its principal industry, the Lyndon B. Johnson Space Center. When she got there, the hallway outside the emergency room was still packed with patients, nurses, doctors, EMS, and members of the Nassau Bay Police Department, all there for one reason—the recent death of Dr. David Harris, prominent owner of Space City Orthodontics in nearby Clear Lake City.

Millie and Gerald supported each other as they were taken into the emergency room. There, on an examining table, lay the crushed and battered body of their son, the end result of a silver Mercedes having rolled over him, crushing and grinding his bone and tissue beneath the automobile's low-slung frame, which was elevated only six inches above the asphalt parking lot.

Life had passed from David Harris only minutes before, but the apparatus used in the vain attempt to save him remained attached. The plastic breathing tubes were still inserted into his body while intravenous fluids in clear tubes were connected to needles inserted into veins, yet the fluid no longer flowed. The couple looked at the son who had been born to them in Newport, Arkansas forty-five years before, now lying dead in the impersonal and public indignity of a hospital emergency room.

David Harris had arrived at the hospital at 9:34 p.m. At 9:48 he had been pronounced dead by an attending physician, likely moonlighting from his day job as so many young doctors now did to pay for their lifestyle.

A paper was put before them to sign. It was an acknowledgment that the lifeless form before them was indeed their son, David L. Harris, of Friendswood, Texas. Now finished with the duty of getting the proper documentation in order, the representative of the county morgue left the couple alone with their son. Minutes later, the body was transported to a building on Houston's south side to be sliced, diced, and dissected in a postmortem that would later be used in the State of Texas' attempt to place Clara Harris behind bars for the rest of her life.

As David Harris lay dead on the hospital table, witnesses remained at the scene being interviewed, as police wrote down their recollections. Some said that they had seen the man hit once, others as many as five times. Still others said that the Mercedes had come to a stop and then backed up, rolling over the body a final time. As wildly different as the witness accounts at the scene were, one thing was an indisputable fact, Clara Harris had killed her husband.

Also at the scene, a woman named Julie Knight picked up her friend Gail Bridges at the Hilton parking lot to take the shaken woman to the hospital.

At 1885 Old Spanish Trail, Houston's morgue lies south of one of the world's great medical complexes, the Texas Medical Center. The cluster of buildings just to the north boasts names like De Bakey, Cooley and M.D. Anderson, names that are household words in the world of treatment for heart disease and cancer. Miracles happened there on a daily basis. But the morgue was a monument to failure, a utilitarian tribute to the science of finding out what exactly had gone wrong to cause the death of every person brought there.

Thousands walked through the building's front doors each year. The female guard had seen it so many times, on so many faces. They were all the same, Black, Hispanic, Vietnamese, Chinese, and Native American. It was always the same. The faces of the bereaved were drained and almost as lifeless as those of the clients who would soon be the subjects of dissection inside, all in the name of justice, fact, and science.

Some were teary, with wisps of moisture around eyes that were blue, brown, black, and hazel. Others were loud, while others were as quiet as the autopsy room itself. The bereaved would be escorted to the family room, a formal seating area where they would await a representative of the morgue, who would escort them to the laboratory where the corpses were kept, each giving mute testimony to its last hours as a living thing.

Some were there because of bar fights gone bad, others

because a marriage had withered to violence. And a portion were there because they had died a natural death, but died alone. In such cases, Texas law demands an autopsy.

It was a place where cops and lawyers came as well, to watch the grizzly business of finding the cause of death for later use in a court of law.

The waiting room was made for grief, filled with the type of elegant furniture that is found in upscale funeral homes. Duncan Phyfe chairs and tables were neatly arranged, a lamp gave off subdued light for the grieving relatives who formed a steady parade for their brief moment in the room before being escorted to see the battered, often mangled body of their loved one.

The cops bypassed this room. There was no need for the niceties of grief when they did their business.

Just outside, the routine administrative business of the morgue was conducted by ten clerical personnel, sitting at their desks in a large room with plate glass windows. Through those windows, the clerks observed the macabre procession of mourners as they came and went from the family room. To them, the parade was routine. Most didn't notice the coming and going at all.

There would be no need for the room for David Harris. It was the other visitors to the morgue who counted now. Police detectives would watch his autopsy, photographing it in full color to be presented to a jury someday in the pristine surroundings of a Harris County courtroom.

There are no niceties in recesses of the morgue. Here death confronts the living in shades of gray and red. The smell of urine and feces permeate the place from the bodies whose organs have shut down, loosening the sphincter muscles of the bowels. The body of David Harris was worse than that of most murder victims. The orthodontist whose office bespoke cheerfulness and hygiene in every corner would have been appalled at what he had become in such a short space of time. Death had not come neatly to him. The shutter of the police camera clicked, recording the indignity of what was left of David Harris.

Death came with the rush of 4,000 pounds of iron, steel, and plastic, hurling him twenty-five feet through the air and across a parking lot onto asphalt after the first strike by his wife Clara. Three more passes by the Mercedes running over his body finished him.

At St. John's, David died lying on his back in the pants, shirt, and belt he had worn that day.

When his body was brought to the morgue, a tracheal tube was still in place in his mouth, a cervical spine collar still in position to prevent the possibility of further damage to the neck, and electrocardiogram pads and defibrillator pads remained stuck on the chest and abdomen. A chest tube remained inserted. Intravenous catheters were still in place, ready to administer life-giving fluids where there was no longer life.

Dr. Dwayne Wolf looked down at the body bag before him, about to see another in a long line of the cadavers that had become his world. He was the veteran of 1,500 autopsies, hundreds of them homicides. His current work load was one to two autopsies per day.

The forensic pathologist was a graduate of Lamar University in Beaumont, Texas, a town more famous as the location of Spindletop, the early 1900s oil patch that ushered in a boom of prosperity for Texas that hasn't stopped to this day. After his 1986 graduation from Lamar, Wolf studied at Galveston's University of Texas Medical Branch and earned an MD–PhD, and served residencies and fellowships at Brown University in Providence, Miami, and then back in Galveston, finally landing a job as medical examiner in Mobile. After two years there, Wolf was in Texas again, working at the Houston morgue as deputy chief medical examiner under controversial M.E. Dr. Joyce Carter.

Wolf is an overachiever whose very body language exudes an aura of superiority, and a disdain for the lesser beings he is compelled from time to time to tolerate. Frequently as part of his job, he is required to take the witness stand. His testimony is complex, difficult for juries to grasp as he speaks using the scientific terms of his trade. As a witness, he is also difficult for prosecutors because there isn't a humble bone in his tall body, not even a humble whisker on his bearded face.

He looks like a tweedy college professor when he enters a room. Wolf speaks that way as well, knowing that he, and he alone, is the authority on what he is about to describe. The autopsy room is his domain, the witness stand is his podium, and the courtroom is his lecture hall.

At 11:28 a.m., on the morning of July 25, 2002, the autopsy of David Harris began as Wolf opened the body bag to reveal the battered corpse of the orthodontist. The body was of average size, stood 5'9" and weighed 164 pounds at death, he observed. The lifeless man had arrived still dressed in the dark pants, gray Jockey underwear with the brand "Jockey" on them, black socks, and black dress shoes he had worn to the Nassau Bay Hilton the night before. The clothing was cut and torn because of the trauma of his death and the resuscitative attempts of emergency personnel who had tried to save him.

Wolf retrieved a pair of broken eyeglasses from the bag, needed now only for evidence to be used later at the trial of his killer. The pathologist noted that part of a hairpiece was still in place and blended with the stubble on his shaved head of dark hair with shades of gray. The forensic psychologist made a mental note of the possible significance of this vanity. Under the toupee, the top of David Harris' head revealed multiple rows of scars, indicating that the prosperous dentist had undergone pricey hair transplantation.

As Wolf continued his examination, he noted both normal and abnormal appearances of the body—the pupils were normal, all of the fingers and toes were present, and there were no needle tracks which indicated that David wasn't an intravenous drug user. Wolf also noted that the dentist, like most American men, was circumcised.

Wolf noted severe trauma to the upper body. The chest was asymmetrical, crushed from the impact that had caused his death.

Harris' head was a mess with a 3 by 4 inch zone of contusions around his ear, or at least what was left of it. There were more traumas to the chin, deep cuts on the scalp, and a large gash to the back of the neck. Wolf observed that the jaw was broken and teeth were missing. Methodically, the pathologist dictated his observations indicating sixteen separate cuts and abrasions on the head and neck.

Five more cuts and abrasions marked Harris' back, with another two on the rear of his left leg. Those corresponded with the damage done in the front of the same appendage.

The attempted resuscitation of David Harris in the emergency room of St. John Hospital was doomed to failure, Wolf observed. The chest was crushed, with ribs broken not only on the front, but also on the backside of the body. While the right lung was intact, the left lung had been destroyed, with multiple fractures from ten broken ribs. Part of the heart was severed from the rest of the organ.

David Harris also had a broken back at the twelfth vertebra, as well as a broken pelvis.

Both arms showed evidence of multiple cuts and abrasions, although neither was broken. Nor were the legs, although, like the rest of David Harris, they were a mass of gaping wounds and red meat.

Clara Harris clearly had intended to inflict as much damage as possible while methodically running over her husband again and again. She was largely successful, but Wolf's examination showed that she had left the brain undamaged as he removed it from the skull casing and examined it in minute detail. The brain that had absorbed twelve years of grade school and high school, four years of college, dental school, and a residency, not to mention countless memories, was intact and undamaged by the impact of the Mercedes.

Not so the tongue. David Harris had bit it as he was hit by the automobile.

Wolf observed that other organs had escaped the trauma inflicted by Harris' wife. The liver, gallbladder and alimentary tract were intact. When he opened the stomach, it was revealed that Harris chewed his last meal very well and hadn't had a drink before he died.

Harris' urethra was separated from the urinary tract. His testes were intact.

The spleen had escaped the trauma of David's final moments, the left adrenal gland had hemorrhaged, but was still intact.

Wolf's autopsy was complete as his assistants took Harris' fingerprints and palm print. A detective from the Nassau Bay Police Department, Teresa Relken watched as she and a helper photographed the proceeding. The dentist's clothing, eyeglasses, and hairpiece were bagged as evidence.

* * *

As the body of David Harris made its trip to the morgue, his daughter Lindsey Harris returned to the mansion with her uncle and her father's friend, dentist Robert Blanchard, in David Harris' gray Suburban. The three had retrieved it from the parking lot of the Hilton where the orthodontist had parked it when he had arrived earlier that evening to meet Gail Bridges. Now, riding home in her father's SUV, there were so many memories—trips to the lake, learning with her father how to play the piano, talks about her future, and her hope that she would someday join his practice as an orthodontist herself. "I love him to death, I miss him so much," she reflected as she rode with the men, quietly sobbing, alone in her thoughts. She would later relate those thoughts to a jury.

When they arrived, Lindsey noticed something strange as the three pulled into the garage. An old suitcase sat by the door, as if someone was about to take a trip. Next to it was a garbage can filled to overflowing with clothes. She looked down as she walked to the door at the clothes and recognized them as those of her father.

The house was filling with people, stunned by the sudden death of David Harris broadcast on the 10 p.m. news.

Convulsed with grief, Lindsey was also hammered by fear because she had been a passenger in the car that had killed her father. She had helped her stepmother "key" the Lincoln Navigator owned by his lover, an act of vandalism. Clara was now in police custody undergoing hours of interrogation.

"I was so scared, I thought we were going to get in trouble," she later remembered.

But her fears were not so great that she didn't notice something strange.

"They were sad, but they didn't act like Clara had done what she did," she said.

Lindsey remembered the frustration she felt just hours before as she helplessly watched her father die.

"I felt so bad that I couldn't help him," she said. "I felt so mad that I couldn't do anything. It was terrifying. I knew that she was killing him. I knew that he wasn't going to be okay. I was only given sixteen-and-a-half years to spend with him. I knew that I wouldn't have any more than that. It was a terrible way for a person to go."

Anger filled her as she thought of what she had witnessed Clara do when the car had stopped.

"She got out and she went over to him and called him baby as if nothing had happened."

Lindsey wanted to be alone, but before going upstairs to the room that had been specially built for her in the mansion, she went back to the garage. She lifted the old suitcase and carried it up the stairs.

"I felt he was there with me," she said.

Houston's Telephone Road begins in the city's seedy east end; an area that saw its best times during the 1920s and has been in decline since. The four-lane street heads south in a straight line to Hobby Airport, a quick shot that will bypass the traffic on Interstate 45 if a traveler is late for a flight. Of course, that traveler will have to pass the used car lots, greasy restaurants, and loan sharks as it cuts through lower-middle-class white neighborhoods, brown ones with their high wrought iron fences and red, white, and green colors of the flag of Mexico, and the black ones dotted with neon signs that announce, "Quick Cash."

The street continues to arrow straight across Loop 610. Then the neighborhoods improve as the social strata of all three ethnic groups moves up a notch. Finally, Telephone Road reaches Airport Boulevard and Hobby Airport sprawls to the left.

The street relentlessly continues its course south after it crosses the intersection. Its east side is covered with a half mile of hangers that parallel Hobby's runways, first used as a municipal airport in 1938 when it was briefly named for the city's most famous aviator, Howard Hughes.

Across the street, diners, used car lots and prairie face the relentless 24/7 facility.

Here, the bustling city of almost 3 million thins out and the street begins to become a highway. Now it takes on the more distinguished name, Texas Highway 35 as it begins to hug the coast, its sometime concrete, sometime asphalt pavement pointing in the direction of Corpus Christi. It quickly becomes a street again, crossing the Sam Houston Beltway, the penultimate ring that circles a city fifty miles across in any direction.

Yet Highway 35 has one last fling at the tawdry side of society as it points south. On the right, a half-mile past the beltway, sits ethnic Houston's answer to the upscale Galleria shopping mall in the city's uptown district. Cole's Flea Market attracts thousands each weekend as vendors hawk everything from power tools to sugary confections made in the colors of the Mexican flag. On Houston's hot summer days, the mall's canvas roofs shade snow cone vendors and merchants who sell slices of tropical fruit to the thirsty.

The nature of the street changes abruptly a half mile away and the crowd gathered inside the clean walls of South Park Funeral Home reflected the contrast of different ethnicities living near one another. The 300 attending

Saturday's services for David Harris were lily white Anglo or Hispanic to the person as they sang "Amazing Grace" in the funeral chapel filled to overflowing.

Friends, relatives, customers, high school chums, old girlfriends, entered the chapel after filing past photos of the deceased in happier days. Mostly the crowd consisted of members of the Shadycrest Baptist Church of Pearland, Texas. It was a close-knit group of very good people. They had come to say goodbye to one of their own.

These were the people closest to David and Clara Harris. They were the ones who came to the church socials the couple sponsored at their Friendswood, Texas, mansion. Now they were gathered in the large auditorium of the funeral home to pay final respects to the man who had played drums to accompany the church's lively choir.

The congregation filed past pictures that showed the prosperous life David had left behind, a life filled with the things a successful orthodontics practice can bring if it is located in one of the nation's most prosperous regions. David was pictured relaxed with his loving children, with his guitar, in family gatherings. The photograph of David's prized Corvette sat on a credenza with the other photos, yet no person was seen in the picture.

Each guest had been handed a funeral notice, reminiscent of church bulletins handed out before services at Protestant churches throughout the South. On its front, printed in soothing pastels of brown, blue, and white, a dove winged its way heavenward, a burst of sunlight shining through to illuminate its flight. Inside the flyer, the two most important days of David's life were announced as a "Service of Thanksgiving." Those dates were the day he was born on November 4, 1957, and the day his wife of more than ten years had hit his body with her silver Mercedes.

The gathering sang staples of the fundamentalist service of Texas Baptists. "In His Presence," and "Written in Red." All of the service was carefully orchestrated to provide comfort to David's grieving family, to give them the promise of the hereafter for him where they would eventually all meet again. This was the service Rev. Steve Daily was ordained to deliver before he would lead the cortège across the street to the waiting cemetery of the South Park Funeral Home where David would be laid to rest.

And there was preaching of the gospel, the kind that stirred men's souls, be it at a revival, in a tent, in an auditorium, or under a tree. Nobody can preach like a Baptist minister.

The coffin was open, and some walked to the front of the chapel before the service to take a last look at their friend. His body looked at peace in the subdued lighting of the funeral home, hardly the broken, crushed, and bloody remains that had been transported to St. John Hospital, then later to the office of the Harris County medical examiner.

Sixteen year old Lindsey had looked at the body of her father briefly at the funeral home. It was so unnatural in appearance, she thought. It didn't look like him at all.

Patriotism wasn't forgotten either, but it was a loyalty not to nation but to a school, the vaunted University of Texas that David had so proudly attended. On the open lid of the coffin, soon to be closed over him forever, the burnt orange emblem of the Texas Longhorns had been attached. The deceased had attended the venerable Austin institution for two years after sojourns at the University of Houston and the small Alvin Community College south of Pearland.

Across the street, a handful of reporters stood watch as the services continued inside the funeral home. The media contingent was small for the funeral of a celebrated Houston murder victim. It was Saturday. Only weekend news crews were available to cover the story. An employee of the business and its cemetery instructed the reporters that if they so much as left the shoulder of the highway they were standing upon, they would be arrested. His instructions were to keep the media at bay so that their intrusive cameras didn't disturb the serenity of the service. To reinforce the warning, he stood about fifty yards away speaking to a Pearland cop.

David Harris went out in true Southern Baptist style, celebrated in one of the denomination's notoriously long services, honored by a funeral that lasted one-and-a-half hours. Shortly before ending, a young girl was escorted from the church, broken by emotion. She was driven away before the casket was rolled out of the service by the funeral director and lifted by the pallbearers into the waiting hearse. Parked in front of the hearse leading the morose parade to the cemetery across the street was a dark green perfectly restored 1953 Chevy pick-up truck. The Baptist preacher, Steve Daily, who led the parade of mourners across the street, drove the truck, his prized possession. David Harris would be deposited into the gumbo soil of Southeast Texas forever.

One person was missing from the service. Clara Harris was out on $30,000 bond for the murder of her husband. She had said goodbye the night before.

She was, however, given the bulletin passed out at the service, its comforting words meant for a grieving widow.

God hath not promised
Skies always blue,
Flower-strewn pathways
All our lives through,
God hath not promised
Sun without rain,
Joy without sorrow
Peace without pain,

But God hath promised
Strength for the day,
Rest for the labor,
Light for the way,
Grace for the trials,
Help from above,
Unfailing sympathy
Undying love

About five miles away, the peace of a quiet neighborhood had been shattered by the invasion of a constant parade of weekend news crews not assigned to the funeral. Since the story had first broken in the local and national press, journalists covering the story had learned that Harris was not alone when he was murdered and had been with another woman when his wife found, confronted, and killed him. Now they knew her name. The world of Gail Bridges, once a housewife in the quiet enclave of South Shore Harbor, changed radically. The lives of a small circle once close to her would change as well.

Gail had played a dangerous game with her life for the past two years, alternating between attempting to present the image of a devoted mom, pillar of the local Methodist church, and wife of a prominent businessman. Now, the two-story brick home in Clear Lake City was being photographed for the nation's newscasts. Still photos would appear on the pages of grocery store tabloids.

Neighbors remembered how others in Clear Lake had gone about their business when another family had been thrust into the news just the year before. A few blocks away from the home of Gail Bridges stood the one story Mediterranean dwelling where Christian fundamentalist Rusty Yates and his wife Andrea once lived. She was internationally famous for drowning their five children in a bathtub and was now spending a lifetime in a Texas prison, her shattered mind racked by memories of how she'd killed the kids to save them from hell. Rusty was contemplating a divorce from the wife he had stalwartly stood beside during her month long murder trial.

During the Yates ordeal, the neighborhood suddenly filled with news vans and satellite trucks. Reporters walked on the closely cropped St. Augustine grass to the front doors and brazenly rang doorbells asking neighbors if they knew the family that had been struck by tragedy. Some responded, others gave the media a cold reception and refused to cooperate with them, refused to answer the most rudimentary questions about the woman and her children who had moved into the neighborhood just months before.

Like the Yates' home, Gail's house looked normal and lived in. Reporters walked to the front door and rang the bell, but nobody answered, even though the house was occupied. Other news crews pulled into the driveway and photographed the pool area with its lawn chairs and blow-up toys awaiting another July frolic by a mother, her children, and their friends.

The home was supposed to be a refuge from the turmoil of the past two years which had resulted from the breakup of the marriage of Gail and her prominent insurance broker husband, Steve. It was a place to get away from the constant rumors that had swirled around the lake about Gail and the ambiguous relationship that she so publicly flaunted with her best friend Julie. Long before the divorce was final, many in League City speculated that the wife of the quietly politically active State Farm agent had a female lover whom she had met at church. The rumors, Steve believed, had hurt his business.

It is possible the truth or falsity of the rumors would never be resolved. Gail and Julie had both vigorously and publicly denied them. Now, caught up in the turmoil caused by the death of David Harris, all of the rumors would fly out of the box again. And this time the rumors could no longer simply be denied. Because whether they were true or not, the rumors had become an unavoidable factor in the tragic events surrounding David Harris' murder and in the nationwide attention generated by the high-profile trial of Clara Harris.

But persistent rumors were not Gail's most immediate problem. Gail was scared, more scared than she had ever been in her life. For days, a vengeful woman who desperately wanted her husband back had threatened her. She knew that Clara Harris was out of jail, free to come for her. She had seen the rage Clara exhibited when she confronted David, a rage so fierce that it would result in his death. Gail was frightened, and so was Julie who had been with her since the murder. Always tightly wound, Julie was now completely undone by the intrusion into the world of her friend Gail. Their former husbands were trying to take their children away from them and now this had happened. Both women were on edge and completely distraught as the press relentlessly invaded their neighborhood, the one safe place they could come to escape the ugliness of small town gossip.

Julie Knight panicked when a blond reporter came to the door of the home. The two women whispered so as not to alert the woman that they were at home as she persistently rang the doorbell again. Julie looked at Gail, and then dialed 911 to report that Clara Harris had come to the home of her friend to finish the job that she had started only nights before when she'd killed David with her Mercedes.

TWO

July 16, eight days prior to her becoming a murderess, was a typical day for Clara Harris. She'd spent it caring for patients who came in a steady stream to the office as they did every day. There was just work, more work in the Lake Jackson office, which was the genesis of the empire that she and David had built. She had bought out the practice of a retiring dentist in April 1993, and had endeared herself to the small rural community after leaving the world of corporate dentistry at Houston's Castle Dental Center where she and David had met. The citizens of Lake Jackson were for the most part workers at the giant Dow Chemical complex in nearby Freeport, fifty miles due south of Houston's sprawl. The workers provided a steady customer base with a dental insurance plan second to none.

The couple had more than doubled the dental facility at 113 Circle Way. Here Clara's practice had done well in a cluster of towns near where the Brazos River meets the Gulf of Mexico after a meander of hundreds of miles from near the Oklahoma border. Nestled in Brazoria County, the area is the birthplace of Texas, the garden spot Texas' founder, Stephen F. Austin, had settled close to 200 years before to entice northerners, weary of the numbing cold, to come south to a land with few rules and only a slight interest by the authorities who ruled in far-away Mexico City.

In this land steeped in history, Clara had built a practice, calling the business Lake Jackson Dental Care, while David sat at home or moonlighted after leaving Castle Dental. She worked from just after dawn until after dusk to build her business. Eventually, Diana Sherrill who capably handled the front office work, and the all-important patient relations vital to a dental practice, had joined Clara. Diana could deal with almost anything, Clara believed. The office oozed charm from the reception desk to the dental chair.

The office operated with efficiency, boasting fifteen employees. Clara handled the general dentistry needs of her patients. Many of those patients were children—children with crooked teeth. Every Monday, the practice was visited by an orthodontist, in this case, the handsome and charming Dr. David Harris. As charming as the staff was, the patients loved David, especially the kids. If the volume of business warranted it, and it usually did, he returned to Lake Jackson every other Tuesday to handle the orthodontic spillover.

Diana was making a good living for Brazoria County, $27,000 plus bonuses, but she admits, "I didn't rely on those bonuses." For the staffer, one year turned into two, then three and four. She became devoted to the couple she called Dr. David and Dr. Clara.

"They had a professional relationship, they worked there as a team," she remembered. "They enjoyed being around each other. Dr. David was very proud of her. He wished that he could clone Dr. Clara and put her in every office."

Diana eventually became close to the couple. She came to their home for parties, and when the Harris twins,

Brian and Bradley, were born, she came to their home and visited.

It wasn't "all work and no play" in the Lake Jackson office for the dark striking woman with sharp facial features. Diana loved her job and looked forward to the time she spent with her employers.

"There were lunches all the time, and I was included all the time," she said, pride filling her voice.

But there were rumors as well, and Diana had heard them.

The rumors were about a budding relationship between David and the receptionist at his practice, Gail Bridges, that had blossomed into a full-blown affair.

One of the workers in the Clear Lake office was Kathy Davis, who managed the office of Space Center Orthodontics, the practice David had started with his wife's help in Clear Lake City. The Baytown, Texas, woman also did double duty running the practice's small office in nearby Mount Belvieu, just across I-10 from her home.

Like Diana, Kathy watched Dr. David and Dr. Clara build their business. She would see Clara Harris often when she frequently came to her husband's Clear Lake office on Fridays.

"He was the love of her life, and it was very obvious," she remembered.

Davis, like most, was charmed by Clara, and although she didn't spend much time in the Clear Lake practice, her presence was felt. Davis saw the good side of Clara, and as far as the office manager was concerned, the good side was the only side to see.

"I never saw her angry," she said. "She is a kind, warm-hearted loving person."

Kathy's niece, Susan Hanson, also worked for the couple from almost the beginning. The Baytown, Texas, mother of three boys is president of Space Center Management, the company that operates the Harris clinics. She was an eight-year veteran of the practice, a nuts-and-bolts businessperson who makes things work financially. She could boast an annual salary of $80,000. Among her duties were human resources, and handling hiring and terminations.

Clara Harris' friend and employee was the go-to person she could count upon, the woman with whom she had so much to talk about. Clara's twins and Susan's four-year-old had been born four days apart. The two moms had plenty in common to discuss.

"We had birthday parties at their home every chance we got," she remembered. If there wasn't a birthday to celebrate, just about any excuse would do to get together at the Friendswood mansion.

Clara was idolized by her husband, Susan remembered.

"They were always loving, and David thought that Clara was the best dentist in the world, the best mom in the world, and the best wife in the world."

And David was always responsive to Clara's needs.

"When she called, he would always run to the phone."

At midnight, the evening of July 24, 2002, Susan Hanson had a call of her own to take. It was a call totally unexpected. It was a call telling her that David Harris was dead, and her friend and employer, Clara Harris, had killed him.

Of all the practice's employees, Susan Hanson had the most regrets about Gail Bridges.

"I hired her," she remembered. "She was to check patients, take payments, and pull charts, as well as to do customer service. She seemed to be savvy about those things when I hired her."

Gail Bridges began employment in the Clear Lake office in August 2001. David quickly took notice of the attractive dark-eyed employee and began going to the front desk as often as possible to visit with her between his hectic patient loads. In February of the following year, he asked her out for lunch at Perry's restaurant

Soon Susan and others noticed that Gail went out of her way to gain the attention of David Harris as he flitted from examining room to examining room, serving eighty patients per day. Soon, the employees learned that Gail Bridges and David Harris were lovers and their anger at both of them became profound because of their affection for Clara Harris.

Diana Sherrill summed up the feeling of most of the couple's employees when they talked about the affair.

"I was offended because Dr. Clara was my friend first of all. I was offended because she was doing the affair in front of the office employees. Dr. David was about to lose the dream of his practice in Clear Lake if there was a scandal."

The dream she spoke of was a one-stop dental supermarket on Clear Lake City Boulevard, the gateway to the prosperous planned community. The two-story building was under construction. It would house not only David's orthodontic practice, but dental hygiene facilities, general dentists and other peripheral specialties of the trade. David had even planned an office for his young daughter Lindsey if she chose to become a dentist.

Susan Hanson was one of the first to observe the changes in her boss.

"I began to notice a difference in David in February. He was not making decisions as well as he had in the past, and he was less attentive to his patients."

Other things began to catch Hanson's eye.

"The relationship was intimate in appearance," she said. And although Hanson was troubled by the inordinate attention she began to see David paying to the receptionist, she didn't tell her friend Clara.

Moreover, the attentiveness that he had always shown his wife began to wane in little ways as well. Now, instead of rushing to the phone when Clara called, he asked that she be placed on hold until he had finished whatever he was doing.

Hanson saw something else that was different in David's behavior, something that nobody else in the office had ever dared to do previously.

"Gail would take any opportunity to interrupt him when he was caring for patients, and he allowed it," she said. "We would never do that, because he wanted to be alone with his patients."

Hanson was also distressed because the apparent affair had become so blatant in the office that even Lindsey Harris had spoken to her about an incident she had witnessed. In the close quarters of the dental office, David's daughter, who spent summers with her father, took everything in. One day, when David dropped a patient file on the floor, she saw Gail Bridges bend over to pick it up, not from the knees, but from the waist. Moreover, when she bent, her bottom was turned provocatively to face David, who was sitting very close by in a chair.

"I told Lindsey that she should talk to him, or someone, about what she had seen," Hanson said.

At that point, Hanson concluded that her boss and Gail Bridges had already consummated a sexual relationship.

Fifty miles away at Clara's practice, Diana Sherrill also noted that David Harris was behaving differently. The change wasn't just in the way he acted. David's physical appearance began to change as well, and he worked out, losing twenty pounds.

Things began to change dramatically when he made his weekly visit to Clara's office, Sherrill noticed.

"He stayed in the back of the office," she says. "He had nothing to do with the office staff anymore, and he didn't give Clara any time anymore, he was always on the phone."

Sherrill remembers first meeting Gail Bridges in January 2002. A few weeks later, she came back to the Clear Lake office for a staff meeting, and then the management team went to lunch together, albeit without Clara Harris in tow.

"We went to David's Suburban, and Gail jumped into the front seat instead of Susan, which was usually the case. Once in the car, her body would lean toward Dr. David. She was hitting him on the chest and flirting with him.

"We didn't do things like that," she stated emphatically. "He was our boss."

Gail's familiarity extended beyond body language. It was clear to Sherrill that the woman had been in the SUV many times before.

"She knew where the change was. She knew where the sunglasses were. She knew where things were in his truck.

"I knew then that there was an affair," she said.

After lunch, Sherrill talked to Susan Hanson and learned other distressing information. David was making a special place for Gail in his new building.

"She was making changes in the new office and Dr. David was making changes for her," she said. "The other workers were nice to her, but they were physically ill when they left work after seeing what was going on."

Gail Bridges also began to do work that Kathy, the office manager, had previously done, increasingly making herself indispensable around the office.

"She seemed to take charge, and Kathy had been there for years and Kathy knew how to do everything," Sherrill said.

Increasingly, "there were lunches all the time, and she was included in the lunches all the time."

As unusual as a receptionist being included in management team lunches was, Bridges was even included on periodic tours of the new facility, now well under construction within sight of bustling I-45.

"We went on a tour of the new office and Dr. David and Gail slipped off," Sherrill remembers. "He had forgotten I was there."

Finally, Diana Sherrill had had enough, disgusted at what she was seeing happen to the two friends she had worked for so long. While the morning of July 16, 2002, had begun no differently from hundreds of others in the office, it was disrupted when her assistant told Harris that she needed to speak with her, speak with her seriously.

Diana was wise in the ways of marriage, and wise enough to see that David's wandering eye wasn't the only reason he had strayed with Gail Bridges. Since the twins had been born four years before, they had become the center of their mother's universe as David was pushed to the rear.

"You need to protect your marriage," she told Clara Harris. "You need to pay attention to Dr. David."

Clara looked at the woman whose olive complexion and black eyes flashed sympathy for her. She stared at Diana in disbelief as she continued to listen.

"Men go through the change of life," Sherrill told her friend.

"She asked me what that was," Sherrill said incredulously. "I was concerned, worried, frightened a little.

"Finally, she asked me if he was having an affair, and I said, yes."

The two left the office, determined to change the appearance of Clara Harris in an attempt to recapture the attention of her husband.

"We went to a salon and got her hair cut and her color changed."

That evening, Clara Harris got home late. Lindsey and her father were at home alone when she arrived at 10 p.m.. David had been playing the new $90,000 grand piano that had been installed in the music room. The mansion boasted two other pianos, a set of drums, and David's gym.

Lindsey loved to hear him play, and her father's love for music had been passed on to her as well. She was a better than average high school violinist, good to the point that her music competed with her duties as a high school cheerleader back home in Columbus, Ohio, where she lived with her mom, Deborah Shank.

Clara came home and went straight upstairs to her room. David followed her. Lindsey didn't think anything of it.

Clara Harris had noticed changes in her husband as well, but was so wrapped up in her children and in her practice, she hadn't had time to think about them. Now she reflected upon what she had been absorbing all along. Yet despite the fact that she now knew that there was something wrong, she still didn't want to believe it.

"We were best friends, very much in love. We were a team.

"I perceived a change in my husband. He was more stressed, more intolerant of the boys, and he got upset with me a few times."

David was angered with his wife because she had co-signed for a vehicle for an employee of the dental practice who had gone into default. The couple had paid the note to maintain their unblemished credit rating.

In May, Clara took ten days off to participate in a wedding in her native Colombia as matron of honor. David was angry that she was going, citing cash flow as a reason for his fury.

"He said that I shouldn't be going, because we needed the money for the construction site."

Then she remembered another change in her husband.

"He used to spend a lot of time playing with the boys," she said. "He stopped doing that. He wanted to be in his music room, either playing the drums or the piano."

Clara also saw David talking constantly on his cell phone, but thought little of it, what with the vast demands being made upon him because of the construction site that was to be the new clinic.

He also snapped at the twins, and "put them in time out frequently."

That night after she and Diana had finished at the hair salon, the two had gone to dinner at 8 p.m. because Clara wanted to continue the conversation about the marriage.

"I thought that Diana was mature and I could talk to her. She made me aware that there was something that I needed to find out, and I demanded it of her."

Diana told her that the other woman was Gail Bridges.

On the long drive from Lake Jackson to Friendswood,

Clara called the person she knew more than anyone else could help her save her marriage, Millie Harris, David's mother. The two talked for forty-five minutes as Clara made the long commute home and told her mother-in-law that her son was attracted to another woman.

At the conclusion of the conversation, Clara Harris didn't believe that there was any truth to Diana Sherrill's allegations.

Yet the questions in her mind returned almost as quickly as Millie had helped her put them away.

The weekend after Father's Day, David told Clara that he wanted to go to the couple's lake house alone, to be by himself.

"That was the first time ever that he wanted to be alone, and wanted to go somewhere away from me."

When she came inside the mansion, Clara immediately confronted her husband.

"Do you love me?" she asked David Harris.

"He hesitated and looked at me with a question mark on his face that told me that he wasn't sure," Clara remembered.

The following morning Clara was about to step into the shower of her private bath when her husband came into the bathroom.

"What is wrong?" she asked him. "It took him a long time, and we sat at the edge of the bathtub."

"Is it that difficult to say?" Clara asked David.

"I think that you have to know that there is somebody else," he answered.

"Who?"

"Gail," he responded.

"Do you love her?" Clara asked, dying inside.

"I don't know," David answered, less than honestly.

"I started to shake," Clara remembered. "I cried, and he tried to hold me. I didn't want him to touch me."

"I'm going to help you," she said.

"What are you going to do?" he asked her, concern now showing on his face.

"I'm going to get an attorney," Clara told her husband.

David grabbed Clara's arms and told her, "I'll do anything not to get a divorce."

Clara ran downstairs where Lindsey was making breakfast.

"I already know," she told her stepmother. "Everybody in the office knows."

Clara ran upstairs and slapped her husband on the face.

"You said that you had been out with her only one time. You said that you only had lunch. You said that you only kissed her on the hand."

"He had told me that there had been no intimacy between the two of them, that he had been lonely. She had grown up there in America, in Texas, and they had things in common. David told me that they talked about snow skiing, and she wanted to teach him how to ski. They had all these things in common," Clara remembered her husband telling her.

Moreover, David said that Gail liked to exercise just like he did. David had weights set up in the mansion, and he used them relentlessly every day. Clara didn't work out.

"I knew I had to lose weight," Clara said. "I called my office and canceled all of my appointments indefinitely."

Clara Harris was convulsed by anger and humiliation, debased by her husband's lies. She was horrified that she had been made out to be a fool in front of every employee in the company. They had apparently known of David's infidelity for months. His own daughter had apparently known.

Yet Clara loved David and immediately determined that she would somehow save the marriage, somehow save a future with a father at home for the twin boys. She stood before her husband and made demands.

"I want you to fire her," she said emphatically, cold steel in her voice.

"Okay," David answered.

"I want marriage counseling," she continued, now becoming shrill as the realization returned that even Lindsey had known that there was more than the one lunch that David had confessed to the night before.

David Harris grabbed her arm with the strength of an athlete and threw her down. From downstairs, Lindsey heard the fighting and ran upstairs, entering the room.

"What are you doing to her, Dad? She just found out. What are you doing?"

David Harris sneered at his wife and daughter.

"You two are perfect," he said. "I am leaving. You will never see me again."

Minutes later, the tension of the moment had abated and the three were downstairs preparing to go to the office together.

Clara decided to ride with David in the Suburban, not wanting him out of her sight a second until Gail Bridges was removed from their life. Lindsey came along with her father as she usually did for her summer job working in the office cleaning instruments and sorting patient files.

Lindsey climbed into the front seat of the Suburban beside her father. Clara got in the back.

Speaking more to himself than to his wife and daughter, David said that he had to find an apartment that evening but it would be tough.

"I have eighty-five cases today," he said.

Lindsey lectured him as the three drove to the office

nestled on the west side of a strip center. As they drove, Clara still was not certain that the man in the front seat had been intimate with Gail Bridges. If he had been, she was determined that it wouldn't happen again.

When they pulled into the shopping center parking lot and came to a stop, Lindsey was the first to get out of the SUV. Next, Clara got out and headed to the front door of the office. She headed straight toward the receptionist's desk. Once there, she approached Gail professionally.

"Gail, I need to talk to you," she said quietly so as not to disturb the patients who already were in the waiting room. "Let's go outside."

But the door was locked, and Clara took Gail's arm and gently but firmly steered her to a back office, hardly private behind a set of French doors, that she shut and locked. Outside, David and Lindsey stood, vainly turning the doorknob to get in as Gail looked helplessly through the glass at them.

"What kind of relationship do you have with my husband?" she demanded of her rival.

"I don't know why you are asking me these questions," Gail answered in her low soft, velvety voice.

"Give me the key to the office," Clara said, reaching out her hand.

"What did I do?" Gail countered. She then called for David through the door.

Clara exited the back room, and walked Gail to the outer door of the office and through it, locking her out.

Clara had fired Gail Bridges from her job as an $1,800 per month receptionist in the Clear Lake office, furious to be paying her husband's lover, and angered as well by rumors in the community that she had jilted her highly respected husband for another woman. Not only was Clara facing the humiliation of having her husband's lover work for her, her woman's intuition told her what was being said behind her back, even among her own employees.

The emotions of the last twenty-four hours were unleashed as Clara returned to the rear of the dental practice and began to cry in the back office. She was quickly joined in her tears by Susan and Lindsey. David Harris kept coming into the room muttering about the 85 patients that were to be seen. He had a new building to be paid for, and the three women were not helping cash flow a bit by crying in a back room.

Clara and Lindsey returned to the mansion, emotionally and physically spent. Clara knew that she needed external help, and often that help came from professionals such as the marriage counselor she had suggested to David the evening before. Often help came to women in crisis in the form of self-help books written with the object of aiding the emotionally ailing to work out their own answers to problems. Clara had heard of two such books and she asked Lindsey to go to the nearby Barnes & Noble at Baybrook Mall.

Her list was short, a book on saving marriage which she didn't read, and *Relationship Rescue*, that she read, authored by Dr. Phillip McGraw, also known as the loudmouth television talkshow host, Dr. Phil.

When Lindsey returned shortly with the purchases, Clara sat down and began underlining portions of the McGraw book as she read, relating how it applied to her own situation.

She called Millie, her mother-in-law, and set up a meeting with David and his parents. The two were the couple's best friends, unbelievably close. At Shadycrest Baptist Church, the four of them sat together in the same pew on Sunday. She and David came to his parent's home a couple of times each week, and the children, including Lindsey, were a constant presence at their grandparents' house.

Gerald Harris personifies Southern dignity and breeding—a gentleman of the old school, healthily endowed with a whopping dose of gracious charm. Tall, his head is crowned with snow white hair that accents his fair skin tinged with rosy cheeks.

Millie Harris is tiny, quick to smile, quick to laugh, and equally quick to verbally tumble any unwelcome intrusion.

The two had spent a lifetime in America's public schools, with Gerald finally nearing the top of the pecking order of the teaching profession. He finished his career as principal of Pearland High School, an upscale suburb just south of Houston.

As a rule, indiscretions in marriage didn't happen in the world of Gerald and Millie Harris. Theirs was a comfortable world filled with church, grandchildren, and more church. The couple's retirement was as blissful as it could be. That bliss would shatter that evening when Clara and David arrived at their home to talk about their marriage. David opened with a lie to his parents, telling the two that he and Clara would be okay, that they would work things out.

Gerald didn't take David's affair lightly, and told him so, sternly warning him that he had violated the sacred vows he had taken ten years before. But Gerald Harris was as quick to forgive as he was to chide, and in the Baptist tradition of "love the sinner, hate the sin," he practiced the word that comes so closely to his lips and those of other men like him—forgiveness. The two couples prayed.

That evening, Clara and David returned to the mansion exuding warmth that had not been a part of the relationship since the twins were born. They retired to their upstairs bedroom for an evening of lovemaking. David was insatiable. He and Clara had intercourse three times before falling asleep exhausted. He also finally told his wife that he had been intimate with Gail.

The following day, Clara began the physical makeover process, the easy part. She went to Victoria's Secret at the mall and bought the most provocative clothes she could find. After that, she made a trip to World Gym, buying a membership and hiring a trainer who would whip her four-and-a-half decade old body back into a semblance of sexual attractiveness. Next, she visited the offices of Dr. Thomas Weiner, the Clear Lakes plastic surgeon of choice and paid him more than $5,000 for breast augmentation. The new Clara would hold on to her husband through whatever means necessary with the aid of artificial beauty aids, and the book by Dr. Phil.

That evening, Clara made a date with her husband.

"I wanted to go to a romantic piano bar," she remembered. "I wanted to talk to him away from Maria [the couple's governess], and the boys. Neither of us knew where a piano bar was, and he was tired of driving."

David Harris pulled his Suburban into the parking lot of the Hobby Airport Marriott Hotel and the two got out, knowing that inside they would find a bar of some sort where they could just sit and talk.

What they found was not to Clara's liking, but at this point she was willing to go almost anywhere to be alone with her husband. The two entered Damon's Bar and Grill, the hotel's 100-seat sports bar, and found a corner table. There, they talked quietly about themselves and their future.

David explained to Clara in language he called "plain

English" what had attracted him to Clara's rival in the first place.

She sat listening, her attention riveted to her husband as he sat across from her relating how engaging he had found Gail. Clara reached for a cocktail napkin and fumbled in her purse for the Mont Blanc pen she always carried. Then, with the efficiency instilled into her during her years of training as a dentist, she reached for another napkin.

On the first napkin Clara would write down what David was saying about Gail. On the second she would write down what he was saying about her. Each napkin would have its own heading: *General Gail*, and *General Clara*.

Under Clara, she wrote that David told her that he found her to be pretty.

Under Gail, she noted that her rival was pretty as well, but made the notation (reasonably).

Under Clara, she scribbled that David found her to be smart.

On the other napkin, she wrote that Gail was smart as well, but again she wrote, in parentheses, the word reasonably.

As David talked, she looked at him, stunned that she was having such a conversation with her husband, stunned that they were sitting in a sports bar next to a busy airport talking of such things. Clara caught herself and returned her attention to what David was telling her.

Clara was educated, he said.

Gail was "reasonably" educated.

But now, the comparison began to turn negative as he described his wife as a "poor communicator." He expounded upon the explanation, saying that increasingly in their marriage he had found her to be negative about his ideas, particularly regarding the construction project they had embarked upon.

Clara believed that the words she had used to David were simply practical and not negative at all. She was stunned that they were interpreted that way.

David claimed that Gail communicated well with both himself and others.

He continued, saying that Clara was "poor" at letting him do the things that he wanted to do.

Again Clara was stunned. David had a Corvette, three pianos, a guitar, a set of drums, and a lake house—what toy had she stopped him from having?

He told his wife that Gail, on the other hand, went along with whatever he wanted to do, no matter what.

Clara continued to write down the criticism, her heart aching as she found out what her husband had been thinking of her deep inside himself.

"You interrupt, while Gail always allows me to finish talking," he told her "You make pessimistic comments, while Gail thinks that my ideas are always correct."

David continued, telling Clara that she was the one who always organized and planned their vacations. It was a resentment that she never knew existed.

Clara had always prided herself on the way she involved herself in conversations with others, particularly using English. The language was still awkward sometimes for her to use instead of her native Spanish. Now David told her he found that she tended to dominate a conversation and didn't allow anyone else to talk, while Gail had what he described as "good frequency" in her participation in a discussion. He cited an example to her of when the two had met their bankers at the mansion for a dinner engagement in which they would discuss the construction project. The couple had joined the financiers in David's Suburban on the way to the restaurant.

"I couldn't get a word in edgewise," he told her.

He also told his wife that sometimes she was loud. Clara had thought herself to be assertive. Gail on the other hand, had a soft, breathy voice that drew comparison to the way the late Marilyn Monroe had spoken.

Clara Harris was hurt beyond belief at what her husband was telling her, yet she didn't let on to him because of the guilt she was feeling. She only thought of what she could do to change herself for the better to improve the relationship with her husband.

David kept talking, acknowledging that Clara did smile more now that he had revealed his involvement with another woman. Gail, he told her, smiled a lot.

Finally David noted physical attributes again when he compared the two women. For Gail, she wrote, "big boobs," making a mental note of Gail's breast implants. For herself she penned, "Will be big boobs."

Under the *Clara General* heading she wrote a word that is ugly to both men and women: "fat." She wrote a different description for her rival: "no fat, perfect body."

Next, Clara won a round when David told her that she had prettier feet and hands, and she was able to write that he didn't find Gail's appendages pretty. In fact, he told her that he found Gail's feet and hands to be "kind of masculine."

Both, she noted on the napkins, had nice hair. Clara had occasionally had highlights placed in her naturally brown hair. Now she made a mental note that the blond hair she had acquired in Lake Jackson when she first heard of David's dalliance was a plus.

He commented also that Clara's eyes were prettier than her rival's. "That made me feel really good."

But the hurt returned when he randomly moved on to the next comparison.

"You are a large person, too big," he told his wife.

Clara mentally returned to David's cruel description of her as being fat.

"Gail and I fit together better when we are making love. She is petite, perfect to sleep with and hold all night."

Clara was hurt in the knowledge that throughout their ten years sleeping in the same bed, David had never held her all night long.

Clara, he acknowledged, had good values and was not a fanatic. Neither was Gail, but neither was she a workaholic as his wife had become since he had known her.

"I was a workaholic, just like him!" she thought. In fact, "the day I found out about the affair, I told him that I would not go back to work so that I could spend more time with him and the boys."

David said that both were reasonable about religion, and that Gail was a good parent raising her children. Clara had seen those children at company functions and had admired them. "I thought those kids were so precious and so well behaved. Those kids were so beautiful."

On both napkins, Clara wrote "equal intellect."

At last, she came to the bottom notation and wrote that David believed that she spent too much money, while he told her that Gail "handles a tight budget."

Clara, on the other hand, "bought too many toys for the boys and too many decorations for the house."

Clara thought about that and remembered that she had curtailed her spending this summer because the couple was short on cash and was pouring what available funds they had into the construction project.

Finally, when the two left the bar to return to the mansion, Clara carefully placed the two napkins in her purse for future reference.

"I can make you happy, David," she told him as he drove toward the mansion.

She determined that when she got home she would again make David forget the other woman in the privacy of their bedroom. She would send the boys to bed early, and then perhaps he would hold her all night long.

THREE

The following day David and Clara rose early to attend a previously scheduled staff meeting at the Clear Lake office of Space Center Orthodontics. He opened the meeting by announcing that his wife would be retiring from her practice immediately.

"I had so looked forward to working in that building we were building," Clara would remember later, "but I wanted to be home to take care of my family." Clara would forgo her successful career to save her marriage and raise her children. She announced that she was about to become a stay-at-home mom.

The day passed uneventfully for the couple as it returned to a semblance of normalcy. The weekend was upon them, and when David returned home that evening, the two of them decided that they would take the family, governess Maria Gonzalez and all, to the beach. The following morning the two loaded up the twins, the governess, and Lindsey in the Suburban. They headed to Galveston.

Galveston's beaches in July come as close as they ever come each year to providing residents and visitors alike with a touch of paradise. The surf, for a brief moment, is clear instead of the murky brown typical of the upper Texas coast the rest of the year. Thus it was when the Harris family of Friendswood crossed the two-mile-long causeway onto Galveston Island from the mainland.

When they arrived at the beach, David found a spot where they could spread out beach towels, set up their ice chest, and enjoy the gentle rumble of the Gulf of Mexico as tiny waves fell upon the sand.

Clara was happy, happier than she had been since she found out that David was cheating on her. She watched him as he played with the children in the surf.

"He was happy too," she remembered.

Finally though, David sat down with her alone as Maria and Lindsey played with the boys in the waters of the Gulf.

"You know, I am going to have to make closure with Gail," he said.

"That is fine with me," Clara replied. "I understand. If you want to talk with her, call her and speak with her on the phone."

"No, I need to tell her in person," David told his wife.

Clara thought about what David was saying, and while she didn't like the idea, she would make a compromise, a suggestion.

"You can meet at a restaurant while I sit outside in the car so that I can watch you," she said.

David Harris knew that that was the best he was going to get from his wife. He dialed Gail's number, but as usual, she didn't answer. Gail Bridges, out of long habit, didn't answer her home phone but returned calls recorded by her answering machine.

David then called her cell phone and she answered, telling him that she was out of town with her kids and her friend Julie Knight.

The conversation was brief because Clara was sitting next to her husband as he spoke with his lover. There was no small talk, no sharing of common interests. David told her that he needed to talk, he had some things that he needed to tell her that he had been unable to communicate since her abrupt firing.

The two agreed to meet the following Wednesday at Perry's Grille and Steakhouse on Bay Area Boulevard.

Clara knew the restaurant well. It wasn't far from the Clear Lake office and was a favorite of area families and professionals. Its banquet room was a meeting place for all manner of groups.

When David clicked off the phone, Clara looked at him with adoration in her eyes.

"I have custom made this summer for you," she told her husband, the future now bright, she believed, for the two of them.

The following day, the family, now united again, went to services at the Shadycrest Baptist Church and sat with David's parents. Later, they had a light lunch at Soup and Salad, and then went home to a leisurely day by their pool, a typical affluent American family.

Monday, July 22, 2002, was to be the beginning of the couple's new life together, with David making his usual Monday trip to the Lake Jackson office, and Clara staying home in seemingly happy retirement, now a housewife instead of a busy workaholic dentist.

After David left the house, she thought about acting upon an idea that had been in her head. She believed that Gail Bridges was only after her husband for his money. Moreover, she had heard rumors about the woman. The rumors had circulated through the Clear Lake area like the swarms of mosquitoes that return each year to the Texas coast. Clara, like most around the lake, had heard that Gail Bridges had left her husband for another woman.

How could she possibly be interested in David? Clara would show him that Gail had no interest in him because her heart was pointed in a different gender direction.

Clara thumbed through the Clear Lake phone book. In the Yellow Pages section she saw an ad with the headline, "Need a Clue? Call Blue." She dialed the nimber of Blue Moon Investigations.

Claudine Favorite Phillips was working the early morning shift at the firm's suite in the atrium office building located near I-45 at 711 West Bay Area Boulevard, one of the four major thoroughfares leading into Clear Lake City, a sprawling suburb near the north side of the manned spacecraft center developed in the early 1960s.

Clara was direct. She wanted the investigation firm to eavesdrop on Gail Bridges, and, if possible get compromising video of her with her friend Julie Knight.

"What is the price, what is the procedure your investigators go through on surveillance cases?" Clara asked over the telephone.

"We charge sixty five dollars per hour, with a minimum of four hours," Claudine answered, her voice matter-of-fact after answering the same question for almost the zillionth time for a possible client.

Slender and intelligent, Claudine Phillips is a favorite of the owners of the detective agency. Her curly black hair and fair skin speak of her Northern Italian descent. She is a solid investigator, so good that soon after she began work with Blue Moon part time, she was asked to come in house for a full daily shift.

College was more important to the shapely young newlywed. Someday, she hoped that there would be a life beyond spying on cheating husbands and miscreant wives. Maybe she would become a professor after she finished her master's degree in English. What little spare time came Claudine's way was spent listening to classic songs on the radio. Then there were the good vegetarian meals with a nice glass of wine that she lingered over with her new husband. Blue Moon paid the bills to enable her to continue school and enjoy a reasonable lifestyle, nothing more.

Claudine told Clara that the "tail" would have other cost factors which she would be charged for as well, such as the 58 cents per mile for distances racked up in tailing Gail.

Clara told the young woman on the telephone that she wanted a video record of the surveillance.

The cost would escalate to an additional $25 per hour, and still photos would be provided, the charge $4 each. Clara didn't flinch. The price was modest for the information she was seeking.

Lucas and Bobbi Bacha, 43, owners of Blue Moon, don't bill their clients. Experience has taught them to get their money in advance in the emotional world of tailing a wandering spouse—get it up front before quarrelling lovers reunite. Clara Harris was no exception. Claudine told the prosperous dentist that should she hire the firm to track the movements of her husband and his lover, she would be required to pay the cost of the hourly surveillance in advance, with the additional expenses to be paid the following afternoon. Clara agreed that the charges were reasonable. She would sign a contract.

"Bring license plate numbers, addresses, and a photograph of your husband," Clara was told.

Bobbi and Lucas Bacha had built Blue Moon Investigations as a team. Lucas was a reserved, cerebral South African, and Bobbi Sue, the expansive daughter of a Galveston street cop. Lucas had spent twenty-one years in the aerospace industry as an engineer and honed his investigative skills working along with thousands of other scientists on the mystery of what happened to the space shuttle Challenger for NASA. He continued his profession after marrying Bobbi, who had earlier formed the agency, and who lives to investigate, a cop's inherited curiosity in her blood. She is a veteran of a thousand Dumpster dives and a thousand boring and sleepless nights. Bobbi first gained national attention when she claimed that she knew where to find the head of Morris Black, murdered and dismembered by New York real estate heir Robert Durst. Despite admitting killing the elderly man, in late 2003 he was found not guilty of the murder by a Galveston jury. Bobbi Bacha has seen all of man's foibles in her nineteen years looking under rocks and peeking through keyholes. She long ago left street work, preferring the computer and sophisticated search engines to expending shoe leather looking for a target.

The two are an inseparable team with offices across a small hall from each other at the east end of the Blue Moon suite.

Yet it is Bobbi who is Blue Moon Investigations. It is her taste, her touch, her ideas, her drive, and her zeal that makes the firm the area's largest. The suite of offices is a blaze of dark blue, her favorite color. Once inside the door, Bobbi Bacha's taste explodes from every surface. The eye is kept busy looking at the organized clutter. Yet somehow, the decorations work. The success of the decorator is painted blue with shades of brown.

The colors are also Bobbi Bacha's favorites to wear, although she will occasionally indulge herself with a splash of purple. With a girlish giggle, the investigator's public presence belies her toughness and street smarts. Bacha, a large woman given to wearing oversized dresses with a shawl draped around her shoulders, sits with a computer to her right, a screen saver depicting Renaissance angels always changing to create a feeling of serenity.

Two sculptures of elephants, one large, the other smaller, sit on top of her computer. On the desk is a coffee cup, decorated with shining bright moons. The moon is depicted everywhere in the office art. It hangs on walls, sits on tables, and is even woven into a throw casually placed on the love seat. The satellite is depicted in thirteen different pieces of art and sculpture in the 12 × 12 foot space.

It was at this place later that morning that Dr. Clara Harris parked her silver Mercedes. She got out in front of the Morgan Stanley office building, walked inside to the elevators on the west side of the first floor atrium lobby, and entered, pushing the button for the second floor, north side, offices of Blue Moon Investigations. She didn't have to wait long in the small receptionist's area. Claudine greeted her. In Clara's hand she held photographs of David Harris and the couple's twin boys.

Claudine offered her a cup of hot Constant Comment tea. The firm prohibited offering coffee to clients, fearing that the caffeine would aggravate nerves already frayed.

"I'm not sure what my husband's plans are for the day or tomorrow," she told Claudine. "I do know that he plans to meet her at some point."

Clara paid the required fee for an initial three days. She instructed the firm that the surveillance was to begin when David Harris left his Clear Lake office at 5 p.m. the following day.

It would be easy to spot the handsome dentist since there was only a front door to the storefront office in a strip center. The modest facility was wedged between two businesses, Thomas Wiener Plastic Surgery and City Nails Tanning.

"Follow him from work," she told Claudine. "I think that he will go to Perry's Steak House on Bay Area Boulevard, but he might go to the Hilton Hotel in Nassau Bay. I just don't know his exact plans. I'll know what his plans are by tomorrow afternoon and I will let you know if there is a change of plans."

Clara continued for twenty minutes, explaining that her husband's alleged lover was a former employee at their dental clinic. She told Claudine that she had personally fired the woman after beganning to suspect that David was involved romantically with her.

"My husband is a good man," she said again and again. "He has just fallen into a trap."

"She wants the money, she wants our money," Clara told the veteran investigator sitting before her, but, "He will never, never believe that."

Clara was emotionally racked by the suspicion of David. She had given him so much, the best years of her life, and she so passionately loved him, adored him, and idolized him. The two had built the house together so that they might raise their family in the ethereal world of living in a mansion, driving expensive cars, tasting only the best of food and providing for their parents in their dotage.

"I confronted him," she continued, speaking in a low, accented voice, the soft lilting South American Spanish of her native Colombia still evident.

"He admitted the affair," she continued, her story pouring out of her to the young woman from the agency.

"He told me that he couldn't leave Gail because she had small children."

Claudine looked at the woman as she had so many before her then handed Clara a handbook titled *Divorce, Texas Style*.

Clara shook her head, refusing to take the book.

"I will never divorce my husband," she said. "I simply want to prove that Gail is deceiving him."

Clara blamed herself and the inordinate time she was spending with the couple's twins.

"I recently had to go back to Colombia, my home country, to handle personal business," she told Claudine. "That gave Gail the opportunity she needed to move in, [on him]. Follow her, not him. He is a victim. Follow her. She is using him."

"You will find them at Perry's Steak House on Bay Area. Follow her, not him," she said.

Now, speaking even more slowly, Clara made certain that her accent didn't get in the way of imparting vital information that she believed about the relationship between her husband's lover and another woman.

"Her name is Gail Thompson Bridges," she continued. "She also has a live-in girlfriend who drives a silver Lexus. I don't have her name, but she is a lesbian. We must prove this to David. Several people have told me that the two women are lesbians. Follow her and observe any activities."

"If you can get close enough to hear any conversations, do so," the dentist instructed the investigator.

"We will get as close as possible," Claudine told Clara. "I can't guarantee any conversations, and we can only record in open areas with a pocket recorder, but this isn't very good and will pick up all of the other noises in a restaurant. We'll try to get as close as possible without blowing our cover."

Claudine was delighted as Clara continued the instructions for surveillance. She was willing to spend and wasn't the kind of client who would come in and only be able to afford a couple of hours of an investigator's time. The surveillance was scheduled for 9 a.m. until 9 p.m. beginning the following morning so that the investigator could observe and photograph activities between Gail and her alleged lesbian roommate.

She told Claudine that she wanted details piled upon details. She remembered to tell the interviewer that Gail was unemployed and would likely spend much of her day at home.

"Give me the daily routine," she insisted. "All of it."

Claudine called another Blue Moon employee, Kathy Ferguson, into the interview and introduced the two women. She told Clara that Kathy would be her contact for daily update calls on the case, which firm policy dictated take place after 1 p.m. the following business day after a surveillance.

The dentist scheduled five hours surveillance on Friday as well, then got the checkbook out of her purse and began writing a check in advance for an initial twenty-two hours of private investigator work. The check was drawn on the couple's joint account with their home address on Pine Drive, Friendswood, in the amount of $1547.98. On it were the names, Clara Harris DMD, and David L. Harris, DDS, MSD.

Clara left the office as quickly as she had come, determined to save her marriage by confronting her husband with the truth about his lover. She wanted him to know that Gail Bridges had left her husband Steve for another woman, and that she had continued the relationship with Julie Knight to the present time. David was being cynically used by a woman with no money of her own other than the child support provided by her former husband, and who, she believed, was almost totally dependent upon her alleged lover.

The Nassau Bay Hilton and Marina tower stands tall on the west side of Clear Lake. The lake is little more than a wide puddle, where the chocolate-colored water of Clear Creek empties into the brackish gray of Galveston Bay. During much of its existence, the lake was only about four feet deep in most places, with a sludge bottom. But coastal subsidence took a toll as subsurface water was drained by the wells of nearby towns that sprang up after the Civil War. Now the lake was deeper.

Clara and David Harris had been married at Windemere, a yacht club adjacent to the Hilton, ten years before on Valentine's Day, 1992. By February 14, early spring has come to the Texas coastal region. There, in the sub-tropical climate, trees begin to bud out and early flowers go into bloom as the area's short winter comes to a fitful end. The end of winter around the lake was the ideal time for a new beginning.

The fourteen floor hotel was now approaching middle age by Houston standards. At 30 years, many buildings would have already been demolished in a city determined to remain new and glistening. To keep up with the times, the owners had refurbished the property in 1996. Yet the Hilton still showed the scuffmarks of a hotel that had long ago seen its best days.

Across busy NASA Road 1, the agency's nerve center bustles with the activities of scientists hell-bent to get man off Earth and onward to other distant planets and eventually galaxies.

The hotel is ideally placed to serve the contractors, vendors, and government officials from out of town who do business at the Lyndon B. Johnson Space Center. It also caters to a modest tourist industry that has sprung up since the early 1960s when the space center was first built during the heady days of the Mercury, Gemini, and Apollo space programs.

America's astronauts have lived in the Clear Lake area for almost forty years. To the rest of the nation, they are heroes. In towns like League City, Clear Lake City, Houston, Dickinson, Kemah, Friendswood, and Pearland, they are just neighbors, as likely as not to be the man or woman pushing a shopping cart at the local supermarket or getting calloused elbows at a nearby watering hole such as Carlos's Beer Garden, a favorite hangout (many of the nation's astronauts were, and are, exuberant drinkers).

Challenger astronaut Judy Resnick once won a chug-a-lug contest at the venerable Houston sports bar, Griff's Shillelagh Inn, a spot founded by inveterate sports fan Michael Griffin, a Boston Irishman famed for dribbling a basketball down Main Street during the city's annual St. Patrick's Day parade.

Across the lake from the Hilton, the South Shore Harbor Resort and Conference Center completes the picture of tall buildings constructed upon the shore of the lake. Newer, and with a health club to boot, the hotel has continually taken business from the Hilton since it was erected by Galveston banking and insurance mogul Robert L. Moody. His grandfather had once been called the richest man in America by *Life Magazine*. The scowling elder Moody's face had glowered in black and white from the cover, its red-and-white square masthead above his right eye.

The old man, and his Confederate hero father before him, had made their fortune in banking and insurance on the barrier island of Galveston. Eventually, the two came to control even the most minute details of the islanders' daily life, then reported it in the Moody owned *Galveston Daily News*, Texas' oldest newspaper. After the death of W. L. Moody Jr., Robert's grandfather, the family fortune passed to the control of his doting aunt, Mary Moody Northen, then finally to his control at her death.

Every bit the visionary businessman his grandfathers were, Robert Moody long thought of developing hundreds of acres of salt grass-covered land on the south shore of Clear Lake just to the east of the old town of League City. The undeveloped prairie would eventually become South Shore Harbor, boasting not only the hotel, but a health club, marina, and country club. Moody's company first bought 1,200 acres for development, then continued to buy until the planned community encompassed 2,200 acres and was the home of 9,800 members of the latter day gentry.

The project was an instant success as Houstonians flocked to buy homes a splash away from some of the country's best sailing on Galveston Bay. The estuary boasts almost constant southerly winds. Other upscale homebuyers such as Steve and Gail Bridges were drawn because the development was in the neighborhood of his insurance agency. There, the two could raise their family as respected pillars of the Bay Harbor United Methodist Church, send their kids to the best schools around, build a successful insurance business and establish friendships that would last a lifetime.

Others flocked to the community like Exxon/Mobil software developer Chuck Knight and his wife Julie. Chuck was a Minnesota transplant, and Texas had been good to him. His multiple degrees enabled him to earn an annual salary of $120,000 after only six months with the company. South Shore Harbor was an ideal place for him and his accountant wife to land.

Julie grew up in the nearby tank town of Deer Park. Both were into their second marriage and wanted to make a go of it in the decidedly comfortable South Shore Harbor. Both chose the life of commuters on Houston's efficient Park and Ride system as they traveled to and from their downtown Houston jobs.

Don and Natasha Warren chose to live in South Shore Harbor for a different reason. Don was a successful League City lawyer. The house in South Shore Harbor was close to home.

Still others were drawn to League City because it and some of the other areas around the lake were hotbeds of the moralistic politics practiced by the religious right. At one point, the religious right prevailed in local elections and took control of the League City mayor's office. Tommy Frankovich, pillar of a local fundamentalist church, adopted a doctrine governing his city under "Godly principles." After relentless ridicule in the press, the regime was tossed out of office following a bitter election campaign.

Most residents of League City are not political at all, preferring to live their lives in the quiet suburban setting surrounded by the region's ample recreational opportunities such as sailing on the lake, the cosmopolitan atmosphere of nearby Houston, good shopping malls nearby, and arguably some of the best seafood restaurants in the nation within minutes of their homes. They wanted to live the good life, looking out the windows of their upscale homes at their neighbor's upscale homes. They were determined to send their children to the best upscale preschools possible with the children of their upscale neighbors. They wanted a place to jog, play tennis, golf, or work out at the South Shore Harbor Fitness Center. This was their enclave, the refuge that success brought them.

Across the lake from South Shore Harbor, Clara Harris called Claudine at Blue Moon Investigations to give her David Harris' plans for the evening, as well as to tell her that she had obtained a photo of Julie Knight. She also now gave the woman David's license tag number.

Lindsey Dubec, the part time investigator assigned to stalk David Harris and Gail Bridges was about to leave the office to begin her surveillance when Claudine stopped her and told her to wait, that Clara Harris, her new client, was coming to the office. The statuesque blond 25-year-old stayed at the office killing time.

Dubec had taken a private investigation course offered by Blue Moon on Saturdays. In several short afternoons' work, the firm claimed that it could teach budding investigators the trade.

At 4:40 p.m., Clara and David's daughter Lindsey Harris walked into the Blue Moon office. As the two sat in the reception's area, Bobbi Bacha walked by the new client to make copies on an unrelated case and saw the well-dressed woman and teenage girl sitting before the receptionist desk, businesslike, as if sitting in the lobby of a bank waiting to see a loan officer. Another investigator also observed the two and asked who she was.

"A client," Bacha said, shushing him so that Clara Harris would not know she was the topic of idle office conversation.

"She is pretty, and dressed to kill—just a joke," she later remembered her employee saying.

"She's a client, hush, she may hear you," Bacha admonished him.

Lindsey Harris was left in the lobby as her stepmother walked into the office to meet with Claudine, who introduced her to Lindsey Dubec.

"Are you going to do my case?" Clara asked.

"Yes," Lindsey answered, flustered a bit because she wasn't accustomed to actually meeting clients, just filing the report of her surveillance after a job was complete.

"Please get close to them to get conversations," she told the investigator. "He is supposed to go to Perry's Grill tonight to see the other woman."

Claudine also introduced Clara to Kathy Ferguson, another Blue Moon case manager.

"I'll be off tomorrow, and Kathy will give you the report if you will call in after one p.m.," she said. "She is familiar with your case and will be able to give you a full verbal update tomorrow."

Clara gave a start, and then began to cry.

"You are my best friends," she sobbed. Claudine thought the comment strange, as she quickly got tissues and offered them to the crying dentist. Clara refused them because there were no tears, she noticed. The woman quickly composed herself, and then left with her stepdaughter. The two drove away in separate cars, observed by Dubec.

The last few days had been difficult ones for David Harris. He was juggling a wife and a girlfriend, working his normal orthodontics practice, running the businesses, and overseeing a major construction project.

He and Clara had drifted apart after the twins came. It was an uncomfortable situation, but one that was a long time in coming. More and more, the two became Dr. David and Dr. Clara, not just the two people who had fallen in love ten years before at another dental practice. Now they were a business entity, joined by commingled assets as much as love.

David Harris needed good relations with his wife. The two had built their business empire largely upon their skills as effective dental practice managers, buying up the practices of seven other area dentists, and then husbanding them as their own. He didn't need public exposure to their troubles at home, and he didn't expect any.

There was an image to consider after all. The Harrises carefully structured ads featured a smiling Melissa Summers, Miss Pre-Teen America, 2001. She was a patient.

The business was booming, growing at exactly the rate the two had projected it would grow. That was made possible because of the easy availability of credit for the budding empire builders. The two were on a fast track to set up as many practices as possible in affluent areas within an easy commute from their Friendswood base. David's storefront practice in Clear Lake alone was pulling in $35,000 per month.

A large part of that was access to minority loans that Clara's maiden name would facilitate. On paper, Clara owned a 51 percent controlling interest in the entire empire. The last thing in the world David wanted was a complicated divorce while the two were building their new 6,000 square-foot-professional building in the high-traffic I-45 corridor between Houston and Galveston. David Harris needed money, and access to plenty of it. Dissolution of the minority-based business relationship could come later, after the facility was built and all of the office suites were leased.

When the building was completed, Clara planned to move her office there as well, and eventually there would be a third Harris working for the empire. Lindsey had already begun to make career plans. Now Clara wouldn't be part of the practice. David had told his daughter that he was reserving space in the building for her practice when that day came. The two would work in the new building together. Clara would no longer be there.

FOUR

David Harris was a nerd by modern American standards, albeit a highly successful one. His language was of the '40s and '50s. His favorite expletive was "golly."

But Harris was driven by a Protestant work ethic burrowed into his being. It was reinforced by the bigger-is-better, more-is-greater, and gaudy-is-tasteful mentality of Baptist preachers who build mega-churches complete with gymnasiums and bowling alleys. Those churches boast their own rock bands because mainstream music played by secular radio stations and musicians was deemed a willful acceptance of a world gone bad. But Baptist preachers also built small neighborhood churches like Shadycrest within the church family; there was no need to go outside. David Harris' world was a comfortable place where, if a person made enough money and lived according to the rules of society, he wanted for little. It was a society that was insular, closed, walled off from the rest of the world. But the walls were easily breached simply by saying a few words and declaring that you were saved.

"Do you accept Jesus Christ as your Lord and Savior?" the preacher would ask the shameful sinner before him.

"Yes," came back the simple reply.

Slate clean, end of story, get ready for a full immersion baptism—another soul had been saved.

Below that level of piety were the others, the great-unwashed sea of un-saved souls waiting to be delivered to the Almighty by the inerrant bible believing, born again and again minions of the Southern Baptist Church. These lesser beings hadn't loudly declared that they were washed in the blood of the lamb, (a curious reference to animal sacrifice). They had not made that walk down the aisle of the church or auditorium or stadium to the feet of the evangelist, hands in the air, to declare their fealty to God.

In recent years many people in the world of David Harris had stopped using the designation *Baptist* altogether and simply declared themselves to be Christian, as though all other denominations, both Protestant and Catholic, didn't matter. A goodly number of members of other sects resented the Baptists' laying claim to the noun with the name of Christ himself embedded in it.

Life in the small Shadycrest Baptist Church wasn't all drudgery. These bible-believing Christians didn't practice the grim solemnity of some of the more dour sects. The church even had its own band, named the Colemans. They were not an official band, but they played their own brand of Christian music and frequently performed at the church. The Colemans' drummer was a successful orthodontist named David Harris. Shadycrest was a fun place to worship. The congregants were so close to each other that were not common blood a requirement, they would have been family. It was an all for one, one for all kind of church, and its pastor, Steve Daily, had been recruited to make it even bigger and better than it originally was.

When the preacher answered the call to Shadycrest, the

congregation consisted of 90 inerrant souls. In a few short years, it had swelled to 250.

It was in this narrow and confined world that David Harris lived his charmed life. He worked hard straightening the teeth of as many as 120 kids per day, then came home to reign as king of the mansion, plan the next expansion of the empire, and then finally go to the church with his beautiful Colombian wife who had grown up Roman Catholic.

Clara Suarez' father had died when she was six, and her mother provided for her beautiful daughter as best she could, designing and making clothes for the prominent members of Bogotá society. School had come easily for Clara, then college and dental school. She started a practice in the capital city, but longed to immigrate to the United States. It was a dream her father had embedded in her when she was a tiny girl. She was eventually accepted at St. Louis' George Washington University Medical School. After graduation, she returned to Colombia. But her father's dream had been for her to come to the United States and work.

She finally emigrated, but in order to practice in the United States, even though she was a practicing dentist in Colombia, she was required to meet the requirements for licensing in her new home. That would entail spending a year in a U.S. dental school and getting a certificate of competence in the field. Clara enrolled in the University of Texas Dental Branch in Houston.

David had planned this life from his formative years. He was always driven by success, and after false starts at the community college and UH, he completed his degree and went on to dental school. He finished second in his class at the University of Texas Dental Branch in Houston. He graduated with a cumulative grade point average of 93.06. David was awarded his doctorate in dental surgery on May 27, 1989. Two years later, on a summer day in June, Clara Harris received her certificate from the Houston dental school which would enable her to practice in Texas. Shortly thereafter, on a whim, she entered a beauty contest. Clara Harris was crowned Miss Colombia Houston. It was a magical time for her.

At South Shore Harbor it was also magical for a time for Gail Bridges, mother of three, upstanding citizen of her community, upscale poster girl for the yuppie lifestyle and owner of a two-story, red brick house in League City's most exclusive neighborhood, South Shore Harbor. Gail and her insurance executive husband, Steve, flaunted their success right down to his-and-hers Lincoln Navigators, his white and hers red.

The two were still almost newlyweds, married July 16, 1998, almost four years to the day before Clara Harris fired a now-divorced Gail from her job in David's orthodontics office.

Steve Bridges, a product of the Sulphur, Louisiana., Cajun environment where he grew up, had been raised Baptist.

"I was there every time the doors opened," he remembers. "In fact, I had a key to the church." The entire family consisted of solid citizens, the pride of Sulphur. His chemical engineer father and schoolteacher mother raised their three boys by the same principles that had been instilled in them a generation before.

After graduation from high school in the small town sitting in the shadow of Lake Charles' oil and chemical refineries, Steve attended Northeast Louisiana University in Monroe. There he worked on the yearbook staff as an extracurricular activity, and after classes, performed as a disc jockey at a local radio station.

Good income came easily to Steve Bridges from the very beginning, he says. After NLU, he was hired by Ford Motor Company in their corporate office in New Orleans because, he says, somebody noticed on his resume that he had grown up on Mustang Street in Sulphur. True or not, Bridges was a rising young star in the Michigan-based corporation. Eighteen Ford dealerships were soon answering to him.

The money was great, more than he had ever dreamed of earning. But success had its drawbacks. He was paying the price for it traveling 1,500 miles each week, and sleeping in a different motel room every night. Steve Bridges knew that he needed to get a life, and quickly.

He took a vocational aptitude test and the results were startling. It told him that he would be happiest working in the real estate or insurance industries. He took the test results literally and lined up an interview with State Farm, winning the opportunity to train with the giant insurer over 200 other applicants vying for the same job.

Bridges took a whopping pay cut and moved back to his old college town of Monroe, then from there to Austin, Texas, where he spent three-and-a-half years learning the insurance trade. The company liked him and he was offered an agency in League City, Texas.

Becoming a State Farm agent is one of the most coveted plums in the insurance game. Across America, these quiet Babbitts are among small-town USA's most wealthy citizens earning between $300,000 and $600,000 each year. The State Farm agent can easily drive any car he likes, and live in the biggest house in town if he so chooses.

But high earnings are a well-kept secret in an industry that keeps such knowledge close to the vest and well within the select club of the anointed, because customers might balk at paying high premiums if they knew how much of their money was going to the agent.

The agency Steve Bridges was being offered was a plum—just outside the gates of the planned community of South Shore Harbor, an upscale address that was almost guaranteed to spin off enormous profits.

Bridges loaded up his possessions and his four-year-old miniature dachshund, Heidi, and made the short drive to his new home. "They promised me that the AC in the U-Haul would work—and it didn't."

Steve Bridges, League City's new solid citizen, arrived in the community on July 31, 1987. He drove straight to his new office. It consisted of nothing more than a slab and four walls. He was taking over from an agent who was scheduled to open the agency, but who had been diagnosed with terminal cancer. Nothing had been done to set up the office and open for business. But typically, Bridges hit the ground running, selling 63 profitable life insurance policies, and a total of 110 policies overall the first month.

Steve Bridges knew only one person in the entire area. His life previously had centered in Sulphur, New Orleans, and Monroe, plus a scattering of cities served with Ford dealerships.

But he had met a Clear Lake woman the year before when he had come to town to conduct a seminar for State Farm area managers. Her name was Gail Thompson. She worked in the local State Farm office in Clear Lake City, across the lake from League City.

"I dropped in on her from time to time," he recalls.

Soon, the two were going out on dates, an attractive couple sitting talking and having dinner at the local Black-eyed Pea and Pappas Seafood restaurants.

"It was beautiful," he says of the courtship today.

Soon the two decided to wed, by "mutual decision."

After their marriage Steve and Gail moved into a home on Apple Street in Rustic Oaks to the west of town, not very far from the lot on a quiet stream where David and Clara Harris would someday build their mansion.

Gail liked the home, but after the children were born she worried about a stairway in the house after one of them almost fell from an interior balcony.

Steve and Gail were both proponents of conspicuous materialism. They liked having money, and they both flaunted it—she more than her image-conscious husband, who in those days dressed for success, wearing a coat and tie almost everywhere he was seen in public.

The town where Steve and Gail Bridges settled, League City, is a churchgoing community, where the pews are filled each Sunday with townsfolk seeking to wash away the previous week's transgressions with an hour of the gospel, or to be seen in the right place by the right people for reasons best kept to them. Steve and Gail Bridges were no different. At first they shopped for a church. They were regular parishioners of St. Mary's Roman Catholic Church for a time because Gail had converted to Catholicism before she met her husband. But the two were still looking for a sect that fit them, and their Protestant roots. Finally the two moved their communion to the Bay Harbor United Methodist Church.

The two shared much in common, such as small-town values and a heritage steeped in Southern Baptist tradition. They became Methodists for no better reason than the fact that the Methodist church was closer to their home and Steve's office than the local Baptist or Catholic church.

Gail had enjoyed a modest but happy upbringing in

Crosby, Texas, a tiny town almost thirty miles to the east of Houston. There her high school years were spent as a popular cheerleader for the football team, as well as a member of the marching band. She also served on the student council and yearbook staff and was active in poetry reading, the local medical career club, and the school's Audubon Club.

Crosby was founded along the Southern Pacific Railroad tracks at the end of the Civil War. It slept for most of the rest of the nineteenth century with a population of 50, the Baptist church and a Methodist church. It had earned the curious nickname Lick Skillet by 1898. During Gail Thompson's formative years, Crosby could boast 2,500 souls, most of whom still attended the two churches formed by the town's founders.

Her father, Oliver Thompson, was liked enough to serve on the Crosby school board as well as perform as a pillar of the First Baptist Church.

Gail blossomed into a beautiful young girl, yet she suffered from a congenital defect, a limp. But like many young girls, she wanted to enter beauty pageants. She fulfilled the dream by entering the prestigious Miss Houston Pageant. Hours of relentless practice yielded an unexpected result. To her parents' surprise, come pageant time, she walked steadily across the stage without the trace of impairment. Gail Bridges had shown an inner strength and determination to conquer her infirmity that few knew she possessed.

After her high school graduation in 1981, Gail went to nearby Baytown Lee College, one of the first junior colleges in the state. From there, the pretty coed attended the University of Southwestern Louisiana in Lafayette, and then the University of Houston.

* * *

Gail was an enthusiastic member of Bay Harbor's congregation, inviting friends and acquaintances to attend the upscale services in South Shore. It was, and is, a church where a popular former minister, Tom Pace, maintained a happy, active, and decidedly well-to-do congregation. "You went to church to see your friends," remembers Gail's former best friend Laurie Wells. "It was a country club church."

Pace, 44, remembers the couple as generous with their money at the church he founded, whose atmosphere he describes as "a suburban mentality as opposed to a small-town mentality." Pace moved from the church to another upscale suburban flock almost forty miles away in Sugar Land in 1995.

Laurie Wells met Gail Bridges in 1989 at a Lamaze class when the two 26-year-olds were both pregnant. They hit it off immediately. For the next year-and-a-half, the women were inseparable.

Laurie Wells lived in nearby Dickinson, married to a man from a family of some local prominence; Steve Wells was 34 when the two met. He lived at home with his mother. He owned his own business, rehabbing homes that had seen better days and were in need of repair. Laurie worked as a travel agent and part time baton-twirling instructor.

Laurie Pitts grew up with her chiropractor father in Tampa, Florida, living the upscale life of a daughter born to a man of some prominence, enjoying jaunts to Ybor City, Tampa's tourist hot spot, for black bean soup at the famed Columbia Restaurant. Her parents divorced when she was young. Laurie moved to Chicago with her mother, and when she became a self-described out-of-control teen, she moved back to Tampa, settled down and became an honor roll student and head majorette at Land of Lakes High School.

Immediately after graduation, Laurie moved to Houston in June 1982, to join her brother, who was opening a chain of Linen-Closet outlets in the booming petro capital. In October, she met her future husband.

The two shared a home, which they had bought in 1983, on Park Avenue, a street that parallels Dickinson Bayou, a picturesque stream whose murky brackish waters are fed by the tides of Galveston Bay. The blacktop street meanders along the edge of the tidal outlet for about a half-mile. Once modestly fashionable by Dickinson standards, today Park Avenue is given to aging residences on the north side, and light industrial businesses along the water's edge alternating with nice homes. Despite Steve Wells' work in the home improvement business, the couple's own home remained unfinished. But the house served Steve's purpose. It was a comfortable place for him, Laurie, and the children, and it was an ideal office for his home-based business.

Their children played together and the Wells and Bridges families joined others from the church for outings to Chucke Cheese's. For relaxation, Laurie regularly joined Gail and her friends in South Shore Harbor for bunco, a popular dice game played by many of the local women.

Typically the bunco game rotated among the affluent homes of South Shore Harbor. The hostesses attempted to outdo each other with game prizes and décor. More often than not, white wine or tequila laced margaritas were served to the women, who sit at three tables, their men banished to another room in the home or to the country club, yacht club, sailboat or fitness center. Players roll dice, a bell placed on one table, and a large fuzzy die or stuffed animal on another. The women sit through six rounds for each set. Points are earned by rolling the dice, the idea being to roll the same number as the bunco round being played. The custodian of the fuzzy stuffed die throws it at the person who calls bunco. At the end of the game, the person holding the die wins a prize.

The round is ended when the first, or "High" table reaches 21 points. At the end of the round, players rotate among the three tables, changing partners and conversation, take a potty break, and mix another drink.

At the end of the time the hostess has allotted for the game, the team with the highest score is the winner. Life among the women of South Shore Harbor—and for Gail Thompson Bridges—was good, if prosaic and predictable.

Laurie and Steve Wells couldn't have picked a better town to raise their children than the one in which he had grown up. For a century Dickinson was a bedroom community of Houston and Galveston white-collar workers, as well as the highly paid laborers who made a good living in the chemical plants in nearby Texas City. The village is known mainly for its dense forest of tall pine trees. The lost pines are the only stand of their kind along the entire 467 miles of the Texas coastal prairie between Sabine Pass in the east, and Brownsville on the Texas/Mexico border.

It was here that Herb Wells moved his family in the late 1950s. He quickly became a pillar of the Howell Memorial Methodist Church; a small red-brick building facing the local elementary school. Holy Trinity Episcopal Church and cemetery is across what, in the early 50s, was the only thoroughfare between Houston and Galveston.

The Anglican church fronts a lawn where each year the congregation holds a Strawberry Festival honoring what was once the town's chief export. The event commemorates the sweet, tart berry despite the fact that strawberries have not been produced in the town since the early nineteenth century.

One of the oldest Anglo towns in Texas, the settlement began in the early 1820s and was eventually named for John Dickinson, who had obtained a land grant from Mexico just north of the present community. By 1850 there was a village along the banks of the bayou, and by 1890 commercial land developers were promoting the sale of land around the little community. That was given impetus when hurricane wary islanders were induced to leave Galveston after the great storm of 1900 killed more than 6,000 residents. Also in 1900, an influx of Italian immigrants gave the small city a cosmopolitan flavor. By 1911, Dickinson could boast three stops on the Houston Electric Railway tracks which ran through the middle of town.

The town was one of Galveston County's most desirable addresses until well into the 1970s. In fact, it was a tax haven of sorts, remaining unincorporated until late in the decade.

Laurie met Steve at a meeting of Alcoholics Anonymous she attended as moral support for her mother. She was impressed with the small business owner, whose principal firm, Welco Diversified, had a good reputation around Dickinson for quality work at a fair price.

Yet, according to Laurie, the two had a troubled marriage from the beginning. Laurie remembers how what should have been a joyous occasion brought bitter tears to her after she announced to her husband that she was pregnant with their first child.

"How much is this child going to cost me?" was Steve's response, she claims. She says that things didn't get much better for the thirteen years that the two remained together. Throughout the marriage Laurie was never a signatory on the couple's bank account at Dickinson's Citizen's State Bank.

"He would shout at me, shout at my mother," she recalls. "He would shout at my mother for eating a baked potato. 'You are taking food out of my children's mouths.'"

Laurie sought refuge in religion. "I bought into the whole ball of wax," she says today. "I can't get through life without God."

The troubled young woman began to have fits of temper with her husband, alternating between anger at him, and withdrawal into religion.

Eventually, Steve Wells moved out of the Park Avenue home the two had shared for so long.

Laurie began to keep a journal, detailing her innermost thoughts to God, penning long rambling letters meant for nobody else to see.

Dear God:

I'm having a rough morning. I didn't want the kids to go today. I wanted them home with me. I know the reason why. I heard Steve's conversation with Kayla last night while I was at bunco. He just drills her and lays into her. It kills me to think that she has to spend the entire weekend surrounded by hate. Why can't he see how much he is hurting our girls, especially Kayla. God, she is just an innocent child. Please protect her. I know verbal abuse can be just as bad, if not worse, than physical abuse, and that's what he is doing to her.

He is also hurting himself, because the kids don't want to be around him, or talk to him on the phone.

I know he blames me, God. He thinks I won't let them talk to him. Yes, I admit when I'm not home I don't want to talk to him, because I'm not here to comfort and explain things to them. When I'm home I tell them they need to call their Daddy and they usually say he's gone to bed, or I don't feel like it now.

Last night on the phone he didn't approve of Kayla watching wrestling with Joanne on normal TV, yet he lets her watch a PG 13 movie where they draw a penis on the side of some guy's face. The language alone was horrible. Not only does he let Kayla watch this, God, but Kalista.

I bet God, he has no idea what the kids are watching—he goes into his room to watch his movie.

Oh God, just help him! Maybe when this nightmare is over he will learn to be a better parent and put the girls first.

Between you and I, Steve is not being a good Dad.

In Jesus name I pray,

Amen

Long before the murder of David Harris, Julie Knight had been accused of being a lesbian by her former husband Charles Knight, and since the death, the old rumors had spread again. Chuck and his former wife had been locked into a bitter custody battle since their separation. Moreover, he was under indictment for allegedly taping the private conversations of Julie and her best friend Gail Bridges. Transcripts of the tapes reveal a warm relationship between the two women; however, their intimacy is open to interpretation, and the questions they raise ultimately do not resolve allegations that the two women have been engaged in a long-term lesbian relationship. Indeed, Julie Knight has threatened to sue anyone who calls her a lesbian.

Yet she has one problem, another former husband who claims that such a relationship is nothing new. Moreover, he and his wife have become close friends with his successor, Chuck Knight and his new wife, Laurie Wells. Julie's first husband, John Eaves, loves his job as a non-faculty executive at the sprawling University of Houston. The job is important. He is in charge of the campus, literally. Eaves is the university's maintenance major domo, the fix-it guy who the administration goes to when the hands-on, blue-collar work of keeping the doors open is needed. Eaves came to the position after working his way up through the ranks. He is respected both on campus and in the greater community where facilities maintenance long ago became a complex and challenging field.

John Eaves remembers his former wife, Julie as being, "a conniving bitch. She'll hold back, hold back, hold back, and then she will screw you."

Eaves still harbors anger at Julie, the rancor, a consequence of their eight-year marriage that ended fifteen years before. "She is quick to do put-downs, and she is quick to make judgments. Once she gets down on you, she is down on you forever."

Eaves gives his former wife credit for one positive trait though. "She is brave enough to go up against just about anybody."

Julie Knight grew up in the Houston Ship Channel town of Deer Park, a suburb on the city's southeast side more noted for the smell of its petrochemical plants than anything else. Near the community, down Battleground

Road, stands the towering 570-foot San Jacinto Monument, a sandstone obelisk built from 1936–1939 as the nation struggled through the Great Depression. It was erected to honor Texas' war for independence with Mexico, and was a work project for Houston's blue-collar labor pool. To its west is Pasadena, the second-largest city in Greater Houston. It has a population of almost 123,000 mostly working-class souls who endure the odor of Ship Channel industries and live under the constant threat of a fatal explosion at one of the plants.

Deer Park didn't thrive until World War II when one of the refineries began to produce toluol, a key component used in the production of TNT.

It was in this explosive atmosphere that Julie, the older of two children, had her turbulent childhood. She went through school and then got out of the house.

Eaves met his former wife in late 1978 when he worked at a Weingarten's supermarket located at the intersection of two busy streets, Shaver and Spencer Highway. "I was unloading a truck and this good-looking girl came up to me and said, 'When are we going out?' I said to myself, Lady, I don't even know you."

But Eaves liked the shapely young woman enough to take her up on her offer. The two eventually married, but money became an issue. "I would come home with a check for $1,700 for a week's work, and then I would go to bed with it in my wallet and wake up the next morning with the check gone and a fifty dollar bill in its place."

Pilferage of his wallet didn't bother John Eaves nearly as much as another foible he says Julie exhibited. He believed that she was bisexual and claims to have witnessed her making love naked with another woman.

In the late 1980s, Julie was still in school often carrying up to 21 semester hours and earning a 4.0 GPA. One evening, John took her to study with another girl who he describes as "an obvious lesbian."

"The girl lived in some apartments behind the Nassau Bay Hilton on Clear Lake," he remembers. "I drove there and parked while Julie went inside to study. I took my fishing rod out to a pier to fish and pass the time. A boat race or parade was going on and I watched for quite some time. Finally, I got bored and walked back to the apartment. I glanced through a window and I saw Julie and the girl on the couch naked and kissing."

Eaves stormed through the door and told his wife that the two of them were leaving.

"We had a big, huge fight," he remembers. "This was not normal. I had planned on making a life with her."

FIVE

Methodists love to get together among themselves. They have been that way since John Wesley founded the Protestant denomination in the Eighteenth Century. Members of Bay Harbor United Methodist Church in League City were no different. Much like their neighbors the Baptists, these parishioners' lives centered on the church and its extended set of social relationships. The Methodists fraternized among themselves with covered-dish suppers, outings, choir practice, Sunday school, house parties, and family excursions to restaurants. It is the nature of things among the devout to spend the bulk of time with like-minded people. The church is also a place in small Texas towns where important business and social connections are made and nurtured.

The Methodists frown upon alcohol. Yet these Christians are far less straitlaced than are their brethren in the Baptist, Church of Christ, and more Pentecostal sects. Methodists accept mankind's foibles as something to be worked upon, not something that will condemn a soul to perdition.

Such was the case among members of Tom Pace's flock at Bay Harbor. Such was the case with Chuck and Julie Knight, Steve and Gail Bridges, and Laurie and Steve Wells. The couples were friends, good friends who were devoted churchgoers. Their kids played together and held parties among themselves and others in the church.

Chuck Knight remembers first meeting Steve and Gail Bridges after he and Julie were invited to come to church by Laurie Wells. Laurie had just met Julie on a commuter bus, Houston Metro's Park and Ride.

"It didn't take long before we were invited to the Wells home in Dickinson for burgers. There were three couples there, the Wells, us, and Steve and Gail Bridges," Chuck Knight remembers.

Knight's first impression of the Bridges was mixed. "They seemed nice, they always seemed nice and they didn't have any outwardly apparent problems," he says.

"Steve was a little more straitlaced than the average person, but he was a public figure, he had an image to uphold in League City, and remember, that was a very, very small town where image counts for everything. He is a State Farm agent. He wears a tie all the time. He pretty much has to be that way because of his position in the community."

Knight was right. Bridges was small-town America personified, a small businessman in a small Texas town. His agency even bought the T-shirts for a local Little League team. Bridges was a do-gooder in the best sense of the word. He had once approached the legendary and intimidating local banker, Walter Hall, to make improvements at League City's Walter Hall Park for the soccer moms in town. The park was named for the owner of the bank. The improvements were made before sundown the same day, and Bridges was a hero. Short of serving on the city council, Steve Bridges was about as high profile as a man can be in the small, tight-knit world of League City.

Chuck Knight's first impression of Gail was more harsh.

"She was a little catty, but then, lots of women are

catty," Knight remembers. "She acted like her poop didn't stink, but lots of women act like their poop doesn't stink."

Chuck and Julie joined the church's young adult Sunday school class, the Pathfinders. Each Sunday, the three couples joined others in the class for fellowship, discussion and prayer, and went to the services in the church to hear Pace's weekly sermon.

Chuck Knight had met his future wife, Julie, at the home of a friend whom he remembers as a matchmaker who promoted the romance among the two divorced but very nice people.

"I remember that she [Julie] came on to me on the way home after she drank too many margaritas," Chuck says. "She had more food on her clothes than in her mouth and I stopped and bought her coffee. On the way home, she asked, 'Am I the kind of person you want to have sex with?' I told her yes, but I thought I had better take her home. I drove her to her mom's house in Pasadena. We dated for about six months, then were married by a JP in Pasadena, Texas."

Chuck was in the bucks, enjoying a successful career, earning the good life that comes with multiple degrees and a good job. He had bought Dom Parignon for the party, perhaps to show off his good fortune to the couple's friends partying at their home at 2010 Cutter Drive.

Julie too was doing well, albeit not as well as she told a close neighbor. Chuck remembers hearing from a friend that he was lucky to have such a successful wife, a wife who was chief financial officer for Zapata Corporation, the oil company founded by the senior George Bush during the heady days of the 1950s when a Connecticut war hero could come to West Texas and be accepted instantly as an oil man. Chuck thought it strange that his wife would tell such a tale, and although she worked for the company, she was merely an accountant. She didn't even hold a CPA.

The couple first attended a Baptist church, but quickly switched to the much more fashionable Bay Harbor Methodist. Chuck and Julie joined the church's young adult Sunday school class, the Pathfinders. Each Sunday, the three couples joined others in the class for fellowship, discussion and prayer, and went to the services in the church to hear Pace's weekly sermon. They mixed well with the other young and prosperous members of the congregation. Both were gregarious, fun. They laughed a lot and easily fit in with the parties being thrown almost constantly by the other prosperous young couples of the congregations. Quickly they began to throw parties of their own, including New Years Eve celebrations that grew in popularity each year that the couple held them..

The parties were well known and much anticipated among members of the church, as well as by the two very sociable hosts. "These parties had become famous. We drank, and we had people from our Sunday school class there."

On December 31, 1993, Charles and Julie Knight's party got out of hand as the evening went on and as members of the class imbibed the beverages forbidden by the church.

The couple also had a wild side, according to Chuck. They liked to show their individuality, despite the piety they showed their friends and neighbors in the church. Chuck had an ear pierced, while Julie pierced her belly button.

As the New Year's Eve party went on, couples loosened their inhibitions and sang karaoke as the clock ticked relentlessly toward the bewitching hour of midnight.

Julie was pregnant, Chuck remembers. She and Laurie

Wells sat on a couch in the couple's living room. As alcohol took effect, the two women lost control of bodily functions.

"Julie and I peed on the couch," Laurie recalls.

"One of the guests got a little too drunk," Chuck remembers. "There were mostly church people there, and he started talking about black men's members, you know, their dicks. Somebody snitched everybody off to the preacher. He told us that we shouldn't have alcohol at Sunday school functions."

After the party, wild by Methodist standards, Laurie says that she was kicked out of the clique of parishioners who surrounded Chuck and Julie Knight.

But the relationship between the Knights and the Bridgeses warmed. The fun-loving Chuck Knight, an electro-geek/computer whiz guy down the street was an interesting diversion from Steve Bridges' world of actuarial tables and mind numbing Texas insurance regulations. The two men liked each other and developed a friendship separate from their involvement in Sunday school class at Bay Harbor.

Julie and Gail also became fast friends, comparing notes on child rearing. To a degree they were raising their kids on a parallel course.

The two couples increasingly became inseparable, doing the fun things that people with similar interests do. Dinner was an integral part of the relationship and the four South Shore residents loved the good life they led, loved a nice evening in a good restaurant with just them, no kids, no other couples, just the four—Julie and Gail, and Chuck and Steve.

But neighbors in South Shore Harbor began to notice something different about Gail and Julie—a glance, a touch, a word here and there that women don't normally use to each other in the course of a platonic friendship. There were whispers, the kind of ugly, catty whispers that happen in a small town where there is little to talk about other than where the next bunco game would take place, the next day's school menu, or what was happening for the week at the church. The whispers grew more intense as time went by. Neighbors talked among themselves that the relationship between Julie Knight and Gail Bridges was something more than two "girlfriends" sharing time together. The talk in South Shore Harbor was that the women were having a lesbian affair.

The former mayor heard it, as did at least one fellow former council member.

One neighbor, a schoolteacher, claimed that he saw the two women kissing each other. Another said that Julie and Gail had shared a romantic kiss at the church itself. A growing number of League City townsfolk believed that something was going on between the two, while the husbands were oblivious.

One friend, Vanessa Dirks, had known Gail well before Julie came along. However, when Chuck Knight's wife came into her friend's life, almost immediately she began to feel the heat of jealousy. "It was as if Julie wanted Gail all to herself."

Julie Knight frightens Vanessa Dirks to this day.

Dirks remembers Julie's appearance at that time.

"She always dressed like a country bumpkin. People would say, 'What's wrong with your friend, that she dresses that way?'"

Dirks lived the good life in her $600,000 South Shore Harbor home, taking her children to the best of schools like most of her neighbors. But Dirks says that she discovered the dark side of Julie Knight as she became closer to her friend Gail Bridges.

Dirks claims, "Julie harassed me and Gail was part of it. I would characterize all of those people as stalkers, Julie tried to run over me in my driveway, and they were very mean to my children. She literally went up the curb after me in her Lexus. I'm afraid of her. I don't want to run into her at night."

Dirks never reported the alleged incident to the police.

"The two women were strange," she remembers. "But both of their husbands were civil and rational people. Both couples were active in the fitness center. Gail was a respected person, an all-American person. They were like the all-American family."

Dirks finally sold her home and moved to another section of South Shore Harbor, she says because the harassment by Julie Knight became so great. "I moved my child to a Clear Lake school because of them. I think that they are real different people. They put a tape recorder in my garage at one point, and I got crank calls in the middle of the night," she claims.

Dirks also remembers that there was talk in the neighborhood about the special relationship that both women seemed to have with each other. "When Gail had [breast augmentation] surgery, she recovered at Julie's house. I just think that they are really weird people. I feel sorry for the kids. Why didn't she stay at home and recover? There are a lot of people in this loop, a lot of people who have been affected. South Shore was like a Peyton Place, a crazy place."

Dirks remembers how immediately after Gail began to appear in public again following the implant surgery, her wardrobe changed dramatically. "She was sexy. After Gail got the implants, she was a different person."

Laurie Wells had a similar experience with Julie Knight over the friendship of Gail, she says. Laurie and

Gail had been close friends, but when Julie came into the circle, she found that Gail was drifting away from the friendship. Eventually, what had been a warm bond had become one of only passing acquaintance.

Both Julie and Laurie used the same day care for their children near the Gulf Freeway, a nickname for I-45, the interstate highway that connects Houston and Galveston. Now there started to be trouble, and eventually, "Julie got my kids thrown out of the day care," Laurie claims. There were problems in ballet class as well.

Things now deteriorated rapidly in the marriage of Chuck and Julie Knight. The two owned a condo near Colorado Springs and over Thanksgiving, 1998, they took a mini-vacation. Sitting in a Pizzaria Uno franchise, his wife stunned Chuck Knight.

"You don't trust me," she said. "You have never trusted me."

The two stayed in Keystone five days, but much of the time, he claims, his wife was on the phone to League City, speaking with Gail Bridges. "She was on the phone three hours a day, and my long distance bill was $300."

Knight wasn't the only one paying hefty tolls to a long distance company for the trip. Steve Bridges gave his wife Gail a $300 pre-paid calling card to use to speak to her friend.

Rumors of the alleged but unproven lesbian affair spread through South Shore Harbor as fast as a Texas blue norther making its way south.

Things were going well financially for Chuck and Julie Knight. When Julie's great aunt Helen Elliott, an 82-year-old widow from Arkansas came to live with them things got even better. With her she brought the lifetime savings that she and her husband, a Smith Barney broker, had socked away for old age. The two had made sure that there would be enough money for Helen or her husband through their dotage. When he died, the elderly woman came to the open arms of her Texas family member.

Julie Knight, Helen's favorite niece, was made trustee of a living trust that Chuck claims amounted to $2.5 million. The elderly woman suffered from senile dementia and needed little more than a warm place to sleep, good meals and a roof over her head as she waited to end her days. By all accounts she was happy in her new home in South Shore Harbor, although she did cause a stir in the normally quiet streets when she once walked down the thoroughfare in front of the Knight home naked.

When Helen moved in, things changed financially, Chuck says. The couple was already making good money, but because his wife was able to spend her aunt's money as she saw fit, things got even better. "She would have me deposit $6,000 a month into our personal account."

Chuck and Julie Knight were living the American dream by any standard. But like many couples, the Knights lived above their means.

"We were spending seventy thousand dollars more each year than I made," Chuck says. "Our American Express bill was sometimes twenty to thirty thousand dollars per month.

"She burned the cash on a Lexus, paying for it in about two chunks, paid about $70,000 for an addition to the home. She would have people come out and fix things, then fix them again.

"And she spent the money on toys for the kids, and clothes. There were clothes still in boxes.

"Sometimes she would get a stretch limo and take friends to dinner," Chuck remembers.

"When we went skiing, she would hire a personal instructor for the whole day, every day we were there," he remembers. "That's big bucks."

One favorite haunt of the couples was Ruggles, an icon of a restaurant in the heart of the city's famed Montrose District, where patrons dine on trendy dishes with a Texas/California flair, along with desserts that can only be described as divine. It was in this atmosphere Charles Knight says that his world began to unravel. New Year's Eve had always held a special spot for Chuck and Julie Knight. Instead of hosting a party, the couple decided to go to the restaurant on December 31, 1998, joining their friends Steve and Gail Bridges.

The night progressed predictably, the girls talking girl talk, and Steve and Chuck making light conversation with the gregarious Chuck doing most of the talking. Chuck glanced at his wife and noticed that her hand was under the table, and then looked up at her arm.

Chuck was a body builder, and he was attuned to muscles and how they appeared—how they flexed. "I noticed that Gail's bicep was turned outward toward Julie. That was not natural for the place where her hand should have been under the table and in the lap."

Chuck Knight put his hand under the table and placed it upon the knee of his wife.

"They both jumped a mile," Charles Knight remembers. Steve Bridges recalls the incident as well. Chuck Knight was profoundly troubled by what he believed he had seen. He had suspected that something was going on. Now he believed solidly that his wife and the wife of his friend from church were engaged in a lesbian relationship. A few days later, he heard a conversation between the two women over the intercom of their home.

"I didn't get to kiss you enough today," he claims that he heard one of the women say.

"Every floor of our house was cordless," he recalls, so it was easy to listen to anything over the intercom. Gail then went on that she didn't like her lips, and Julie said, no, they are perfect. "I like them just the way they are."

Later, Knight went into his wife's bedroom and confronted Julie.

"What the hell is going on?" he asked.

Julie Knight was standing in the closet.

"She collapsed in a big pile," he says. Charles Knight demanded that his wife go to a therapist.

Bridges had noticed the strange reaction of the two women at Ruggles, but thought little of it at the time, oblivious to what Knight was convinced was going on. On January 15, 1999, Martin Luther King's birthday, Chuck Knight went to Steve Bridges with the revelation that he believed that their wives were lovers.

"At first he didn't believe it," Knight remembers. "He did by the time I was done."

Knight says that his friend then began coming over constantly, to the point that he had to tell him to stay away. "I said, 'You need to go home and tend to your thing. I need to stay home and tend to mine.' I wasn't mad, but I needed him to go away. He just kept coming over.

"Again I tried to get Julie to go to a therapist, but she told me, 'If I walked to the edge of the cliff, I won't come back,'" he recalls.

Finally, the Knights entered counseling. What Chuck claims he heard there shocked him. "Julie told me during a session that she had fondled Gail's vagina."

Chuck now told stories to anybody he saw about his wife and the wife of his friend.

Steve Bridges claims that he didn't relay stories of the alleged lesbian relationship at all and kept his mouth shut about the affair Chuck was alleging publicly.

Today he says, "It was there for all to see. I've had so many people tell me that they saw them kissing in the parking lot of the grocery store, here and there. I didn't have to tell any stories. They were seen, man, they were seen."

"They would lick whipped cream off each other," Chuck would tell friends.

"The two of them went into a tanning booth together, a booth for one person," he told others.

In April 1999, Knight says that the therapist told him to get out of the marriage.

By this time, he was afraid for his life, he now claims.

"I heard Julie and Gail ask, 'Where is Dr. Kavorkian when we need him?'" he says today.

In early May, Julie Knight moved out of the fashionable home she shared with her husband. "But she kept coming back."

"I slept in the guest room with a chair propped against the door knob," he says. "Julie asked Gail to have me killed when I was in Orlando," he claims today.

On other occasions, Chuck slept behind the couple's upright piano cuddling a baseball bat, he says.

Following the scare, Knight filed a complaint with the local police on April 1, 1999, alleging a terroristic threat made by his wife, but no charges were subsequently pursued by authorities.

Gail and Julie left something behind when they moved out of their homes—the tapes Chuck Knight had made of their conversations—tapes that would ultimately result in a wiretap indictment against him.

Transcripts of the tapes reveal a relationship between Gail Bridges and Julie Knight that to the casual reader may sound like intimate conversations between two lovers. The two dispute the allegation, saying that Chuck

Knight spliced them together in such a manner so that they make the two appear in the worst possible light.

In a conversation, Gail asks Julie, "I miss you so bad, honey. Do you miss me so bad?" The tapes reveal a conversation in which Julie speaks of an abortion. In one of the most suggestive lines in the transcript, Julie says, "I'm going to walk in the house, take a shower and crawl into bed and find you there waiting for me."

The two women speak then of forbidden fruit.

"Oh God, that sounds good. What'd we do?" Gail continues.

"I don't know what we did, but he should have never tempted us with this if he wasn't like gonna let us have it. All I've got to say about it," Julie responds.

"You sure it was him tempting?" Gail asks.

"Really, Satan?" Gail answers.

"Think about it now," Julie says.

"Could be, could be, could be, could be Satan," Julie answers.

"All I know is, it's a perfect fit," Gail says to Julie. "Anywhere you put it, it fits."

"Put it on me anytime you feel like it, darling," Julie says.

"And I do," Gail tells her.

To the casual reader the words on the transcript sound as if Satan has given them the gift of forbidden fruit, or even lead to a more graphic interpretation, the discussion of the use of a sex toy.

The transcript again reveals the women's purported intimate relationship when Julie calls Gail from the frozen food section of a local supermarket.

"Oh, pineapple sherbet, ooh, cherry limeade sure be yummy. Guess what part of the store I'm in?" she asks.

"Frozen foods dairy," Gail answers prosaically.

"I'd rub it on your body and lick it off," Julie tells her, leading the conversation to more intimate realms.

"Uh-uh, cold now," Gail responds, disinterested.

"I recall somebody telling me they's gonna bake me a cake and smear it all over my" Julie says. "And eat it. I'm getting there baby, it'll happen okay. I just feel like poo-poo. My throat is as dry as the Mojave Desert."

"That's the way mine was. Took two bottles of Gatorade."

"And my teeth feel like something crawled across it and left their trail behind," Julie continues.

"Lemons, cleaned mine and flossed them," Gail tells her friend.

"Ooh and you can share that with me now," Julie responds, continuing to speak provocatively to her friend.

Minutes later the two use the word that has caused them so much grief.

"You are a whiney baby, a grumpy whiney baby," Julie says to Gail.

"Cold now," Gail responds, still complaining.

"Can't help ya. Wish I could. Unacceptable. Unacceptable. Un-natural. It's un-natural. For me to want to help you. It's un-natural for me to want to take care of you if you're hurting or sick," Julie chides.

"I know," Gail says.

"Lesbians. What a word," Julie responds.

"I know, what is that? Funny," Gail says.

SIX

The separation of Gail and Steve Bridges, Chuck and Julie Knight, and Steve and Laurie Wells caused a sensation in South Shore Harbor. The local Methodist congregation was rocked to its Wesleyan foundations by the allegations regarding some of its most prominent members. Gail and Julie added fuel to the conflagration of rumors regarding them when they moved out of their homes. Julie Knight took up residence at Las Palmas, a gated enclave on El Camino Village. Gail Bridges moved in across the street from her.

Chuck Knight had hired Blue Moon Investigations to tail his wife in early 1999 for a brief two hours, but paid the fee for the firm's required four-hour minimum. He got a report the following day stating that the surveillance had been unsuccessful.

The Bachas, owners of Blue Moon, have a simple philosophy that bypasses the complexities of ethics regarding conflicts of interest that govern other professions. Once a case is closed by Blue Moon, it is over, and the firm is open and eligible for hire by anybody, including the person they had previously investigated. The firm's owners claim that switching clients and sides is within the ethical boundaries set by their professional trade group. Other private investigators dispute that claim.

Such was the case when Julie Knight hired the firm several months later to tail Chuck Knight, Blue Moon's old client, and his new girlfriend. Laurie Wells, her old rival for the friendship of Gail Bridges, was now estranged from her husband Steve and was dating Julie's former husband.

A Blue Moon investigator tailed the two to Brandon, Florida, where they were visiting Laurie's family. She and her lover were videotaped on a rental car shuttle at the Florida airport on their return home, then again at George Bush Intercontinental Airport upon their arrival in Houston. Today, the two are married and expecting a child. They laugh that they unwittingly escaped Blue Moon's surveillance for several days of lovemaking in Sarasota.

But the Blue Moon video would prove Chuck Knight's and Laurie Wells' undoing in their later divorce and custody battles, which dragged through the Galveston County courts for years and still continue today.

Knight vs. Knight and *Wells vs. Wells* proved to be two of the nastiest family court battles in the history of Texas. Both Charles Knight and Laurie Wells ultimately lost custody, and even visitation rights to their children in a Galveston venue. Moreover, both had angered the judge, Susan Baker, and their jury, by their antics in the courtroom. Their custody battle took a decided turn for the worse when attorneys for Julie Knight produced Blue Moon video of Chuck and Laurie taken during their clandestine trip to Florida. The attorney for Steve Wells in turn portrayed his client as the soul of stability, the ultimate loving small town dad. Importantly, Wells believed himself to be just that, cut from the cloth as his father Herb.

By August 1999, Chuck Knight knew that his former wife planned to destroy him when she answered an interrogatory in their case.

Julie refused to answer questions regarding whom she had had intimate sexual contact with and what health care providers she had seen in the last five years. Moreover she would not answer questions of who she had purchased gifts for in amounts more than $200. However she answered in detail why it was in the best interests of the children that Charles Knight not be appointed by the court to be managing conservator. The answers were not pretty and may have further angered Baker, an ardent feminist once active in the Democratic Party of Galveston County.

Julie said in the interrogatory, "Charles Knight has also made every effort to contact each and every parent of our children's friends and inform them that he believes that I am a lesbian and that their children should not be around our children or me."

Knight admits that he told anybody who would listen that he believed his ex-wife was a lesbian.

She also said, "My children have cried for hours because their father and Steve Bridges have told them that their mother did not love them, and that Steve Bridges was going to be their new mother." She also answered that her daughter had asked her what a lesbian is because "that is what her daddy calls me."

Julie Knight then got down to business in her attempt to destroy her former husband by answering the questions in his own written interrogatory.

"In late 1987/early 1988, against my wishes my husband inserted a banana into my vagina while I was menstruating, took it out, ate it and called it 'strawberries and bananas.'

"On numerous occasions, my husband has requested that I hold his head down so that he could perform fellatio on himself.

"My husband has asked me to urinate on him and in his mouth or into a champagne glass for him so that he could quench his thirst. He made this request of me on numerous occasions, even though he knew that I was repulsed by this request.

"My husband purchased and presented me with a strap-on dildo. He requested that I wear it and insert it into his rectum. He also requested that I wear it and insert it into his rectum while I pretended that he was Gail.

"On numerous occasions, my husband has initiated sex against my will while I was on the telephone with a friend. He would tell me to pretend that I was having sex with my friend while he proceeded to have intercourse with me."

Julie's reference to being asked to have imaginary sex with a friend while her husband was allegedly forcing his affections upon her paint Chuck Knight as a boor at best, and a rapist at worst. It also begs the question of which friend she is referring to having a telephone conversation with as she engaged in sex with her husband.

"My husband was relentless in his requests that we have sex with another woman. He also made countless requests that I have oral sex with my friend so that he could film it and sell the video on the Internet. He requested that my friend and I get on the bed and that he would get in between us and take photos."

But Julie, in the interrogatory, acknowledged that there was some unusual contact between her husband and her "friend."

"He would suck on my friend's toes and he drew a tattoo on her. He has painted my friend's toenails on several occasions. My husband would also invite my friend over to watch movies and then begin sucking on her toes."

She continued saying, "My husband was constantly trying to convince me and my friend to tongue each other so that he could watch.

"My husband was constantly requesting that my friend show him her bare breasts. My husband offered, on several occasions, to pay for my friend's breast implants so long as she would let him touch her breasts and look at them whenever he requested.

"My husband and his friend frequently attempted to get me and my friend intoxicated so that they could convince us to perform oral sex with each other so that my husband and his friend could watch and film the oral sex acts and sell it on the Internet."

Charles Knight emphatically denies the sexual allegations made by his former wife in the document.

The interrogatory was only the beginning of the problems of Charles Knight and Steve Bridges. Julie Knight, Gail Bridges and Steve Wells took seven tapes to the office of Galveston County Criminal District Attorney Michael Guarino charging that Chuck Knight and Steve Bridges had illegally taped private conversations between the two women.

In January 1999, a Galveston County grand jury indicted the two men, stating that they "did then and there intentionally intercept and endeavor to intercept a wire and an oral communication, to wit: the telephone conversation of Julie Knight, by installing a recording device to the phone line at her residence."

The indictment against Steve Bridges was later dismissed, and he quickly reached accommodation with

Gail. The indictment against Charles Knight remained active for years.

Lindsey Harris had spent much of the ten summers since her parents' divorce with her dad and his new wife Clara, in Texas. The Hilliard Davidson High School cheerleader had come to like the woman, even reaching the point recently of referring to her as "Mom."

She had been four years old when her parents divorced and she had grown accustomed to David's new life with Clara as she grew older. Now, at 16, Clara had been a large part of her life for ten years. She watched her father and the woman grow in their relationship.

"They loved each other," she remembers. "They told each other that they loved each other all the time. They got along very well."

When her twin brothers were born, Lindsey began to notice that Clara didn't pay as much attention to her dad as she had before because she was always doting on the infants.

In fact, David had told Lindsey recently that he wasn't getting any attention at all from his wife. When Lindsey had arrived at the mansion in late June, she noticed something different. Before, she had felt that she was a part of the family. Now, Clara's life constantly revolved around Lindsey's half brothers.

She noticed something else. There were photographs of the twins "all over the house. There was none of me."

When Lindsey first arrived at the office for her annual summer job in June, she met Gail Bridges for the first time and she liked her instantly.

"I thought she was really nice and really pretty," she recalled. "She was petite and bubbly. Her hair was perfectly in place and her nails were done."

Lindsey noticed something else. Susan Hanson was

"nice to her face," but behind Gail Bridge's back was another matter.

Lindsey's first recollection of anything going on between her father and Gail occurred when "I saw him put his hand on her leg. At the time I didn't think anything of it."

As she saw David and the woman more each day, she realized that the relationship between them was beyond the way a professional treats an employee.

"I was really confused, he wasn't like that," she said. "Gail was the aggressor."

On July 16, 2002, Lindsey was at home with her father.

"He was playing the piano and it was getting pretty late and we were getting worried [because Clara wasn't usually out at that time of night]," she recalls.

When Clara came home, David followed her upstairs and Lindsey stayed downstairs on the computer. She heard them talking but didn't think much about it.

The following morning though, Lindsey was again on the computer when she heard yelling upstairs. The two were fighting again.

"I felt really bad for her," Lindsey remembered.

The girl and her stepmother almost immediately developed a bond that the two hadn't enjoyed before. "We became very close," Lindsey says. "We went shopping. She told me everything. It made me feel important."

Lindsey had suffered her own frustrations regarding the affair and had confronted her father. His attitude made her even more confused and frustrated. "He told me that I don't understand because I don't live there," she remembered.

As Lindsey, Clara, and David got into his Suburban, Clara told the girl and her father that she was planning to fire Gail when they arrived at the office.

David protested. When they were at the office, Lindsey was the first one through the door.

"I was really upset," Lindsey later said. "I was lashing out at Gail and she was acting like it wasn't a big deal."

When Clara Harris came through the door, Lindsey saw her take Gail by the arm and escort her to the back office.

"She was very mad, but she was professional," Lindsey said.

As David and Lindsey Harris watched through the glass of a set of French doors, Clara Harris fired her rival. The teenager looked at her father.

"He looked very hurt," she says. "He looked very sad and he didn't want Gail to know."

After the firing, after the crying, David and Clara Harris went to a noon luncheon meeting. After all, the two had a business to run.

The following day, July 18, Clara told Lindsey that she and David had a long talk the night before, talking late into the night. He had told her in detail where he and Gail had gone, and what they had done. Clara related to Lindsey that David and his lover's favorite places were Perry's Steak House, a Chinese café, the Aquarium Restaurant in Kemah, a room at the Westin Galleria, and the Nassau Bay Hilton. She confirmed to her stepdaughter that her husband and Gail bridges had a sexual relationship.

On Monday, Lindsey Harris first learned from Clara that her father was going to meet with Gail at Perry's the following Wednesday at 6 p.m. to formally end the affair.

"She was kind of nervous about it. She had doubts," Lindsey said. "She kept doing her hair and kept going shopping. She was nervous."

Lindsey assured her stepmother that everything would be okay, but Clara continued to be stressed about the meeting.

There was a good reason. David had told his wife that he missed Gail Bridges.

Tuesday, July 23, 2002, Lindsey would spend the day with her stepmother, the friendship and common pain brought on by David's infidelity a bond between the young girl and the older woman.

The two of them got into Clara's silver S-Class Mercedes and drove. Eventually, they were on NASA Road 1, the lake to the south and its residential neighborhoods and small businesses to the north. They approached the Hilton, and Clara instructed Lindsey, who was driving, to pull the car in. The two parked in the smallish parking lot in front of the hotel and went in.

On a whim, Clara walked up to the afternoon desk clerk, Garrett Clark, and asked to see a room.

The clerk gave her the key to a mini-suite, and Clara and Lindsey entered the elevators located on the east side of the lobby and went upstairs.

"We went there to see where they went," Lindsey later recalled. "When we got into the room, she was calm. She said, 'Well, I guess this is where they spent their time.'"

Clara looked out the window of the room at Windemere, the yacht club below. It was there that on Valentine's Day, 1992, she and David had been married. She wiped a tear from her eye.

The two went downstairs again, down to the hotel's restaurant, the Marina Bar and Grill, on the south side of the lobby, and ordered lunch. Clara wept quietly, finally overcome by confronting the fact that her husband and the woman she had so recently fired had likely made love in a room much like the suite she and his daughter had just left.

"I told her it was wrong," Lindsey says. "But I told her I still loved him."

Lindsey and Clara left the restaurant and began to drive again. This time Clara instructed Lindsey to drive to Bay Area Boulevard and park in front of the Morgan Stanley Dean Witter office building.

Clara called Blue Moon Investigations to say that she was on the way. During the drive, Lindsey recalls that Clara was "nervous, angry, confused." When the two finally arrived at the offices of the private investigators, "she was calm but then she started to cry."

"I didn't know why we were at Blue Moon," Lindsey said. "When I figured it out, I felt that they were invading his privacy."

After the two left the office of the investigators, they returned to the mansion.

Julie Knight was at Gail's helping her hang blinds on July 24, when David called. He begged to see her again that evening at their old haunt, Perry's Steak House. She reluctantly agreed, but changed the meeting place to the Hilton.

Julie cautioned Gail Bridges not to go, but to wait to see David again until after he was divorced. Gail related to a friend that Julie told her that she had a vision of a "mad Colombian woman coming after her with a knife or something."

Gail retorted that she was a big girl and that David would be with her at the hotel. Gail said that she thought the Hilton would be a public place, and after all, she and David would be discreet. She told Julie that the meeting would be innocent. She would not spend the night with David. She would just sit in the lobby and talk.

That evening Gail Bridges made the short drive from her comfortable two-story home in Clear Lake City to the Hilton. She didn't have much left from the marriage to Steve Bridges besides the children.

When she arrived at the hotel she pulled into the parking lot on NASA Road 1 and briefly thought about parking in front of the hotel as she had always done. This time, however, she pulled around back, parking in a space with a clear view of the boat basin behind the hotel, and beyond that, the view across Clear Lake all the way to the high Kemah/Seabrook Bridge.

On July 24, 2002, Clara was extremely nervous as the hour approached for David's 6 p.m. meeting with Gail.

Lindsey watched as Clara answered a call from Susan Hanson.

Susan gave Clara directions to the home of Gail Bridges, located at 15914 Lake Lodge Drive. Gail had bought the two-story house in a fashionable neighborhood not far from the Johnson Space Center for $211,000. County appraisal records show that she owes a balance of $159,200 to Countrywide. A block away at 15900 Manor Square Drive was the $155,560 home of Julie Knight.

Susan had been following David to Gail's home after work. She called to tell Clara that she had lost him at a light, but had the address for her.

Clara was upset and crying, Lindsey said, as she listened to the conversation.

Clara and Lindsey again got into Clara's Mercedes and

went looking for David and Gail. The two pulled into the parking lot of Perry's, but there was no sign of the couple.

They then drove to the home of Gail Bridges and pulled into its deserted driveway. Nobody appeared to be home, but Clara got out of the car, went through a gate and peeked into the side door of the garage looking for David's car. The garage was empty.

"She was on a mission to find out where he was," Lindsey said. "She was crying."

The two continued Clara's mission, driving to Tommy's Patio Café, a spot David had mentioned when he had ticked off the haunts where he and Gail met. The two were nowhere to be seen. "She was now confused," Lindsey recalled.

Clara remembered that she wasn't the only one looking for David Harris and Gail Bridges. She dialed the after-hours number of Blue Moon Investigations and left a message. Clara now got on NASA Road 1, the picturesque drive along the north shore of the lake. Clara wasn't sightseeing though, as so many did when they made the drive between the two ends of the short highway between the small towns of Webster and Seabrook. The Hilton, she guessed, was probably on David's agenda of likely places to stop that evening.

Clara couldn't contain herself. She had pushed for everything she had ever gotten in life, and this was no different. It was time to push again, despite Blue Moon's rule about not calling until the following afternoon. Clara was a client of the firm and believed that she was in a position to demand a response at any time, day or night. After all, she had paid the fee, cash up-front. There was no answer, so she left another message.

"She was still determined to find where he was," Lindsey said. "I was driving, and we drove next to the

Kemah Aquarium. They were not there either. She was still confused."

The two crossed the high bridge on Texas 146 that separates Kemah from Seabrook, then turned left and headed back west on NASA Road 1 toward Friendswood.

"We were going to forget about it and go shopping," Lindsey remembers.

Then things changed with a telephone call that would ultimately lead to the loss of David Harris' life. At 8:30 p.m., as the two were heading to the mall, Lucas Bacha returned the second of Clara's messages. Although he was unfamiliar with the details of the case, he was aware that the firm had assigned an investigator who had been reporting in. Bacha told Clara that her husband and the woman were at the hotel and currently under surveillance, not knowing that the client was already there.

"They are on the fourth or sixth floor," he said. "Be patient and you will get a full report tomorrow."

"A man said he knew where my dad was and that he couldn't tell her until the next day," as Lindsey remembered the call. "He did anyway."

Clara Harris' world came to an end at that moment. All of her hopes and dreams for a lifetime with David crashed around her, consuming her soul with the deadly fire of jealousy. From that moment on, Clara's charmed life would never be the same. The infidelity of David Harris with Gail Bridges was all-consuming, eating at her gut and pitting her soul in a deadly battle with her desire to have him back and her desire to separate Gail from him.

Lindsey could see the change come over her stepmother, but she could do little besides humor the woman.

Clara Harris clicked off the cell phone and dialed her number at home. She told the governess, Maria Gonzalez, to pack her husband's best clothes in the couple's oldest suitcase and place it outside the door in the garage, and to throw the remainder of his clothes in the trash.

"Go back to the Hilton," Clara then ordered Lindsey.

"I'll go there," the teenager replied, thinking that she wanted to comfort her stepmother.

The two parked the Mercedes in the middle of the front row of parking spaces just opposite the hotel's entrance. They got out and walked directly to the front desk.

The desk clerk, Garrett Clark, recognized them from the day before. Clara asked for her husband's room by name, and then when he said that there was nobody registered by that name, she asked if they were registered under Gail Bridges' name. Again, she was told that there was nobody registered at the Hilton by that name.

"My son is sick," she told Clark. "I must find my husband."

Clark again told her that there was nobody registered by that name at the Hilton.

He didn't lie. When he had taken the cash from David Harris, he hadn't bothered with the niceties of asking for his driver's license, asking for the license number of the car he was driving, or having the man sign a registration card.

Garrett Clark had taken the cash from David Harris and handed him the key to room 604.

The two women walked to the back of the lobby, past the Marina restaurant and out a back door of the hotel onto a small concrete porch leading to the pool, marina, and parking lot. They walked down the steps in the direction of the hotel guests' cars neatly parked side by side. In one section of the lot, the pavement was white, paved with concrete next to the hotel's loading docks. This was employee parking. The other half of the lot was black, paved with asphalt, reserved for hotel guests and visitors to the restaurant, lounge and meeting rooms.

Clara and Lindsey didn't have to look hard. Parked in the center of the small employee lot facing south was the black Lincoln Navigator owned by Gail Bridges.

Clara Harris exploded, running toward the car. She grabbed the rear windshield wiper and bent it in half, then scratched her car keys along the side of the luxury SUV. She bent the front wipers as well. On the bumper hitch, Gail Bridges had purchased an insert decorated with the image of a heart. Clara looked angrily at it, and broke off the bottom tip. Finally, Clara took the keys to her silver Mercedes and began to scratch the word adulterer.

Clara's fury was spent momentarily. She walked again toward the back entrance of the hotel. Nearby, families frolicked in the July Texas sun as they splashed and swam in the Hilton's pool, not noticing the angry woman in the parking lot. Beyond the pool, sailboats bobbed in the small marina next to the hotel, their halyards' metal parts tinkling against the boats' aluminum masts in a pleasant sound heard at every yacht club worldwide, the yachts-man's wind chimes.

At the glass back door leading to the parking lot and pool, Lindsey and Clara devised a plan to smoke David out of the sixth-floor room. Inside the hotel, guests were filling the Marina Bar and being seated in the restaurant. It was a typical summer day at the resort hotel.

The women had decided that one of them would call and tell David that one of the children was ill. It was a good plan, because one of the twins, Bradley, frequently suffered from asthma attacks.

Lindsey dialed the number of David's cellular phone.

He answered, standing in the upstairs hotel room next to his lover.

"You need to come home," she said. "Bradley's sick."

David answered that he would head to the Friendswood mansion immediately.

Clara and Lindsey waited a minute, then another. Finally, Clara could stand it no longer as she watched the elevator alcove to no avail.

This time, Clara called her husband, ordering him to come home to care for his son. David answered that if the child was so sick, why didn't she head to the hospital and he would meet her there? No, she insisted. It was his responsibility to come home.

David told his wife that he was on his way.

By this time, Clara Harris had gone through the glass doors to watch the elevator as she called David.

Lindsey Harris knew that there was trouble on the way. She had the presence of mind to get her stepmother outside again.

"If there was going to be a fight, it wouldn't happen inside," Lindsey recalled thinking.

"She was calm until she saw Dad and Gail come out," she remembers. "She ran inside. She was ready to go inside and fight."

Clara exploded again, this time at the woman who came out of the elevator hand-in-hand with her husband.

"She began hitting Gail," Lindsey Harris says. "She tore her shirt off. It was a big fight."

Thirty minutes before the fight broke out Clara Harris had turned to her stepdaughter and uttered words that would contribute toward sealing her fate.

"I could kill him and get away with it for how he has been acting," Clara told Lindsey, anger boiling inside her.

SEVEN

Garrett Clark had worked for the Hilton for the past six months when he took cash from David Harris, and handed him a sixth-floor room key in return.

Clark didn't like dealing with cash customers, the transaction caused more work for him because the Hilton's computer system was not really set up to accept cash, he said. "You trick the computer. You do a check-in, check-out on the same day. It cancels itself out of the system."

He was three hours into his 3–11 shift when he checked in David Harris. Clark watched as Harris and a woman with black hair went to the elevator on their way to room 604.

Fifteen minutes later, the two came back to the lobby, and then walked to the restaurant area of the hotel. Five minutes later, they went back to the room.

The afternoon had been routine as it turned into early evening. The cash transaction was the high point of another day at the desk for Clark, a break in the monotony.

At 8:30 p.m., he heard screams in the lobby and looked up from his work. Clark saw Clara Harris pulling the dark straight hair of Gail Bridges as she wrestled her to the hotel floor. He saw her punch her rival in the face with closed fists. The desk clerk leapt over the registration desk, his tall frame flying through the lobby of the hotel toward the two women fighting near the elevators.

Clara lunged, screaming, "You bitch, he's my husband!" She flew at Gail, the emotions of a lifetime of dreams shattered in a moment in the impersonal environs of a hotel lobby.

"This is David Harris, and he's fucking this woman right here," she screamed as she hit Gail and tore at her blouse, eventually ripping it from the woman's body. Hotel employees rushed the couple to separate them, but Clara would break loose and go at the woman again.

At one point, an enraged Clara Harris bit Gail on the leg.

The two grappled over the blouse, pulling it from opposite ends, one obsessed with the hatred of a woman scorned, the other engulfed in blind mindless fear of someone who had already threatened her life just days before. Gail's phone had been under siege, Clara's cellular phone records would later show. The dentist had been relentless in calling her rival. Clara pummeled Gail's head so hard that months later, she still complained that she nearly passed out and was seeing stars, and that her leg still showed a scar from Clara Harris' perfect dentist's teeth.

John Tyler, a 31-year-old public affairs officer at Houston's Baylor College of Medicine was in the lobby of the hotel after attending a church service there.

"I ran in and it was a scuffle happening right inside the doorway," he said. "I ran in there and the woman was beating on another woman and screaming, 'You bitch, He's my husband!' Nobody thought to call the police as David Harris stood helplessly watching his wife, out of control in her fury at him and at Gail Bridges. Finally, he grabbed his wife as Tyler watched him get her in a head-lock and lift her from the body of her rival.

David Harris had made the mistake of trusting his wife with the fact that he was having an affair, and even comparing the attributes of Clara and Gail in the sports bar at the airport. He had assumed that she would handle the matter intellectually, businesslike, like she did everything else in her life.

David Harris needed good relations with Clara. He didn't need this kind of public exposure added to their troubles at home.

Garrett Clark got between the two women, shielding Gail's body with his own as Clara turned her fury on him, assaulting him in the face with her fist.

David Harris didn't intervene, standing to the side of the fray as Clark took the hits.

Lindsey screamed "I hate you!" at her father while hitting him with her purse

Food and Beverage Director Evangelos Smiros, a Greek immigrant who had come to the Hilton from a Galveston hotel a year and a half before, hearing loud noises, looked at his watch as was his habit when something of importance was happening on the property, and noted that the time was 8:30 p.m.

"There was screaming, yelling," he remembers. "There were more than one person yelling, but it was [primarily] a female voice. I initially thought it was teenagers playing in the lobby."

Smiros carried a two-way radio, in constant contact with other managers on the property.

"M.O.D., please come to the lobby immediately," the radio squawked, calling for the manager on duty. Smiros rushed from the bar area to the lobby.

"I saw her screaming and yelling, and I saw another woman who had been assaulted," he remembered. "Her clothing had been torn off and she was trying to cover herself."

The woman he saw was Gail Bridges, her neat black hair now disheveled. He had seen her in the hotel with David once before.

"She seemed frightened," he said. "She was kind of shaking."

By this time, David Harris had pulled his wife off of the body of Gail, whom Clara had knocked to the marble floor. Clara was now five feet away from her rival, her husband ten feet away. Garrett and the bell captain on the 3–11 shift, Blake Doran, 22, separated the two women.

Doran had been on the phone in the back office behind the front desk when he heard the screaming and saw Clark leap over the front desk.

"She was pointing at David Harris," Smiros recalled. "She was saying, 'He's fucking the secretary.' "

Doran remembers Clara Harris saying the words as well, shouting them at her husband.

Smiros stepped between Clara and her husband's lover.

By now, Smiros, Doran, and Clark had been joined in the lobby by the manager on duty, Jose Miranda.

"I asked her to leave the building, and I told her to calm down. Once outside, they were under the port cochere and David Harris was at the front door," Smiros related. "He kept screaming, 'It's over, It's over!' "

Smiros looked at the face of Clara Harris.

"If looks could kill," he remembered.

Meanwhile, inside the hotel, Garrett Clark helped Gail Bridges collect her things.

"Her blouse was off, she was scared for her life, and she was shaking," he remembers.

"Please get me to my car. I have to get out of here," she told Clark.

David Harris walked ten paces behind the desk clerk and Gail Bridges as they went through the front doors of the hotel and walked left along the sidewalk that borders the building, and then walked along a high wall that separates the employee parking and loading area from the front lot. At the end of the wall, the three hastily moved toward the black Lincoln Navigator. Immediately, despite her fear and shock, Gail Bridges noticed something amiss with her car.

She had loved the Navigator. When she was married to Steve, "Old Ed" as she and Julie jokingly called the serious-minded insurance man. There was something special about the luxury SUV that had seemed to fit Gail.

Now something was wrong. Someone had vandalized her car. The realization of who had done it added to Gail's fear and anger, and she only wanted to get out of that parking lot, only wanted to go home to the comfort of her house with its pool and its two stories filled with her things and her kids. She also had a friend nearby who could help her calm down.

Outside the front of the hotel, Evangelos Smiros escorted Clara and Lindsey Harris to the waiting silver Mercedes. He opened the driver's side door and the distraught woman got in, while her stepdaughter, still crying and red in the face, sat down on the passenger side of the car.

Clara Harris started the car, put it into reverse and backed out, turning the rear of the car to the right. Suddenly Smiros was stunned as she threw the Mercedes into gear and spun the tires, burning rubber on the hotel's asphalt parking lot.

"She was screaming again, crying, hysterical, out of control," he says of the woman he watched as she drove the roaring car down the parking lot.

Smiros began to run, cutting across the lot at an angle as if to head her off. Clara then turned left and was driving toward the hotel, he sprinted toward her, only to reach the Mercedes in time to bang his fist on the trunk and run behind the car.

"Stop, you are going to hurt somebody," he screamed futilely at her.

It was evident to Spiros now that Clara had no intention of leaving the hotel property as she passed first one, then a second, and finally a third exit from the parking lot. She raced around the end of the high wall.

As Smiros reached the wall's end, he saw the Mercedes turn sharply around a Black Lincoln Navigator and take aim at the man he had seen in the lobby of the hotel. Smiros heard what he describes as "a thump" as the car struck the orthodontist.

"Oh my God!" the Greek immigrant screamed.

Garrett Clark says that David Harris acted frantic immediately before he was struck by the death blow of the Mercedes.

"He was more concerned for Gail Bridges than he was for himself," he remembers.

The desk clerk and Gail had arrived at her Navigator, and David, according to Clark, was standing in the parking space immediately next to, and slightly to the left of the SUV as he opened the door and she got into the driver's seat.

The desk clerk was helping Gail into the front seat of her car. The tall hotel employee could see over the top of the Navigator, and he saw a nightmare coming at him.

"I saw her driving very fast around the corner and accelerating toward me," he said.

Clara Harris turned the wheel sharply to the right,

grazing the rear of Gail Bridges' car, then grazing Garrett Clark's hip.

Garrett swirled and looked directly into the face of David Harris.

"I saw bulging eyes, a terrified look in his eyes," he remembers. "I saw the Mercedes hit David Harris, then come to a complete stop."

The body of David Harris was thrown 25 feet across the asphalt to the other side of a median, coming to rest near a concrete curb.

"She proceeded to drive over the first median, then across the parking lot, then in circles she drove over the body three times, then did a reverse, then forward again. As Clara Harris drove, her intent to kill her husband evident to Clark, he heard the young girl he had seen inside the lobby screaming, "Stop, please stop, stop the car." Clark said that Clara ran over David twice more after he heard the screams of her stepdaughter begging her to stop.

Clark says that the voice of Lindsey Harris wasn't the only one heard coming from the Mercedes.

"I heard her [Clara Harris] cackling, or laughing as she drove the last two feet before she hit him," he remembered. He later told police that she continued to laugh as she drove the car over her husband.

To his recollection, Garrett Clark believes that Clara Harris may have run over David as many as five times, three times rolling over him as the car moved forward, one time as she backed over him, then another as she drove the car forward again before coming to a complete stop, parking next to the body lying prostrate on the ground.

Clark's statement to police was taken within fifteen

minutes of the murder of David Harris as he leaned in pain from his own injury against the black Lincoln Navigator of Gail Thompson Bridges.

"She was not incoherent," he later said.

Hilton night manager Jose Miranda too had begun his shift at 3 p.m. that day. Like the others his day had been routine, and like Smiros, he heard his hand-held radio crackle with a message that there was trouble in the lobby. He jumped up from his seat in the Marina restaurant where he was doing his daily paperwork. Miranda's watch showed 8:45 p.m., running faster than the others.

By the time he reached the lobby he saw two people lying on the floor.

"My first thought was that somebody had a seizure," a not uncommon occurrence in a busy hotel. He quickly realized that it wasn't a medical emergency he was dealing with, but a fight. He bluffed, telling the assailants that the police had been called as his employees cleared the lobby.

He then went out the front doors, noticed Clara being escorted to her car, and started walking down the sidewalk.

"Here she comes," he heard as he was almost hit by Clara's Mercedes, which he saw round the wall on the hotel's west side.

Running now, he reached the wall's end. When he made the turn, Miranda was devastated by what was happening. David Harris lying on the ground, Clara Harris running over his body, then he watched her run over him again and again. Inside the car, he too heard the terrified screams of Lindsey Harris as she pleaded in vain for the woman next to her to stop killing her father.

Other witnesses, such as League City businesswoman Norma Ramos, had earlier watched Clara and David briefly make eye contact in the parking lot as she heard Lindsey Harris scream, "I can't believe that he is doing this to us."

Ramos then heard him tell his wife and daughter, "This is over, no more, it is ended. You have to realize that this is over. This is the end."

When she heard the impact of the Mercedes hitting something behind the hotel, Ramos told a friend, "Something terrible has happened, call 911."

Vacationers Julie Creger and her fiancé Robert Williams too heard a commotion as they sat by the hotel pool. Then simultaneously, the two heard the chilling words, "Oh my God, he's been hit."

EIGHT

Blue Moon investigator Lindsey Dubec parked her gray late-model Toyota Camry opposite the end of the wall protruding from the hotel and separating the large front parking lot from the two smaller ones in the rear. Earlier, the PI had parked in the lot of the shopping center outside David Harris' orthodontics office and watched him go to a nearby Bank of America ATM. He had then gotten into his Suburban and driven directly to the Hilton. Dubec noted for her report that he arrived at 6:18 p.m. The license number of the SUV, 3NYN88, was duly noted. After he went inside, she circled the lot and spotted Gail Bridges' car parked in the employee parking area near the hotel service section. At the office, she had been given a photo of a smiling David Harris wearing a light jacket and a sweater. She was also given the license tag numbers of his Suburban and Gail's Navigator.

The vantage point was strategic. To the casual observer and to the targets of her investigation as well, the young woman was just another tourist taking videos of her vacation and the hotel in which she spent it. She stationed herself next to a street that ran to the side of the hotel. Across it, tennis players lobbed serves back and forth oblivious to her. A couple of hundred feet south was the entrance to Windemere, the yacht club behind the Hilton.

Her training from Blue Moon had been sketchy—a half day on Saturdays for three weeks—then a field trip out with the chief investigator, and bingo, Lindsey Dubec was a bona fide Blue Moon investigator making $10 per hour and glad to get it. By the time she was assigned the surveillance of David Harris and Gail Bridges, the young woman was a veteran of 30 cases.

For her, the surveillance of David and Gail was just another day at the office. At 6:57 p.m., Lindsey Dubec hit the jackpot for the client, a prominent dentist named Dr. Clara Harris. She observed David and Gail walk out the back door of the hotel to the other woman's car where they stayed twenty minutes, the time being duly logged by Dubec.

The two had been in the bar. He and Gail had had to talk about their relationship. Both were troubled. Both were in love. David told Gail that he was far from ready to break things off with her, that they could still see each other. Gail, despite her reputation in and around League City, was an old-fashioned girl, her small-town upbringing still tugging at her. She told David that as long as he was married, a relationship with him would be out of the question, period. Then she got up, emotion swelling inside her, and walked out of the hotel to her waiting black Navigator. David followed her. The two talked as the sun was setting on Clear Lake, shimmering silver on the water.

At sunset, the sun reflects on the water to give the scene a magical fairy tale beauty, and then each night after the sun goes down, lights twinkle around the lake as boaters travel its waters in the moonlight. After a few minutes talking and watching the sunset, Gail and David walked back into the hotel, this time not stopping at the bar.

As Dubec waited, her friend Andrea Thompson arrived at the hotel to keep her company. The two women talked about skipping out on the surveillance, playing hooky for a little while. They agreed that a trip to Perry's would look like Lindsey was on the job if they were by chance caught by someone from Blue Moon.

Andrea decided to help out her friend and followed Gail and David back into the hotel and watched as David Harris registered with Garrett Clark at the front desk. He then walked briefly back to the Marina to meet Gail, then the two of them walked to the elevators. Out of the investigator's sight, David looked at the number on the key and punched the button to take his lover to the fourth floor.

After David and Gail disappeared into the depths of the hotel, Andrea returned to her friend waiting outside telling Dubec what had happened. The two waited, talking about the things that young women in their twenties naturally gravitate to in conversation. Comparing notes and ideas, they talked about the cheapest venue to hold a wedding. "Think," Lindsey told her friend, "of the money you would save just by going to a justice of the peace."

Lucas and Bobbi Bacha had left their office at 7 p.m. For the two investigators, leaving the office never meant leaving the business. They locked the office and rushed to get home to feed the kids. The family planned to spend a brief evening at Bobbi's parents' home while Lucas installed a new fax machine for Robert Trapani, her father.

On their way out of the office, Lucas and Bobbi noticed that the cell phone of the night shift investigator, Natalia Heckman, had been left behind. The owners forwarded calls from the main office line to Lucas' cell phone. When the calls to his phone started to become frequent, he called Heckman and told her that she had forgotten her phone and asked her to go to the office and get it and start taking calls. The woman went back to Blue Moon and picked it up.

Unaware of the commotion inside the hotel lobby, Lindsey Dubec waited, her surveillance quiet. But outside the front door of the hotel, a young girl now sat on the hard concrete of the sidewalk. Lindsey Harris had heard her father tell Clara "It's over," as she sat cross-legged, crying. Finally, her stepmother took the girl by the arm and said, "Let's go," taking the keys to the Mercedes from her. When the two got into the car, Lindsey looked at Clara Harris and saw that she was still angry, her face distorted from the fight inside.

"She backed out," Lindsey remembered. "She wasn't saying anything. I knew that she was mad because she was red in the face, and she had this evil look on her face."

As Clara gunned the engine and roared down the parking lot, the teenager saw a Hilton employee dodging the Mercedes to get out of the way. "He would have been hit if he didn't get out of the way.

"I was hoping that we were going home," she remembers. But Clara wasn't turning the car to the parking lot exits onto NASA Road 1, or the street paralleling the tennis courts.

"Stop, go the other way!" Lindsey Harris shouted at her stepmother.

Vacationers Julie Creger and Robert Williams reached the battered body of David Harris before anybody else.

"He lay with his feet on the curb and his head away from the curb," Julie remembers. "His right leg and arm were drawn up like a stroke victim."

Immediately, Creger, who was trained in CPR and first aid, knew that she was looking at a very serious injury.

She watched as Clara Harris knelt by her husband and heard her say, "David, look what you made me do."

"She was crying," Creger remembers.

"When I approached, I thought that he had already expired," Creger recalls. "I pushed Clara away. I put my hand on his chest and said, 'You can't move him.'

"There was something coming from his mouth and nose, and his eyes were closed. I looked down to see if blood was coming from his ears, but he didn't have any ears. I put my hand behind his head and reached my hand into his mouth. His jaw was tightly clenched. His teeth were loose. I couldn't get his jaw unclenched. He was breathing, but it was terribly labored breathing, it was wet breathing.

"At this point, I knew that there was nothing more that I could do," she remembers. "He was dying, and there was nothing I could do. I told him to keep breathing. I told him that it was going to be okay."

Creger then became aware of Lindsey Harris, crying nearby.

"She was hysterical, hyperventilating. I told her to shut up and calm down, he didn't need to hear her cry like that," she recalls.

"She was looking at her dad, and she asked me if he was dead," Creger remembers. "I told her no. Whatever I was going to tell her was not going to help her in any way."

Lindsey would later say that it angered her that she was lied to. She was smart enough to know that her father had just been murdered.

Creger looked over at the Lincoln Navigator and saw a disheveled woman with dark hair sitting in the driver's seat. She walked over and asked Gail Bridges if she could put Lindsey Harris in the back seat.

"She had her head in her hands, with her knees facing out of the car," she remembers as she and Lindsey walked up to the Navigator door.

Gail called Lindsey by her name. Now Creger turned to her.

"Lindsey, who did this?" she asked.

"My mom, I mean my stepmom," she answered.

"Did she mean to do this?" she asked.

"Yes," the young girl answered as her father lay gasping his last breaths.

While Julie Creger comforted the dying man's daughter, Robert Williams knelt by David. He had been right behind his fiancée as the two got to the body of David Harris. He heard Clara scream at her dying husband, "Now you see what I can do."

"Get away from my daddy, that's my daddy," he heard a girl scream hysterically as Julie walked away and put Lindsey Harris in the Navigator.

"I heard fluid in his lungs and when I looked at him his ears, looked as if they were ground off."

Williams reached down to the chest of David Harris.

"I felt no ribs on the lower side of his chest, and I didn't find his right lung expanding at all. I couldn't feel three ribs on the left side," he remembers.

"David was moving his neck left and right as he struggled for breath," Williams remembers.

"Breathe, breathe, look at me," he shouted at the dying man. "David, your daughter is watching."

David responded slightly to Williams' entreaty.

As the drama had begun to unfold in the lobby, Lindsey Dubec and her friend Andrea sat in the Toyota waiting for something to happen, waiting for their prey to emerge from the hotel. The two sat passing the time as they continued to talk about marriage, their own someday. It was ironic that Lindsey Dubec was earning money to help the potential disintegration of the marriage of someone else as she chatted with her friend about future nuptials.

The breakup of the marriage they were to film didn't have anything to do with them. Lindsey had long ago learned that the business of being a private investigator was nothing like it was portrayed on television and in the movies. It was mostly boring drudgery. It had nothing to do with her. She was just earning a paycheck.

Suddenly, Dubec realized that the people coming down the sidewalk from the front of the hotel were the subjects she was supposed to catch on tape in her surveillance video. She noted the time as 8:50 p.m. for her report. Dubec fumbled with the camera, picking it up from the front seat where it lay between her and Andrea.

The steering wheel was in the way as she clumsily raised the camera to her eye.

"I turned on the camera, then turned it off," she said as she described how clumsily she had handled the device. "I saw a car coming at a high rate of speed and driving crazy," she said. "It drove past us, and then left along the side of the wall."

Lindsey Dubec didn't see Clara Harris hit her husband with the Mercedes and run over him. She was too busy again fumbling with the camera, then was too busy attempting to catch the action on tape as she watched the scene, which she described as "blurry" through the viewfinder.

In fact, Dubec fumbled with the camera so much that it took ten seconds for her to begin filming after the Mercedes first hit David Harris.

After Clara Harris stopped the car, Lindsey jumped out and walked to get a closer look at what had happened.

"I walked up to him, and then I walked away." She was sickened by what she saw.

The investigator returned to her car and called the office and spoke with Natalia, the Blue Moon investigator now back on duty.

"I told her that the subject, Clara Harris, ran over her husband," she said. "She told me to cooperate."

Rattled beyond words, Lindsey Dubec and her friend drove next door.

"Andrea was hysterical and I had to get her under control. She was screaming. I had to straighten her out," she remembers. "I called Mr. Bacha, but there was no answer.

"Five minutes later, I went back because I was a witness," she said. "One minute after I came back, the cops came."

Dubec's cell phone began to ring. Lucas Bacha was calling for an update.

Nassau Bay Police Department dispatcher Kimberly Maldinado was accustomed to the voices of frantic people in crisis situations. It was her job to remain calm and deliberate. When the call came in from the operator at the Nassau Bay Hilton at 8:49 p.m. that evening, she thought that the call was probably nothing unusual, just a disturbance at the popular hotel, perhaps a routine dispatch regarding a guest who had had too much liquor in the Marina bar.

Nassau Bay Officers Mike Reyna and M.D. Staudt were sent to the scene. Six minutes later, the two cops radioed Maldinado that they had arrived at the Hilton, and then gave her a license number to run on the computer.

One minute later, the dispatcher's radio crackled with the police officer's words telling her to "Send EMS, call the fire department, and call Life Flight."

When Mike Reyna arrived at the hotel, people waved at his patrol car motioning him to the back parking lot. He parked his car, got out and got sketchy details from the crowd that had gathered in front of the hotel. He then walked round the long wall and looked in the direction of Gail Bridge's Navigator.

"I saw a crowd," he said.

He then walked closer. "I saw a man down."

"He appeared to be unconscious," the cop observed, not getting closer than ten feet from David Harris.

Clara Harris was kneeling next to him, hotel employees holding the woman by her arms.

Reyna's fellow officer, Staudt, arrived, and Renya told Clara to come with him. He placed her in Staudt's car.

"She was upset," he remembers. "She was really upset. She was crying. She was sobbing."

Reyna noted that although hysterical, the woman looked sober. The cop also noticed that Clara appeared to calm down once she was in the patrol car for a while.

"She took deep breaths, and just sat there," he remembered.

Detective Teresa Relken of the Nassau Bay Police Department was at home when she had received the call to come to the Hilton. The pretty young cop had worked her way up through the ranks, starting as a police dispatcher and volunteer firefighter with the nearby Santa Fe and Dickinson departments, and then as a campus cop at the University of Houston at Clear Lake.

When she arrived, Relken walked the crime scene and glanced into an ambulance where she noticed the body of a man about to be transported. The attendants quickly closed the door and the vehicle moved out, sirens blasting, although the distance to the hospital wasn't even a mile.

"I didn't know if he was dead or alive," she said.

The detective was now on the scene and in charge. She

began barking orders to the patrolmen who had arrived at the Hilton that they were to take the witnesses to the Nassau Bay Police Department.

Relken made note of the vandalism done to the Navigator, and saw the rear windshield wiper lying on the ground behind the SUV. She also saw that the car had been hit, and that it had scratch marks on its side. Nearby, the detective made a mental note of a silver Mercedes, its right front fender damaged.

There was blood on the asphalt and tire marks on the grass of the median separating the sections of the lot. Relken saw a blood-stained button lying on the ground, car keys in the grass, and a bloody towel.

Near the car lay testimony to the vanity of David Harris. Part of his hairpiece had become dislodged from his head and the expensive toupee suffered the indignity of lying upon the ground—now a piece of evidence.

Relken began to lay down the markers in order to give a permanent record of where each piece of evidence was found.

At 12:45 a.m., she arrived at Cristus St. John Hospital to begin the grisly process of photographing the deceased. There, she found Millie Harris sitting alone with the body of her son.

"His ear was shredded off, and he was bloody. There was a tube in his mouth. There was bruising on his shoulders and legs and on the back of the head. There was blood on the back of his head."

Officer Mike Reyna had his hands full. He had a major accident on his hands, and a possible homicide to boot. He was dealing with a parking lot full of people and what's more, there was a likelihood that he would have to work with at least one grieving family member.

After he placed Clara Harris in Staudt's patrol car, he returned to the "crime scene," and found the crowd gathered around the body of David Harris in disbelief at what they had witnessed, and were continuing to witness.

A tall, youngish man walked up to him as he surveyed the scene, noticing the two women in the Lincoln Navigator. The man, Garrett Clark, handed him the keys to the SUV. Reyna told the desk clerk, as well as Gail and Lindsey Harris to get in his patrol car. He would transport them to the emergency room at Clear Lake Hospital.

Reyna looked at the disheveled woman with dark hair who appeared to have suffered some sort of physical attack.

"She was going in and out, she wasn't responsive," he remembered. "She kept telling me that she was cold. I brought her a blanket. She kept going in and out of consciousness."

Detective Relken returned to the scene of the homicide and completed her work before going to the Nassau Bay Police headquarters where Clara Harris was taken in handcuffs. Her arresting officer noted that her crying and occasional hysterics ceased when he placed her in the back seat of his patrol car and then cuffed her.

After her interrogation, in which she made an incoherent rambling statement claiming that she had killed her husband by accident, Relken transported Clara Harris to the Harris County Jail where she was charged with the murder of David Harris.

Relken then left the jail and headed to the morgue. She had an autopsy to watch.

Bobbi and Lucas Bacha had to catch their breath after the murder, and the best place to do that was over a cup of flavored coffee at Denny's. The two tucked the kids in for the night and drove to the late-night eatery across the street from the Nassau Bay police station. The two frazzled investigators recapitulated what little they knew of the events of the night again and again as they waited for Blue Moon's chief investigator Jeff Moore, and his girlfriend, Missy to arrive.

When they got to the restaurant, Jeff told the couple that Lindsey Dubec, the firm's investigator on the scene, was doing about as well as a person who had just witnessed a grisly murder could be expected to be doing. She was so shaken by the event that she was already beginning to block details of what she had seen out of her mind. Fortunately, she had video taped the entire killing, he believed, from start to finish. Moore had given the tape to the police.

Moore told his bosses that when he'd arrived on the scene he heard the agonizing screams of Lindsey Harris. He had been called by Bobbi Bacha after she had been notified by Natalia that a tragedy had occurred.

"It pierced your soul," he told them, emotion filling his voice.

The scene was chaotic, as Moore related it to his bosses. Members of the EMS were holding down 16-year-old Lindsey, and as he looked in her direction he heard a Nassau Bay cop make a joke about her state of mind. He looked at the cop in disgust, a bad impression of the policeman that got worse as the crime scene investigation progressed. When the girl was able to get her shattered emotions in check, she gave a statement to the police. Moore said that he watched as the same cop kept interrupting the girl, telling war stories, conduct that he considered totally unprofessional.

Lucas was unaware that he knew the victim of the crime as he listened to Jeff Moore describe the evening's events.

The chief investigator handed the Bachas the Harris file, which he had snatched from the office on the way. The two scanned it, missing the fact that the victim, Dr. David Harris, had worked on Lucas' teeth the Friday before his death. Lucas Bacha wears braces. Moreover, they didn't notice that another name on the report, Belinda Gail Thompson Bridges, was, in fact, Gail Bridges, friend of both a former client and of the Bachas themselves who had spent a weekend in New York with them the previous year.

All that they could think of at the time was the current client, Clara Harris, and why she would do such a thing. Questions raced through the minds of all three as they attempted to make sense of something that was fundamentally senseless—as senseless as the murder by auto of the husband of a prominent client in the parking lot of a posh resort hotel. The investigators talked until about 4 a.m., when exhaustion made its inevitable demands on bodies racked by emotion and worry.

Fatigue at last took its toll, and the two couples left the restaurant. Jeff got into his dark blue Jeep, and Bobbi and Lucas got into their white Durango. In the parking lot, Moore pulled up next to the couple.

"You know, no matter how we try to put buffers in place, if someone wants to kill someone or hurt someone, they will find a way," he said. "It looks like this woman was going to do what she did and no one could stop her. She obviously had a plan. You just can never predict a person's actions."

NASA Road 1 was quiet as Lucas pulled the Durango onto the normally busy street. Bobbi Bacha, as is her wont, looked up at the moon all the way home, thinking about fate and how it can't be controlled.

The following day, Bobbi Bacha's concerns were profound. The very future of the business that she and Lucas had worked so hard to build could be at stake.

"Thoughts were racing through my mind like, Oh my God. Clara must have followed our investigator, or she hired someone to follow us following her husband," Bobbi Bacha remembers.

"What if she was planning to kill him and followed our PI to find him and kill him?" Bobbi thought.

Bobbi Bacha questioned her husband again about his telephone conversation with Clara Harris just hours before, knowing that there would inevitably be legal questions about the conduct of the firm that night.

"What did you say to her?" she probed.

"The usual," Lucas answered. "I did not give her the name of the hotel, but she somehow knew. I told her they are in a hotel on the fourth or sixth floor. I told her to be patient, and she would get a full report the following day."

"Clara asked Lucas if they were at the Hilton Hotel" Bobbi later recounted, "and Lucas said that 'they are at a hotel, the case is going well, and we will have all of your evidence the following day.' Clara even asked if we were taking photos, and Lucas said that, 'We will if we can.'"

The conversation, as Bobbi Bacha related it, would be inconsistent with the later testimony of both Lindsey and Clara Harris.

Lucas continued, "It was Thank you, thank you, and call over."

"Lucas even began to question what he said," Bobbi remembers today. "But after eight years of doing this, answering these calls, he would never not follow protocol."

The couple re-examined the case file and talked to Claudine, who had initially interviewed Clara Harris and accepted the case for Blue Moon.

"Claudine said that Clara told her about the hotel and the restaurants and everything, and found the notes stuck in the photo pocket of the file," Bacha recalls. "Claudine said that Clara only wanted us to listen to conversations and acted as if she really did not care about the adultery, as she knew it was going on."

For Bobbi and Lucas, there was plenty to worry about, and the two investigators knew it. Their business had grown to the point that it was the biggest investigative firm south of Houston, and it was now threatened. Inevitably questions would arise regarding how Clara Harris had found her husband at the hotel. If investigators had tipped her during an active investigation, it could mean big trouble and the threat of suspension or complete revocation of the firm's state license.

The two owners had never encountered a situation like this. They and their corps of thirty-eight investigators had spied on hundreds of quarreling couples without incident, without a cheating spouse lying on a cold stainless-steel table in a morgue as the body of David Harris was now doing. Surveillance of the unfaithful by Blue Moon's investigators accounts for a whopping 30 to 40 percent of the firm's income.

Other types of cases brought in substantial income to the firm as well. Often family members wanted to know who their child or parent was dating. Then there were missing persons cases, a somewhat frequent staple of the company's business.

Bobbi Bacha prides herself at having a bloodhound's nose for finding missing family members. She has found children long ago given up by their birth mothers for adoption. The investigator made a name for herself by finding missing siblings and even heirs to fortunes. She claims a success rate of 98 percent, and Internet technology as well as computer databases are only making the job easier and more efficient, she says.

Another huge chunk of business comes from insurance companies' attempts to unearth false claims, as well as competitive intelligence cases. These are cases investigating franchisees to make sure that the mother firm gets its due share of profits and fees from their "trusted partners."

Once in a competitive intelligence case, the Bachas sent a suspect firm in Dallas a fake flyer offering to clean its office for free. The franchisee took the bait, their greed so great that they were willing to take almost anything if there wasn't a charge. Bobbi and Lucas got in their car and headed up I-45, bought cleaning materials and a vacuum cleaner along the way, and legally walked into the business and cleaned it. They also cleaned out all of the company's trash, placed it in plastic bags, and brought it back to their conference table in the Clear Lake office and sorted it. The trash revealed that their client's suspicions had been on target and financial records thrown in the garbage revealed that the firm's management was hiding assets.

Much to Bobbi and Lucas' amusement, the company was unsatisfied at the job the two had done in cleaning its office. They called back and complained that the windows were still dirty.

Bobbi came to the business naturally after watching her father, veteran Galveston cop Robert Trapani hone his skills. He knew the language of the streets, knew how to get an illiterate burglar to 'fess up with little effort using the force of words, not violence.

If he caught one burglar, but the other escaped, "Trap" knew how to get results.

"Tell me now," he would say. "Tell me now who your friend is, who is running down that street there? If you don't, I'm going to take you downtown and put you on the lying machine," he would say. The fear of the machine sometimes broke the suspect by itself as he sat confined to the blue vinyl back seat of a Galveston police car.

Now, twenty years later, and with thousands of cases behind her, Bobbi remembered her father's street cop determination and patience.

"What would Trap do in a case like this?" she thought as she sat with Lucas and Jeff Moore in the noisy restaurant.

As she learned more about the Harris murder, she knew that the press would be calling her soon. She was becoming accustomed to dealing with reporters—and liked them.

Her baptism of fire with the media was the case of Robert Durst, the errant son of Manhattan real estate magnate Seymour Durst. Blue Moon Investigations was hired by the family of Morris Black, a drifter allegedly murdered, then butchered. by the cross dressing millionaire, who had been implicated in at least two other murders including that of his wife and a close companion. The *New York Post* and the *New York Daily News* were having a field day with the story, as were the local Texas newspapers and television stations.

Black's torso washed up in Galveston Bay, but the head remained missing. On a tip, Bacha and a team got on boats and hit the water. They found two female wigs, women's clothing, unopened makeup and what looked to them like bloodstained carpet, all of which she gave to the Galveston cops. Unfortunately, Black's head was still absent.

But it didn't remain missing for long. Bacha heard that .

a fisherman had seen a head with eyes staring up at him while fishing in shallow water at low tide. Again, the firm's armada hit the water and searched for the head of Morris Black. Bacha believes that she will find the head and reunite it with the torso.

Bacha enjoyed the publicity that the Durst case brought to her, and it was good for business.

Bobbi Bacha's long experience told her that danger was lurking ahead with the press on the Harris case. But she was not ready for the blindside that was to come to her the day after Clara Harris was released from jail.

"When the news announced via the Nassau Bay Police Department that the PI had led Clara to the hotel, we were outraged, and at the same time puzzled that Clara would lie about the fact," Bacha says. Bobbi and Lucas Bacha collected their emotions and looked at the situation with an analytical eye. "Clara was going to try to use us as a scapegoat somehow to justify her actions. Then when we heard that Parnham was Clara's attorney and he said that something must have triggered what happened we suspected that he too was also going to try to blame this on us—telling Clara where to go.

"Clara was in handcuffs, but she was thinking a logical thought by saying it was an accident. Hearing that Clara was telling the police we told her where her husband was at was totally untrue.

"We began to suspect that Clara was beginning her defense, but we were also confused because we thought she went nuts somehow. We knew that she was not tipped off by us and she gave us all of the addresses. Our PIs and investigators were still in shock when she called our office less than forty-eight hours later asking for a refund. This is when we began to get suspicious of Clara Harris' real motives."

As the morning following the murder wore on, the investigators again glanced at the name of the girlfriend of the late Dr. Harris in their file but had no reaction to it whatsoever. They had never heard of Belinda Gail Thompson Bridges before Clara Harris had walked into their office. They had no idea that the woman the firm had been hired to tail was the alleged lover of their former client, Julie Knight, the wife of another previous client, Charles Knight. The two had no idea that they knew, and even liked, the young mother of three.

There was no story about the murder of Dr. David Harris in the *Houston Chronicle,* the newspaper that billed itself as "Houston's leading information source," the day after it happened. The murder had occurred just as the newspaper was hitting its final deadline of the day. Instead, local coverage was consumed with relating that fatal police shootings in the city had spiked, surpassing the total number of similar deaths for all of the previous year. The district attorney, Chuck Rosenthal, denied that the city's cops manifested a cowboy attitude, while three groups, the National Association for the Advancement of Colored People, the League of United Latin American Citizens, and the American Civil Liberties Union all called for the establishment of a civilian review board in the city, as they had for decades.

But the following morning, the death of the popular Friendswood orthodontist provoked a firestorm of coverage. The headline in the *Houston Chronicle* read: "Livid wife leaves car parked on husband/Argument ends in hotel-lot killing." Local television coverage made the newspaper account look tame.

Houston television competes for the most vivid crime-scene action. No pathos goes unnoticed, and coverage of fires, murders and floods is the nightly staple. One station, KTRK, boasts longtime consumer reporter Marvin Zindler. He is a white toupee-wearing octogenarian who was the inspiration for the Broadway hit, *The Best Little Whorehouse* in Texas. In a series of commentaries the crusading loudmouth had once single-handedly forced the closing of a rural bordello and became a star.

Nothing satiates the appetite of a Houston viewer more than a good murder, and Clara Harris and her S-Class Mercedes provided them with enough of a feast to chew upon for the entire summer, into the fall, and ultimately through to the new year.

News of the murder shocked the patients of David and Clara Harris in the communities where they owned practices, around the lake, and in Lake Jackson, as they saw it reported on television.

NINE

Gail Bridges was rattled to the depths of her soul as she lay in the hospital, lucky to have escaped the fatal collision with the silver Mercedes that may have been meant for her. The small-town girl from Crosby, who only a few years before had had everything, was now reduced to fighting the aches and pains inflicted upon her in a hotel lobby by a vengeful wife fighting not only for her husband, but for the empire that they had built together. Gail had been in the way, an obstacle that needed to be removed. Clara's goal, her only goal when she had seen Gail, was to separate her from David.

Gail was completely aware of the threat that she posed to Clara Harris. From the beginning, David had told her that he had informed his wife of the affair and in fact had been providing her with the locations of his extracurricular activities with his lover. David told her that he believed his wife was comfortable with the arrangement, knowing that the two would never go to Gail's home because of the presence of her children. The marriage was open, and she had nothing to fear from a jealous wife.

Gail knew, as she lay in the hospital, that before his death, David Harris was living a hell on earth in the mansion on Pine Drive in Friendswood. Clara no longer slept with him, he told her. Moreover, she had become increasingly short with both him and his daughter, Lindsey. He described his home life as "Friday the 13th, every day." He told Gail that the only peace he could enjoy anymore was that which he found with her.

Finally, things became intolerable and David Harris told Clara that he was going to leave her and marry Gail Bridges. Clara exploded, he said, chasing him out of the mansion in his underwear. After things calmed down, David called Gail, without Clara knowing it, and told her of the eruption, and that he didn't understand why Clara had reacted so strongly, since she already knew most of the details of his affair with Gail.

Then Clara had come into the office and fired her, and David was helpless while she was doing it. He had stood outside the French doors of the back office watching as he looked for the keys to the room. Gail Bridges left, confused, hurt, angry and betrayed. She had not been happy at the office except for her friendship with David. The rumors that she was a lesbian had followed her, she later told a friend, and she believed that her co-workers stared at her, "as if she was an alien."

Gail was under the impression that Clara had heard the rumors about her and Julie and believed them. David had confronted her about the rumors himself.

"I just can't believe that you are a lesbian," he told her. "You do not act like I would expect."

All of this welled up inside Gail as she lay in the hospital, beaten by Clara Harris. She remembered the anger and betrayal she felt as she had driven away from the clinic, anger that she had been fired and embarrassed in front of her fellow workers, betrayal that David had lied to her about the openness of his marriage to Clara and the ease with which his impending divorce would be accomplished.

Gail was troubled as well because she had told David

that she had no intention of continuing the relationship until his divorce was final, and then maybe she would consider seeing him again. Until then, she wanted nothing more to do with him.

Gail ran the tumultuous period through her head again and again, confiding her thoughts to a friend months later. Clara had called her home repeatedly threatening to kill her. She said that she was perplexed by Clara's action because she had believed that her affair with David had been common knowledge for months to everybody including his wife.

Gail had been frightened at the time, she later related, terrified by the threats. She had turned to the one friend whom she knew she could count upon. Gail Bridges and Julie Knight left immediately for a long weekend in with the kids in Corpus Christi to give Clara Harris time to cool down and so that Gail would be out of the way and halfway down the coast to Mexico in case the dentist was determined to follow through with her threats.

When the two women returned the following Tuesday, David desperately wanted to see Gail, was calling her but she had thought it over and had decided that she didn't want to see David Harris again, now or ever. She later told a friend that she believed that he was lying to her and using her. But David kept calling, telling her that he loved her and didn't want to lose her.

Then David leveled with his lover. He told her that he would have divorced Clara two years prior were it not for the issue of the division of the considerable estate the two had established through their highly lucrative dental empire. Further, he told her that he still had financial issues to settle with his wife before a divorce would be possible.

David retorted that he was no longer in love with Clara and that the marriage was over.

* * *

The Texas 146 bridge was high so that sailboat traffic could pass under it. On the southeast side sat the Kemah Boardwalk, a restaurant and recreation destination built by developer Tilman Fertitta, a local entrepreneur and founder of the Landry's restaurant chain.

Gail went inside the hotel and waited for David, tense, but not fearful that anything untoward would happen.

David arrived shortly thereafter and sat down with her, immediately saying that the only time that he felt relaxed was when he was with Gail.

Gail was uncomfortable, and a little frightened at meeting David. She had been threatened by his wife, after all, during the course of the past few days. She didn't like the feeling but she had made the mistake of falling in love with David Harris.

When he had arrived at the Hilton, David Harris was agitated as he settled into a chair near Gail. She assumed that he had been with his wife.

"I had a lunch from hell," he told her. "I want to apologize to you about Clara locking me out of the office and firing you. I had no idea. I'm also sorry that she told Lindsey about us. That is unforgivable."

David also told Gail that Clara had bought his daughter a cell phone. Why? he wondered. Clara had never been close to Lindsey, he said. He then professed his love for Gail and told her that he wanted to continue seeing her.

The two talked, sitting in the lobby, enjoying the company of each other, enjoying the pleasant atmosphere of the resort hotel.

Finally, it was time to leave, and David walked her out the back door of the hotel to her Lincoln Navigator waiting in the parking lot. When they reached the SUV, David got in and the two continued talking, she remembered.

Quickly, the July Texas heat took its toll and Gail started the engine of the luxury automobile, pointing a vent toward her lover.

David was still hot and he told Gail that he wanted to go back inside the hotel. Texas summers can be their hottest in the late afternoon, and even in the most expensive of cars, air conditioning systems are often inadequate. The two returned to the hotel lobby and talked some more, she told a friend.

David was persuasive. He convinced Gail to go to a room with him. David walked to the front desk and registered under his own name, Gail remembered. The desk clerk gave David the key to room 604. The two lovers talked an hour more.

David's cell phone rang, and he saw the number of Lindsey's new cell on the display of his own. He was surprised to see that number because his daughter wasn't in the habit of calling him on his cell phone.

David told his daughter that he was on the way home, explaining to Gail after he hung up that one of the kids was sick.

Gail was suspicious. She was still on guard, frightened by the barrage of calls from Clara Harris threatening her life less than a week before.

The phone rang again, and this time Gail could hear Clara Harris screaming in the background, even from across the room.

Clara asked David where he was, and he told her that he was on NASA Road 1 and that he would be home soon. He then asked his wife why she didn't take the child to the emergency room if he was so ill. Clara answered that David needed to come home and take care of the child, not her.

David clicked off the phone and looked at Gail.

"I do not understand why anyone would want to harm you because you are so kind and good," he told her.

The words made Gail wonder if Clara had told her husband that she intended to kill her, just as she had threatened her on the phone the previous week.

Although the two had not made love in their time in the room, David had made himself comfortable. Now he dressed, and on the way to the elevator, he asked Gail if he could buy her a Coke. He was aware that she was taking medication that required fluid intake.

The doors of the elevator opened. David and Gail entered joining a man and a small boy holding a black balloon. The balloon floated over David and he played with it and talked to the boy. He also said that he loved being around Gail. At the first floor, the elevator eased to a stop and the doors opened.

For a brief moment, the world was wonderful for Gail as she clasped her lover's hand.

Gail was looking at David, and she instantly noted a change in his demeanor as they got out. He was holding her hand in that unusual way of his, up in the air. She followed his eyes and saw that Clara and Lindsey were waiting for him. David walked toward his wife and she began hitting his face. Trained in jujitsu, he easily averted the blows. Clara then locked eyes with Gail. Like a lioness on the Serengeti, she pounced, striking the lover of her husband in the face so hard that Gail's vision blurred as she was knocked to the ground. Clara grabbed Gail's hair and pounded her head into the hotel's marble floor repeatedly.

Gail's blouse was torn off, but she doesn't remember that part of the melee. She only remembers screaming for help, being nearly unconscious, and finally, Clara being pulled off her and held by several men. In a feat of almost superhuman strength, she knocked the men over like dominos and again knocked Gail Bridges to the floor. Clara crawled along the floor and bit Gail's leg as she called her a bitch and screamed that she was sleeping with her husband.

Clara was again pulled off, and Gail remembers the sight of her back as she was being escorted from the hotel.

David and Gail gathered their belongings. The contents of her purse were scattered all over the lobby floor, and Gail remembers that she was frightened that Clara would come back in and attack her again as she picked up the incidentals she carried with her that day.

The desk clerk, she recalled, had handed her the blouse that had been ripped from her body. He told her that he was security for the hotel and that he would escort her to her car. Almost unconscious at this point, Gail followed, telling herself to move her legs, move the body to get to the car and get out of there. She could hear David running behind them as they neared the parked Navigator. She saw that the side of the car had been keyed, the taillights broken, and the windshield wipers bent.

"Look at my car," she told David.

"I am sorry, I am so sorry, Gail," he responded.

The desk clerk, Garrett Clark, reached for the car door and opened it, but Gail Bridges nightmare continued. Looking beyond him, she saw a silver Mercedes driving straight at them. Through the windshield of the car, Gail saw the eyes of Clara Harris, blazing in their hatred as she aimed the car at her husband. She didn't see Lindsey in the car as Clara targeted David with the vehicle.

Somebody pushed her into the seat. The rest is a blank.

Gail did not see the car strike David Harris. She only remembers seeing the Mercedes go over a median. She says that at the time, she believed that David had run after

Clara to stop her and had not been hit by the car but had escaped the deadly vengeance of Clara Harris.

The next thing Gail knew was that a hotel security guard told her to get to a ramp behind the hotel.

"You will be safe there," he said.

"I just want to go home," she told the man from the front desk. "I just want to go home to a safe place."

"The police will never let you leave, lady," he said. "Not after this accident."

"What accident?" she screamed, emotion welling inside of her.

From a distance she heard another voice, the voice of a young girl calling her name.

"Gail, Gail," Lindsey Harris called. She saw David's daughter coming toward her and hid her head, frightened that she would be hit again.

"Gail, I'm not going to hurt you," the young girl said. "She killed my dad. Clara killed my dad."

The two erupted, their emotions overcoming them, filling them with their newfound grief for the man they loved, lying bloody and battered on the asphalt of the Nassau Bay Hilton parking lot.

Finally, collecting herself somewhat, Gail was able to speak.

"How did you find us?"

"Clara hired an investigator and they told her that you were at a hotel."

The two held each other and cried. Finally, Gail asked the girl if there was anyone she could call for her. She responded, calling Lindsey's mother, and her grandmother, Millie Harris.

She told David's parents that Lindsey needed a ride home and that their son had been injured in the accident.

* * *

Clara Harris' exit from jail with attorney Dee McWilliams was as unceremonious as her entrance. When she came into the building, she was whisked past a tiny crowd on the steps only to answer shouted questions from reporters that the killing of her husband was an accident. She walked out under a modest $30,000 bond.

Female murderers are treated with some deference in the Harris County Jail, a small city within itself, perhaps because so many of them are themselves victims of domestic abuse. The state didn't consider her to be a flight risk. The dentist was a first-time offender, and she was a prominent member of the community. In short, Clara Harris had too much to lose by escaping the borders of her adopted country.

Clara Harris was lucky, far luckier than many murderers who enter the Harris County Jail. The facility at one time or another has housed a full third of all inmates on Texas' death row, the state that leads the nation with its efficient killing machine situated in a small room in the little college town of Huntsville.

The charge against Clara was murder, simple, uncomplicated murder. It would not be muddied by an appeal by prosecutors for the death penalty. It would not be complicated by other minor charges such as assault for her attack on Gail Bridges. She would not be charged with reckless driving as a result of the collision of her Mercedes with the parked Lincoln Navigator. No, there would be no death penalty because none of her other crimes rose to the felony level required by statute in the Lone Star State.

Texas law requires that for the supreme punishment to be imposed by a jury, more than one crime must be committed. In the case of Dr. Clara Harris, there had been only one killing, with no other mitigating crimes that would elevate her charge to the level that would put her own life in danger, as it had for Andrea Yates the year before. The Clear Lake homemaker was tried for her life because she had killed her five children, and each killing was counted as a separate crime.

Andrea Yates had been lucky indeed, because for the better part of the latter half of the Twentieth Century, and now on into the Twenty-first, the Harris County District Attorney's Office was known for its deadly efficiency.

Despite stumbling and bumbling by lead prosecutor Joe Owmby in the Yates case, the state had secured a conviction of the woman whom both defense and prosecution agreed was hopelessly mentally ill. The jury, however, refused to impose the death penalty, not able to stomach sending such an obviously impaired person to death row. Yates was given life, and in Texas that amounts to 40 years before an inmate is eligible for parole. Andrea Yates would likely die in prison.

The entire spectacle of the Yates trial prompted revulsion at the bloodthirsty nature of the Harris County DA's Office when Owmby told the jury that he was proud to be asking them to kill Andrea Yates. The jury argument prompted American Civil Liberties Union regional director Annette M. Lamoreaux to write, "their prosecutorial discretion has spiraled so out of control that they are the ones who don't know right from wrong. Will someone not stop these people? Please."

Dr. Clara Harris was lucky, indeed. She had not been charged with capital murder. The worst thing that could happen to her was that she would spend the next 40 years in prison—alive.

For much of his life attorney George Parnham's world has been spent with men, first as a young seminarian in

New Orleans, then later as a first lieutenant in the U.S. Army, later still raising his four sons, and even today acting as a doting grandfather to five grandsons. He also has one daughter and a granddaughter. At age 62, George Parnham is settled in, a successful criminal lawyer with posh offices on the eighth floor of Houston's Lyric Centre, a building built by an affable promoter who went to prison, a victim of the go-go days in Texas when a developer could do anything if he knew the right people at the right savings and loan.

The building is tasteful, sitting near Houston's Wortham Center, home of the Houston Grand Opera. In front of the Lyric is a violin sculptured in concrete. The builder was making a statement to other developers in Houston's growing downtown with its Emerald City skyline. Joe Russo was telling the world that his building, at least, would not be just a monument to cash and energy, but to another side of Houston as well—its deep commitment to the arts.

It is in this environment that George Parnham, a one-time convenience store clerk, lives, works, and practices law. He is the only college graduate in his family, the only lawyer. His mother was working in a restaurant when she met his father who was the dishwasher. Parnham was born in Fort Lauderdale, and then moved with his family to Georgia where he lived until he was 12, when he left to attend seminary and study for the priesthood.

"I worked in the hills and gullies of Alabama until I was nineteen, working with sharecroppers and that sort of thing," he said in a 1992 profile in the *Houston Press*.

Texas produces some of the best trial lawyers in the world. Men like the late Percy Foreman and Warren Burnett turned criminal law into high theater as they practiced their craft in "the pit." Today, others carry the banner proudly, lawyers such as Roy Minton of Austin, and Houston lawyers Richard "Racehorse" Haynes, Mike Ramsey, Dick DeGuerin, Rusty Hardin—all have achieved near legendary status among their peers and the press.

Minton is a master of endearing himself to a jury. Haynes wears down witnesses and juries with relentless detailed low-key questions until he catches each in his snare. Ramsey utilizes a folksy down-home competence. The diminutive DeGuerin, the most flamboyant outside of the courtroom is a master of procedure on the inside. And Hardin, perhaps the best of the lot, always dresses in brown suits to set himself apart from natty blue-suited prosecutors whose snotty high-toned questions often put off the blue collar juries who pass judgment upon his clients.

Parnham founded Parnham & Associates in 1971 after working for a year with famed Houston criminal defense lawyers Clyde Woody and Marian Rosen. He took whatever cases came along, often struggling to collect on the Texas cut-and-shoots, a staple of any young criminal lawyer's practice.

Then in 1976, as America celebrated its bicentennial, George Parnham, by no means an expert on wills or probate, abruptly moved to Las Vegas to represent the Mormon Church and a man named Noah Dietrich who had been named executor of a will claimed to be that of Howard Hughes, the eccentric billionaire born in Houston. The document had been found at the church's headquarters on Temple Square in Salt Lake City, Dietrich claimed. The young Houston lawyer lived in the gambling capital for a year and a half, and then spent seven months in trial trying to prove that the will had indeed made the church the eccentric billionaire's heir.

One year to the day after Hughes' death, an editor took a long shot and dispatched a young journalist who had been covering the courts for the *Houston Post*, George Flynn, to Glenwood Cemetery to mount surveillance of the grave of Hughes. The reporter was to write about who showed up. It was a beautiful day, Flynn remembers. "I parked a good way from the grave and just waited. A car pulls up and it was George, all by himself. He walked up to the grave to pay his respects and stood there for a few minutes. Finally, I went up to him and asked what he was doing there. He said that he would drive out there occasionally to just clear his head."

After pouring himself into the case, Parnham lost. The court found that the will wasn't in the handwriting of Hughes.

However, the case of the Mormon Will was the young lawyer's introduction to the heady high-stakes game of big time law, the sort of case that could make or break a reputation. Despite losing, Parnham had acquired the addiction, the all-consuming drive that could make his name a household word in his chosen profession. He didn't plan to make his name as a probate lawyer.

George Parnham aspired to join the Texas lions of the pit, lawyers whose mere utterances are repeated by their brethren as if what had come out of their mouths was from holy writ. It was in this heady league that George Parnham attempted to carve out a niche in the Texas bar. The Houston lawyer wanted to be known as the acknowledged master of the insanity defense. He wanted to be the go-to guy who can unlock the jail for those accused of even the most horrendous crime because at its commission they were not in control of themselves and could do nothing to prevent their actions. From representing cases in Houston, with any luck at all, Parnham would develop a national reputation if the right case were to come along.

The right case came to George Parnham in 1994 when he successfully defended Calvin Bell, accused of wounding two Houston police officers at Piney Point Elementary School during a shooting rampage.

In his successful defense of Bell, Parnham overcame jurors' bias that attorneys resort to the insanity defense when there is nothing better to present to a jury. To be successful, a lawyer must prove that his client had a prior history of mental illness. To do this, the lawyer must present a timeline of the accused's incarceration as well as the treatment for the illness. Such a defense ultimately would boil down to a battle of experts.

An acquittal in such a case does not automatically mean that a defendant will be free to leave the jail. Instead, he is sent to a maximum-security mental institution where he is periodically examined. If ever found to be sane, a Texas judge has no choice but to approve the inmate's release. Calvin Bell was ultimately released back into society. In lectures before legal groups, Parnham calls his insanity defense, "helping the jury comprehend the inconceivable."

The successful defense of Calvin Bell insured George Parnham's reputation as one of a handful of trial lawyers in the nation who was capable of making such a defense work.

Parnham's successful defense of Bell insured that his reputation was made among his peers, other lawyers and judges.

Eight years later, he cemented the reputation at the national level with the defense of Andrea Yates, the mother of five who had killed all of her children, the oldest 7 and the youngest an infant, after undergoing treatment for months for postpartum depression. She had just been released from a League City mental hospital after being taken off the drugs that had kept her at least partly functional. Yates spiraled into the depression after years of following a fundamentalist preacher who had urged the successful couple to sell their house, buy a motor home and become traveling cult evangelists preaching an apocalyptic message that the end was near.

Andrea's husband, Russell Yates, was a dominating figure who took biblical exhortations that he should rule the family as literal fact, undiminished by scholarly interpretation. A NASA engineer, Yates had only recently given up living in a motor home and had bought a house in a fashionable neighborhood in Clear Lake City. Andrea was to be a stay-at-home mom responsible for home schooling the couple's children. At trial, testimony revealed that she had only two hours per week to herself away from her husband and children.

On a sunny June morning, Andrea Yates packed her husband off to work at the nearby manned spacecraft center, then methodically drowned all of her kids, laying four of them on a bed, and leaving the fifth, a 7-year-old named Noah, lying face down in the dank feces, and vomit-filled water of the family bathtub. She then called her husband at work and told him to come home, hung up the phone, and called the Houston Police.

After the dust settled and she was safely in police custody, Andrea Yates' family called George Parnham.

The man they hired had by now perfected his carefully crafted image, that of quiet competence. In the pit he can be at once gentle and grandfatherly, and just as quickly a prickly snappish adversary to witnesses who testify against his client, yet all the while never raising his voice in anger.

He could also be forgetful, an absent-minded professor who stumbled through his questions seemingly sloppily, yet often endearing his client to the jury. In the pit, Parnham reminded some of actor Peter Falk's television character Columbo. After the seemingly nonsensical questions of a witness, Parnham frequently had one last thing to ask, and it was sometimes a zinger.

Most often, though, he is Everyman, the gentle soul whom anybody would love to have as his or her grandfather, the man with a full but closely cropped gray beard tending to white. The aging lawyer's right arm is ever at the ready to place around the client's waist or shoulder, his empathy for their pain evident for all to see.

Parnham's image and technique has been crafted in a thousand courtrooms before a thousand judges in a thousand cases. It, like that of most Texas trial lawyers, is almost totally contrived, merely another tool in his mighty arsenal of writs, motions, and other legal instruments. The image is as carefully crafted as any role on Hollywood's big screen, but while the actor must entertain and sometimes educate the multitudes, the actor in the pit must maintain the attention of only twelve of his fellow citizens long enough to create reasonable doubt regarding the guilt of his client. Parnham's great skill is establishing the trust of a jury, making them believe that he and he alone has a superior knowledge of the intricacies of an insanity that drives men to kill their fellow beings, a knowledge that a Harris County prosecutor couldn't possibly possess.

It was to George Parnham that Clara Harris turned after she ran down her husband again and again in the parking lot of a resort hotel, all the while that the act was being captured on video.

TEN

Two days after the killing, July 26, 2002, during a six-minute hearing before Judge Carol Davies, Clara's bond was again confirmed at $30,000. While awaiting trial, Clara Harris would be free to go about her routine in an almost normal manner.

When she arrived in court, Clara sat quietly in a chair with its back against the wall at the rear of the small courtroom as the judge worked the docket prior to her 10 a.m. hearing. Clara appeared to watch the proceedings as a white man with a black wife stood before the judge. The man had turned himself in to law enforcement after being on the lam for fifteen years. He had become tired of looking over his shoulder, he told the judge. His wife took the stand on her husband's behalf, telling Davies that her husband had been a law-abiding citizen for all of those years. She also told the judge that her husband was her sole support. The former prosecutor, who now sat on the bench of the 177th District Court, appeared sympathetic to the former fugitive. The state took a hard-nosed approach to the matter, however, in keeping with the tough reputation of the Houston DA's office. Davies looked at her watch, and recessed the man's hearing so that she could get to the business at hand, the initial court appearance of Clara Harris.

The courtroom was packed to overflowing by media already aware of the national interest in the murder case. Davies called the name and case number of Clara Harris. Parnham stood behind the bar, the rail that separates officers of the court from the public. He walked to the back of the room and took Clara's arm and escorted her to the space directly in front of the bench.

The defendant was pale. There was not a hint that she spent time around the pool behind her palatial Friendswood home. She stood before the judge, thin, erect, wearing a black suit, her blond hair pulled back. She wore a huge ring on her left hand. Prosperity dripped from Clara Harris.

She was told that she had been charged with murder, and faced a maximum sentence of 99 years, or even life in prison, as Mia Magness read the charge to the court. The prosecutor read that she had hit David Harris with her Mercedes and hurled him twenty-five feet, crossed two medians, then run over him three more times. She then said that the woman standing before the judge had reversed the car and backed over him again.

Parnham took Clara's arm and held her by the left elbow as the wealthy dentist was again read her Miranda warning.

Davies first official action in *State of Texas vs. Clara Harris* was to issue a protective order on behalf of the surviving victim on the events on the night of July 24, 2002, at the Hilton. Clara was to make no telephone calls to Gail Bridges, send no letters, and have no personal contact, and was not to get closer than 200 feet from her home. Arraignment was set for August 23, 2002.

After the arraignment, Clara's fate would be in the hands of a Harris County grand jury, a body of twelve generally elderly volunteers with plenty of time to spare. There is nothing democratic about the choice of these jurors, whose only job is to make a finding of probable cause to stand trial. They are chosen for no better reason than that they know somebody of some importance who has been hand-picked by a judge presiding over the grand jury for a term. These appointees job: to recommend people for grand jury service. The only requirement: that they be upstanding citizens with no felony convictions in their past.

Working people have little time to serve on grand juries, but retirees in Harris County volunteer in droves, happy to have a chance at fighting back at the criminals that they so fear. Indictment is virtually automatic. Typically, a grand juror will hear up to 1,500 cases in his three-month term. Presentation of most cases to the jury by prosecutors is quick, in many cases less than a minute. It is the grand jurors' decision to find a no-bill, which means that in their judgment, evidence was not sufficient to warrant a trial. If members of the grand jury found a true bill, then the defendant would face a trial by a jury of their peers. Rarely are Harris County defendants no-billed. Even more rarely are either they or their lawyers afforded the opportunity to appear before the body.

It would take prosecutors almost ninety days after this first appearance to bring the case of the murder of David Harris to the grand jury. Clara Harris would inevitably be indicted with a true bill.

Clara had stood before the judge with calm dignity, supported by the gentleman who was now her lawyer. She was free to go, and as she walked down the left aisle of the courtroom she stopped before her father-in-law, Gerald Harris, and squeezed the elderly man's hand. Tears filled the eyes of David's father.

On the sidewalk outside the courthouse, Clara was escorted to a waiting car, while Parnham walked to a bank of cameras and microphones.

"It is an overwhelming tragedy for the family, his children, her side of the family," he said. "Members of both sides are grieving. This is a mutual tragic event. He was loved as a husband, a son, and a father. All parties understand that this will never end."

Parnham told the press that he had just met his client and that "I am not sure of the fact situation."

But the savvy lawyer who had so skillfully defended Andrea Yates had nothing better to tell the press than what Clara herself had told police immediately after the death of her husband. "This was an accident."

Bringing the brief news conference to a close, Parnham said that "This family needs to get this young man buried."

The Houston Police Department dispatcher received the call at 5:45 p.m. Friday. A distraught woman named Julie Knight was on the line saying that two individuals had walked to the door of the residence of Gail Bridges: a tall African American male, and a blond woman who Knight believed to be Clara Harris.

By 6 p.m., Mia Magness and the office of the district attorney were informed that Clara Harris had possibly violated the judge's protective order that Clara have no contact with Gail.

The following Monday, a bond revocation hearing was convened in Davies' courtroom on cause number 918964, *Texas v. Clara Harris*. Again the courtroom was packed with media. However, Magness diffused the situation, saying that the preceding day she had spoken to George Parnham regarding the matter that had caused them all to be back in court.

The prosecutor said that her office learned that the two people had been persistent in trying to get somebody to answer the door at the Bridges' home.

"They repeatedly pounded on the door, and based on the information that we had at that time, we were very concerned about the safety of Mrs. Bridges. However, we now believe that the two individuals at the residence were overzealous members of the media. Ms. Knight mistakenly identified the person as Mrs. Harris."

Parnham further explained to the judge, "At that time, Clara Harris was in my office being interviewed."

In light of the testimony, Davies immediately dismissed the motion to revoke Harris' bond. However, the judge again warned the dentist to stay away from her late husband's lover.

On the courthouse steps, Parnham told the media "I'm going to make sure that somebody is with her. It is an emotional time for her."

Dan Rizzo, Magness' boss, speaking for the DA's office said, "We do not apologize. We did the right thing."

Parnham had not exaggerated when he told the judge that Clara Harris was a danger to herself. In fact, Susan Hanson had taken charge of her boss, had taken the dentist to her home in nearby Baytown. Increasingly she had become concerned that Clara was becoming suicidal. She called the lawyer, frightened that the situation was getting out of control.

Parnham knew what to do. He called his old friend, Dr. Pricilla Ray, a forensic psychiatrist of national repute.

Clara Harris was now under the care of a physician—and after all, Parnham had made his reputation as a lawyer who specialized in the insanity defense.

Importantly, Ray was known throughout the community for her skill and her civic work. She was also known for another reason. The psychiatrist was the wife of Tom Sartwelle, one of the nation's top insurance defense lawyers.

Tough little Mia Magness is a product of the Harris County District Attorney's Office, molded as an intern by the unyielding prosecutors who in turn were molded by Houston's longtime district attorney, Johnny Holmes. During his terms in office, Holmes, who sported a handlebar mustache, had created the almost mythic image of a prosecutor who took no prisoners. Many of those he challenged would spend years in the penitentiary or die on a white-sheeted gurney in Huntsville.

As tough as the prosecutors in Houston were—some might say they were the toughest in the land—they were also good. They knew a good case when they saw one, and they knew talent in the raw when they saw it as well. Such was the case with Magness, who had done her undergraduate studies at Texas A&M, finishing in 1989.

For postgraduate studies, she went down the highway to the University of Texas Law School, an institution with a century-old reputation for producing some of the best courtroom performers in the world. After graduation, Magness returned to her natural home, the Harris County DA's office.

During her ten years working there, she tried more than seventy-five jury trials, first in the misdemeanor courts, then in the more serious felony courts.

She worked in the public integrity unit, ultimately assisting the Houston Police Department bust, and then try a slew of rotten cops involved in narcotics trafficking.

In Harris County, prosecutors are assigned to specific courts, and generally stay there trying the cases that come before that court. In Magness' case, she was assigned to the 177th District Court of Judge Carol Davies, a former prosecutor who had enjoyed a stellar career under the legendary Holmes.

Magness' immediate superior, Dan Rizzo, heads the DA's trial division. He is a Texas import from Ohio. The affable prosecutor was graduated from Baldwin-Wallace College in Berea, Ohio, in 1979, and then went on to the Cleveland-Marshall College of Law. Rizzo oversees eighteen assistant district attorneys. He is a veteran of more than 150 jury trials, notable among them Houston's famed Thelma and Louise robberies, as well as the city's Torso Killing.

Both would do their dead-level best to place Clara Harris in a Texas prison for the rest of her life. They planned to try the case together, with Magness doing the heavy lifting, and Rizzo at her side to assist any way he could.

Less than forty-eight hours after running over her husband, Clara Harris wanted her money back from Blue Moon, and had the president of her corporation, Susan Hanson, call Bobbi Bacha saying that the contract that the dentist had signed was now null and void because it had not been completed. Susan Hanson wasn't getting anywhere with the demand, and ultimately placed her boss on the phone to try to get the refund. The women were in a panic, because the corporation was cash-strapped in the wake of the death of David Harris. It couldn't have happened at a worse time, from a business standpoint. The couple had been pouring assets into the construction project at what was to be the new office. Now, the possibility existed that some, if not all, of the company's cash assets might be frozen. Clara Harris and Harris Clinics needed money, and needed it desperately.

Bobbi Bacha was recording when Clara Harris came on the line to ask for a refund for the services shortly after noon, July 26, 2002. After five minutes of small talk, the dentist got down to business.

"One last thing, you know I paid for Wednesday, Thursday, and Friday. I did not get to read your contract whether I was entitled to a cancellation refund."

Stunned, Bacha told her in her best little-girl voice that Clara wasn't entitled to a refund because she had violated the terms of the contract by showing up at the surveillance.

"The way the contract reads is that if the client shows up on the scene like you did, all retainers and monies are not refunded, and I will tell you why.

"As you found out the hard way, when there is a client on the scene, it jeopardizes the client. And so, therefore, there is no refund on this case and we may actually have an additional bill for you, because it's going to probably cost us some legal fees and things to go to court."

But it was Clara Harris' turn to be stunned when she learned from Bacha that her actions that night at the Hilton had been videotaped, and the tape of the "accident," as she called it, had been turned over to the police.

"Videotape?" Clara asked, defeat evident for the first time in her voice.

"Yes, ma'am. We have everything, you know, but we don't have it in our possession because of the incident that occurred," Bacha said.

"So, he [the investigator] was there through all the tragic parts?" Harris asked, starting to see the hopelessness of her situation for the first time.

"The investigator did video everything, because you hired us to video the subject," said Bacha.

"There was a videotape?" she asked again.

Bacha said that yes, the police did have a tape, but she didn't know what was on it because she hadn't seen it.

Before the conversation ended, Bobbi Bacha offered her condolences to Clara Harris. Then the investigator's maternal instincts kicked in and she asked the woman how the twins were doing.

In Houston, a couple was oblivious to the news when they heard that a Clear Lake dentist had run over her husband. Charles Knight and Laurie Wells had fallen in love. It began at a birthday party at Chuck E. Cheese's, and had blossomed during their trip to Florida together. Both of their marriages were behind them, and although *Knight vs. Knight* and *Wells vs. Wells* had been bruising, the two were trying to make a new life together.

When Charles moved out of his home in South Shore Harbor, Laurie Wells moved into an apartment with him in League City. Later the two moved to Houston. All that they had now was their love of each other. Their spouses had long ago won the custody battles over their children. The two planned to get married.

They had found a new church as well. Always religious, they had returned to the Baptist Church, this time in a big way, attending one of the nation's top Southern Baptist congregations, Houston's Second Baptist Church, which served as the benchmark for would-be megachurches. Its pastor, Dr. Ed Young, is a smiling velvety-voiced Southerner whose syrupy platitudes are dispensed with annoying regularity on television commercials in the Bayou City. But he is a success, and a huge one. Moreover, his parishioners adore him.

It was into this world that the two had moved—moved into a small but well-appointed apartment in the city's high-toned but traffic-snarled Galleria shopping district.

And it was here that the phone rang on a Friday evening shattering their worlds when Chuck Knight's cousin called to relate what he had seen on the news.

"Did you hear about the dentist who was run over by his wife?" the man asked.

"Yeah, so what?" Knight answered, wondering why his cousin would be asking a question like that.

"It was Gail Bridges who was with him."

For a moment, Charles Knight was speechless. Then he yelled, "Laurie!"

Steve Bridges was at home the morning after the murder when a friend came to his house at 7 a.m. to tell him that his former wife had been involved in a police incident. The man said that another friend, Michael Fondren, had told him that Gail had been with David Harris the evening before and that his wife Clara had run him over and killed him in the parking lot of the Nassau Bay Hilton.

Bridges had his children with him because it was his month to care for them. He immediately called a neighbor who quickly helped him dress the kids. The two loaded the SUV with clothes and toys. Steve Bridges and his kids headed to Louisiana, home to the safety and comfort of those he held most dear.

In Houston, Parnham was learning things fast from the media. Soon the airwaves were filled with the old allegations that David Harris' lover was bisexual. The moment George Parnham heard of the alleged lesbian relationship between Gail and Julie, he determined to unearth as many of the details of that affair as possible as part of his defense strategy for his client, Dr. Clara Harris.

The story first broke in the *New York Post* the Monday following the funeral of David Harris, when the newspaper revealed that Gail Bridges and Julie Knight had made a trip to New York for a January 14, 2002 taping, and had appeared in disguise on a segment of *The Sally Jesse Raphael* show. The program was titled, "My Husband Spies on Me." The program ultimately aired the following April.

Soon, the story was bannered in newspapers across the nation, and became fodder for tabloid news programs and late-night comics.

For their appearance on the *Sally Show*, both women had worn dark, heavily rimmed sunglasses and wigs. Gail donned a wig with straight blond hair, and Julie sported shortish dark hair. Both had bangs and wore dark suits. Most important, both denied that they were lesbians as their husbands alleged. They gave their names as Lisa and Leslie.

"My Husband Spies on Me" was actually a twist on words, because although Chuck Knight had made tapes of the women's private conversations, it was the women who were spying on their husbands at this point in their marriages. Blue Moon's Bobbi Bacha had set up the television appearance when a producer called from the show saying that they planned to present a segment about husbands spying on their wives, and did she have any clients who were doing that?

Ever willing to accommodate the media, Bacha thought

of the two women whom she describes as "socialites." She approached them and both agreed to be on the program as a lark, Bacha says.

Bobbi and Lucas Bacha, Gail Bridges, and Julie Knight hit the Big Apple like a Gulf Coast hurricane and had the time of their lives, riding around in limousines as guests of the show and mugging for the camera in the back seat as the driver shot photographs of the four of them.

Now, in the wake of the death of David Harris, a photo of the two women as they appeared on the program hit the media. Its implications were not lost on George Parnham. The oldest lawyer trick in the book is to try everybody in sight except your client. The alleged affair of Gail Bridges and Julie Knight played right into that strategy for Parnham as an added bonus to his intention to place the unfaithful and callous David Harris on trial.

Carol Davies, 63, judge of Harris County's 177th District Court, is jokingly called "Aunt Bee" around the twenty-floor courthouse because of her resemblance to the character on *The Andy Griffith Show*. At first, the image she presents from the bench is that of a kindly elderly grandmother, which she is, dispensing justice with compassion and mercy—the judge every felon would love to face, if the felon didn't know anything about judges in Texas' largest county. Couple the matronly image with a strong Southern accent in which one syllable-words are almost always turned into two and even more. But there is hardness beyond the façade. As a former prosecutor, she tried 150 cases for the no-nonsense Harris County DA's Office.

On the court's Web site, www.justex.net/crim/177/, a pleasant-looking Davies, wearing bright red lipstick and sporting a butch haircut, appears in the court's official photo. The picture in no way resembles the woman who sits on the bench today. The photo appears to have been taken years before. It is an image of the Carol Davies who once was.

Davies, despite her appearance and demeanor, is as harsh as they come, an offer-no-quarter red-meat conservative appointed to the bench by Governor George W. Bush in 1995 and elected outright for the first time the following year. Like all Texas state judges, she faces the electorate every four years.

A native of Victoria, Texas, Davies' legal career began in 1981, when, fresh out of the University of Houston Law School, she worked as a briefing attorney in Houston's 14th Court of Appeals for a year. Prior to that, she had been a housewife after dropping out of the University of Texas before graduation. For a time, she worked as a legal secretary. Davies moved to Houston in the early 1970s and after the kids were raised, she returned to college, getting a degree in philosophy. It was then on to law school and her brief stint with the appellate court.

She then joined Johnny Holmes' district attorney's office in 1982 for a thirteen-year stint, rising to head the office's Major Fraud Division. The *Houston Chronicle* described her in a 1996 endorsement for election as a "lifelong and active Republican."

In a 2001 poll of the Houston Bar Association, more than half rated Davies as only poor to acceptable, with a bare 43 percent rating her outstanding. A Houston criminal lawyer, who declined to be identified because he frequently practices in her court, said that she got such mediocre ratings because "she's mean.

On the bench, Davies is given to flashes of anger and

involuntary body language when something raises her ire.

It was to Davies' nineteenth-floor courtroom, one floor below the huge room where her trial would be moved, that Clara Harris was summoned at 9 a.m. on July 28, 2002, after Mia Magness was notified that Clara Harris had possibly been banging on the door of a terrified Gail Bridges.

Clara Harris and George Parnham again wove their way through a swarm of press on their way to the courtroom. The case had by now become the number-one murder in the land, attracting the attention of both syndicated and network television programs alike as the Mercedesmurder held the public spellbound. Again, Parnham was facing banks of television cameras camped outside the courthouse, as reporters would hang on his every word. Overnight, a small city of satellite trucks filled a parking lot across the street.

Parnham and Harris entered the courthouse and stood in the throng of lawyers, their clients, and the public and one by one all went through the four metal detectors set up in the lobby. They again walked down a short hallway, and then turned right into the elbow-to-elbow crowd that was jammed in a space too small as they waited for an elevator to take them to the nineteenth floor.

Outside the courtroom, more cameras filled the corridor outside Davies' court. Once in the courtroom, Clara Harris saw welcome faces. Sitting there waiting for the hearing to begin, friend and employee Susan Hanson and David's father, Gerald Harris, had come to show support.

A stern Judge Carol Davies called Parnham and his client before the bench. Mia Magness spoke to the court.

On the sidewalk outside the courthouse, George Parnham began laying ground work with the press for a possible insanity defense, suggesting that the mental state of Clara Harris was very fragile at the moment.

"I'm going to make sure that somebody is with her at all times. It is an emotional time for her."

ELEVEN

The effect of what Lindsey Harris had witnessed could not have been more profound. When the 16-year-old returned to Ohio with Debra and Jim Shank she was not the same girl who had loved to play the violin. She was no longer interested in such silly and trivial high school activities as cheerleading. And Lindsey Harris had lost the dream of joining her father in the practice of orthodontics in the office he was designating as her own in the new building.

No, Lindsey Harris had grown up into a beautiful yet troubled young woman. Her almond-shaped face surrounded by long straight dark hair expressed the sadness she felt. She had matured instantly in the parking lot as she saw her father lying on the asphalt of the Nassau Bay Hilton. She had grown up when she saw the woman she now called "Mom" bending over the prone body, pleading with her father to just breathe until help arrived.

Lindsey's loss of interest in music, and cheerleading was compounded with another loss. The girl had always been a good student. Now, her grades plummeted.

Life for Lindsey Harris now consisted of simply living through the next months until the trial. She chose to do nothing of the sort. Lindsey Harris chose instead to slice her wrists, finding two suicide attempts to be a more agreeable alternative to living with her memories.

Life for Clara Harris was simple as she adjusted to her widowhood. She continued to live in the mansion with Maria Gonzalez and the twins. She continued to go to church with her friends from Shadycrest. She was surrounded by the love and affection that poured from the Baptists. They had forgiven her for killing David almost as soon as the act was completed.

Clara also stepped into a new world, a world filled with lawyers. The considerable estate of David and Clara Harris did not belong exclusively to the widow of the deceased orthodontist, she quickly learned.

On July 31, 2002, silver-haired attorney John A. Davis Jr. filed suit in a Galveston federal court on behalf of his client, a minor named Lindsey Harris. The suit named not only Clara Harris, but her brothers; Lincoln Benefit Life Company; Space Center Orthodontics; American Orthodontics; David Harris DDS, MSD; Bay City Orthodontics; Harris Dental–Lake Jackson I; Harris Dental–Lake Jackson II; Harris Baytown I, II, and III; Harris Dental-Sugar Land; Harris Dental–Stafford; Space Center Management; Space Center Real Estate; Bank of America, and finally, the estate of David L. Harris, deceased.

For the first time, press and public alike learned just how vast the holdings of David and Clara Harris were.

Debra Shank was suing on behalf of her daughter Lindsey to protect her and her two half brothers (Clara and David's twins) interest in the estate of their father. The suit aimed to prevent the children's inheritance from being gobbled up by legal bills generated by Clara Harris' defense against the charge of murder.

David had named the woman who killed him as his sole heir. She was also named as beneficiary of an insurance policy issued by Lincoln. The suit states that those proceeds had been assigned by David as collateral for a loan and would revert back to Clara after the loan was paid.

Under Texas law, Clara could not financially benefit from killing her husband. Upon conviction, she would lose everything she owned, and all of the property should go to Lindsey and her brothers.

Davis contended that the suit be acted upon immediately by Judge Sam Kent because, "Defendant Harris is already calling meetings amongst interested family members and others to discuss the fate of Defendant Corporations and real property assets associated with the Defendant Corporations and . . . Disposition of such property could occur at any moment and Defendant Harris given the mounting civil liabilities and criminal defense costs, has the motivation to act quickly to deplete the estate."

Davis further contended that Clara was already attempting to squander cash rightfully belonging to the children in her defense.

Davis asked Kent to issue a temporary restraining order to prevent assets, which included not only the mansion, but vacation homes in Texas and Colorado, which he said rightfully belonged to the children, from being spent on lawyers like George Parnham and his associate Dee McWilliams.

Kent scheduled a hearing in his cavernous courtroom in the art deco federal building on Galveston's Rosenberg Avenue for August 1, 2002.

A sea of cameras and satellite trucks were camped in front of the white sandstone building. Gerald Harris, David's father, sat in the crowded courtroom.

Seven lawyers sat at the long counsel tables before the high bench where Judge Kent presides in a court with a history stretching back to before the Civil War. In this jurisdiction, cases had once included the return of fugitive slaves. During the War Between the States, the court had heard treason cases.

McWilliams was there for Parnham's firm, and a Galveston County lawyer named Tony Buzbee spoke as local counsel on behalf of Lindsey Harris. But there were other lawyers there as well, including one representing the interests of the insurance company.

Kent, a tall man, entered the courtroom and took his seat before the lawyers and spectators, and listened as the lawyers immediately asked for the restraining order, saying that Clara Harris had attempted to contact her stepdaughter.

Kent would have none of the argument, and referred the issue to the Harris County District Attorney's Office, saying that "There are real First Amendment considerations respecting communications."

Then Davis got the victory that he wanted. Judge Kent granted his temporary restraining order until a local probate judge could appoint an administrator. He said that the routine business of Clara Harris and her late husband's estate could continue.

Clara Harris poured herself into her defense, going to the offices of George Parnham for pre-trial conferences with her lawyer, and his associate, Dee McWilliams. The two also brought in another lawyer, Emily Munoz Detoto, a talented young newlywed who would handle Clara Harris' presentation before the jury. Sitting on the sidelines and ever ready to do the attorney's bidding were Mary Parnham and J. J. Gradoni, the firm's investigator of choice.

Judge Davies had scheduled the trial to begin on January 21, 2003, showing no interest in delaying Clara Harris' meeting with justice.

The minutiae of the case were gone over again and again, in hopes that the defense would find a flaw in the state's case. Parnham had soon developed a possible defense on the actual nuts and bolts of the killing itself, after repeatedly watching the Blue Moon video, dissecting it in his mind's eye as he watched the taillights go in a circle crossing the median, and allegedly running over the body of David Harris.

Behind the closed doors of the law office, Parnham began to assemble the team that he would quarterback for the trial. His first choice was his stalwart law partner and closest friend, Wendell A. Odom Jr. The tall, angular lawyer would handle the admissibility of evidence; there was plenty that the defense of Clara Harris wanted to get admitted—and, equally important, wanted to have kept away from the eyes of the jury.

Parnham had ruled out an insanity defense. Psychiatrist Dr. Pricilla Ray was brought into the meetings to aid the defense in their preparation for questions regarding the state of mind of Clara Harris leading up to and at the actual time of the killings. Ray serves on the active staff of two of the nation's premier hospitals in the world-renowned Texas Medical Center, Methodist and St. Luke's. Equally important, Ray was Clara Harris' psychiatrist.

Veteran pathologist Dr. Paul B. Radelat, a physician and lawyer, would serve as the defense's expert in its attempt to diffuse the certain testimony of the Harris County Medical Examiner who'd performed the autopsy on the grisly remains of David Harris. Radelat brought an array of skills to the defense. Handsome, soft spoken, likable, the distinguished lawyer/doctor was believable on the witness stand and would back up what he said, no matter how outlandish the allegation.

Accident reconstructionist Steve Irwin, a handsome Dallas traffic engineer, would handle the complex defense chore of spinning the killing before the jury in such a manner that it would be believable that Clara Harris had not run over her husband multiple times, and had, in fact, not murdered him at all. It was to Irwin that the defense would turn to refute the Blue Moon tape and to sell the jury on Parnham's theory that the killing was nothing more than a terrible accident.

Robert Hirschhorn and Nora Dodson, nationally respected jury consultants with Lewisville, Texas–based Cathy E. Bennett and Associates would aid the lawyers in selection of a panel who did not appear to be openly hostile to Clara Harris and who would, at the very least, tell the defense that they had an open mind on the case.

Rounding out Clara Harris' legal army were Parnham's stalwart legal assistant Winnie McNamara Howard, and intern Mark White.

The conferences were long and frequent, and the Colombian American dentist was an active and intelligent participant in her defense.

Prosecutors would present their standard case, the tried and true scenario played out in courtrooms across the Lone Star State for generations in murders both simple and complex. The state's witnesses would consist of officialdom, such as cops and forensics experts, the people who make Texas' criminal justice system so efficient and often so deadly to defendants.

But Mia Magness and her boss Dan Rizzo would also

have another advantage over the defense. David Harris had been killed in front of a lot of people, bystanders who had heard the commotion and watched the Mercedes run its deadly circles over the body of the dentist. They were horrified by what they had seen and the prosecutors knew that their eyewitness testimony would be potent for whatever jury was assembled.

The duty of finding and interviewing these, the most important witnesses in the case, would fall to investigator Lieutenant Milton Ojeman, a tall and handsome lawman who always appears in court in a trademark suit and cowboy boots. Answering to the former cop, and now DA sleuth, were six additional investigators whom he could call upon if the need arose.

Ojeman's field work produced witnesses who would then come into the DA's office in downtown Houston for meetings with Magness, and sometimes Dan Rizzo. Magness met with each of them at least twice, learning the details of what they had seen that night in the parking lot and lobby of the hotel. As she conducted the interviews, the savvy prosecutor evaluated each on how they would appear to the jury when they took their place on the witness stand.

All the while, Magness maintained a full trial schedule as chief prosecutor in Davies' court, while Rizzo did his daily routine supervising the office's trial division.

Of all of the characters in the tasty soup that is the Clara Harris case, one of the most intriguing ingredients is Houston attorney Valorie Davenport. The longtime lawyer for Julie Knight in her bitter and strange divorce and custody proceedings against Charles Knight is a larger-than-life character with a talent for hyperbole as long as the Rio Grande River.

She now represented Gail Bridges.

Davenport doesn't walk into a room she sweeps into it. She is passionate in the representation of her clients and is sometimes a powerful spokeswoman. She is loud. She is willing to go to almost any end to destroy her opponent, within the canons of ethics. In front of the right judge, the technique works.

Davenport is a large woman, hard to miss in a crowd. She is given to heavy makeup, flowing clothes made of soft fabric, and dark colors. Her dark blond hair has little luster.

Valorie Davenport is at her most spectacular, and strange, before a television camera. Looking into the camera's eye, she lights up; her natural instinct for performance takes over, and, like other star-struck performers, politicians mostly, the lawyer will orate as if speaking to a crowd of thousands whose very existence depend upon the woman's every word. Davenport's bombastic demeanor is meant to intimidate, and it does, but sometimes reveals a vivid imagination and good acting skills, but little more.

But Davenport was good enough to rescue Galveston millionaire Bobby Moody's chestnuts from the fire when she sued a bogus fish farming scheme and its attorneys on his and three other investors' behalf. Ultimately, a Galveston jury awarded the men $34.7 million in actual damages, and $40.7 in punitive damages. The actual damages were later reduced to $20 million.

Davenport was at her best in the case, playing a Texas good ole girl before a Texas jury. Part of the suit was against a national law firm, Miami-based Greenberg Traurig which was represented by lawyers with thick New York accents. The Web site, law.com, reported on Davenport's performance saying, "The homespun Texas native berated the Park Avenue defendants and peppered her presentation with homilies like 'even a blind hog can find an acorn.'" Later in the case, she referred to the lawyers using words like "privileged, Manhattan Park Avenue lawyers," "who attended private schools and wear $3,000 suits, $500 shoes and silk stockings."

Davenport was shameless in performance during the six-week-long trial, even purposely mispronouncing the names of the Jewish attorneys. She reportedly called the law firm she was suing, Greenberg Trog, instead of pronouncing the name properly as Tror-ig. She sometimes said "Goldberg" instead of Greenberg, and called Greenberg attorney Robert Kirshenberg by the name "Kirshenbaum" in front of the Texas jury. Her tactics prompted complaints by opposing counsel as well as defendants in the courtroom.

In an article about the whopping judgment Davenport had won, law.com even reproduced a photo of her wearing a cowboy hat and standing in front of a Confederate flag. But it was Clara Harris who continued to be in the news, not the publicity-hungry lawyer with the down-home tactics. She did, however, have a client involved in the case, and that was enough to get her before the cameras.

She would remain an irritant for months to come.

Investigators were beginning to learn details of the life of Clara and David Harris. Important for the district attorney's office, they were learning of the massive temper of the distaff half of the relationship. Lindsey Harris told the investigators that her stepmother "just blew" when she didn't get her way.

Gail Bridges also related that she had heard from David that Clara had a monumental temper that sometimes got out of control when things didn't go her way.

As the investigators delved into the private personal world of Clara Harris they found more than they had bargained for. Blue Moon, for example, now had a new client, Valorie Davenport, the attorney who was representing Gail Bridges and Julie Knight.

Gail Bridges almost certainly had a tort, a damage suit to file against the estate of her former lover and the wife who'd murdered him. After all, she had been assaulted in the lobby of a hotel and almost run down by the woman. The insurance settlement could be lucrative for Gail and her children, as well as the lawyer who represented them.

It was wise to hire a private investigator on the case to see what would turn up, and who knew more about the players in it than Bobbi Bacha and her Blue Moon investigators? Bobbi Bacha already had a warm relationship with Gail and Julie. Now, she was working for their lawyer as well.

Soon, her investigations were yielding results. What she claimed to be turning up was shocking beyond anyone's imagining. In a report to her client, Bacha told Davenport that Clara Harris was herself involved in a longtime affair with David's close friend, Michael Fondren.

Fondren had spent four years in a Texas prison after conviction on possession of cocaine with intent to deliver. He was released in 1998 and is serving the remainder of his 20 years as a parolee. Bacha claimed that she had two sources who said that Fondren and Clara Harris were lovers. He denied the allegations, telling a reporter, Laura Elder, of the *Galveston County Daily News* that "Those are all lies" when she asked him a series of questions.

Was Fondren in the parking lot of the Nassau Bay Hilton when Clara Harris confronted her husband and Bridges? Elder asked. Before trial, his name was clustered with other parking lot witnesses in the prosecutor's subpoena list.

Did Fondren work for Clara Harris at her Lake Jackson Dental Practice? the young journalist wondered.

Was Clara Harris having an affair with Fondren when she ran down her husband David Harris on July 24, after catching him at a hotel with Gail Bridges? the reporter asked pointedly.

Bacha had another bombshell to deliver on Davenport's behest. Blue Moon was asked to investigate the January 30, 2000 death of Fondren's wife, Roberta. The forty-one-year-old woman was found dead in the bathroom of her Alvin, Texas, home. Vomit was splattered on the floor. The Brazoria County coroner had ruled that Roberta had died a natural death due to "asphyxiation, aspiration of gastric contents." More simply stated, Michael Fondren's wife had choked to death on her own puke.

Brazoria County contracts out its autopsies to the adjoining Galveston County's medical examiner's office. When the report came back, Mrs. Fondren tested positive for carisoprodol, a drug used to help relieve muscle aches and spasms. The drug has sedating properties as well. The Galveston coroner's office, however, ruled that Roberta had died a natural death.

Bacha wasn't satisfied. She asked the Galveston ME to reopen the case.

When asked about Bacha's allegations regarding the affair that was alleged to have taken place between the wife of David Harris and his boyhood friend, George Parnham called them "trash." He continued saying that "It doesn't rise to the level of comment. It's just a continuation of the same type of baseless character assassination."

Mia Magness wouldn't comment on the allegations either, maintaining the typical posture of a district attorney in mid-case. Brazoria County authorities never pursued Bacha's claims.

Since the beginning, Bobby Bacha had sought to get a copy of the video Lindsey Dubec had shot of the death of David Harris. She had been continually turned down by the Harris County DA's office. In a November 2002 pre-trial hearing in the Harris case, Bacha sought to get her video tape of the murder back again, stating that since the district attorney's office and the defense had copies, so should she. The conference before Davies had been called to establish ground rules for the admission of evidence at trial. It was solely a meeting between the prosecution and the defense. When Bacha and her lawyer sought the attention of the court, it quickly became clear that the judge believed that the investigator was an interloper without standing in the case.

"Returning the video will impair our ability to empanel an impartial jury," Magness argued. "The issue of due process dictates that the video not be returned to Blue Moon. I have a copy of that videotape."

Sitting in the courtroom's second row next to her husband, the demonstrative Bacha sighed and threw up her hands. Parnham then charged that the firm shouldn't get a copy of the video because audio tapes of Clara Harris asking for her money back had been given to the media. He claimed that the release was prejudicial to his client receiving a fair trial.

Audiotapes of the dentist asking Bacha for a refund had, in fact, been played over and over on the sensational local television newscasts.

"The video tape, thank God, was in the possession of the police," Davies interjected, frustrated that the media had obtained the audiotape. Davies ordered that the tape of the alleged murder be brought to the custody of the court immediately.

Bacha wasn't finished. She wanted to turn over new audiotapes to the district attorney's office. On them, she claimed, were conversations she had had with two unnamed women who she says confirm that Clara Harris was indeed having an affair with Michael Fondren. The two women never corroborated Bacha's assertion.

Davies also was annoyed by the presence of Valorie Davenport, representing Gail Bridges and viewed the lawyer as yet another interloper in her courtroom, one with even less standing than Bacha.

In a grandstand play before the judge, Davenport made a dramatic and stunning allegation, saying, "My client may not live past this trial." Gail Bridges, in fact, was still living in fear from the telephone threats that Clara Harris had made to her before she'd killed her husband.

Davies looked at the woman sternly from the bench.

"You have no standing in this case," Davies told Davenport.

The lawyer continued, saying, "Mr. Parnham has subpoenaed Gail Bridges' and Julie Knight's records from Blue Moon."

Bobbi Bacha now rose from her seat in the courtroom's third row. She had become familiar to many Houstonians because of frequent appearances on local newscasts because of her search for the missing head of Morris Black in the sensational Robert Durst case.

"I recognize this lady from television," the judge continued. "My question, since you have interjected yourself . . ." Davies said before being interrupted.

"We recently have developed some new evidence," Bacha said, fervently attempting to get the information

ABOVE David and Clara Harris with their twins. *(Courtesy of George Parnham)*

LEFT A happy family man, David Harris smiles for the camera. *(Courtesy of George Parnham)*

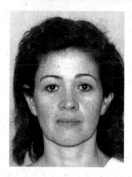

TOP Dr. Clara Harris' car after the incident. *(Courtesy of Steven Long)*

ABOVE Gail Bridges' car after being run into by Clara. *(Courtesy of Steven Long)*

LEFT Mugshot of Dr. Clara Harris trying to smile. *(Courtesy of Department of Criminal Justice)*

Charles Knight, Laurie Wells Knight and their son Kody.
(Courtesy of Steven Long)

TOP Gail Bridges and Julie Knight talking candidly on "Sally Jessy Raphael."

ABOVE Gail and Julie together on a skiing trip.

OPPOSITE PAGE

TOP The Nassau Bay Hilton. *(Courtesy of Steven Long)*

CENTER Perry's Grille & Steakhouse, where Gail and David frequently met. *(Courtesy of Steven Long)*

BOTTOM Windemere. *(Courtesy of Steven Long)*

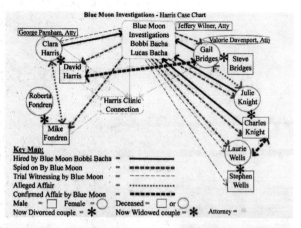

Blue Moon Investigations - Harris Case Chart

George Parnham, Atty
Clara Harris
David Harris
Roberta Fondren
Mike Fondren
Harris Clinic Connection

Blue Moon Investigations
Bobbi Bacha
Lucas Bacha

Jeffery Wilner, Atty
Valorie Davenport, Atty
Gail Bridges
Steve Bridges
Julie Knight
Charles Knight
Laurie Wells
Stephen Wells

Key Map:
Hired by Blue Moon Bobbi Bacha =
Spied on By Blue Moon =
Trial Witnessing by Blue Moon =
Alleged Affair =
Confirmed Affair by Blue Moon =
Male = □   Female = ○   Deceased = □ or ○
Now Divorced couple = ✳   Now Widowed couple = ✳   Attorney =

TOP Bobbi Bacha's Clara Harris Case Chart. *(Courtesy of Bobbi Bacha)*

ABOVE LEFT Clara Harris and George Parnham, her defense lawyer, at a courthouse news conference. *(Courtesy of Steven Long)*

ABOVE RIGHT Judge Carol Davies, from the court's Web site. *(Courtesy of Harris County Courts)*

OPPOSITE PAGE
TOP Lindsey Harris and her mom and stepdad, outside the courtroom after the verdict. *(Courtesy of Steven Long)*

CENTER LEFT Private investigator Bobbi Bacha, outside a Harris County courtroom. *(Courtesy of Steven Long)*

CENTER RIGHT Steve Bridges, husband of Gail. *(Courtesy of Steven Long)*

BOTTOM Julie, Gail and Bobbi riding in a New York limousine. *(Courtesy of Bobbi Bacha)*

TOP The Harris defense team holding a press conference.
(Courtesy of Steven Long)

ABOVE Parnham and his team leave the courthouse in utter defeat.
(Courtesy of Steven Long)

that Clara Harris had had an affair with Michael Fondren, and the tapes she thought proved it, into the record.

"That sure is interesting," Magness interjected, learning of the alleged affair and tapes for the first time.

Bacha continued, telling the judge that she had five or six audiotapes in her possession that represented new evidence in the case. The contents of the tapes would, she believed, prove that Clara Harris and Michael Fondren were having an affair.

Then, in a Freudian slip, Davenport attempted to explain to the judge who Bobbi Bacha was, and what she was doing in the courtroom, saying that Blue Moon is "working for Gail and Julie Knight."

The room erupted in chuckles as reporters and spectators realized the implications of what the attorney had just said.

Clara Harris watched the sideshow being played out before her as the skirmish continued.

Davenport wasn't finished.

"The health, life, safety, and well-being of my client in these matters are critical to the life of my client. My client may not live past this trial. Gail Bridges will be a witness in this case. She became involved in an adulterous affair. It is the same as a rape victim who wears short skirts. She is not listened to."

Davenport had opened Blue Moon to an assault by subpoena and the assailant was George Parnham, who told the court that he wanted Blue Moon's records on Gail Bridges, Julie Knight, Steve Bridges and Chuck Knight. But Davies quashed the attorney's request for a subpoena, while ordering Bacha to preserve the contents of the files.

Parnham could not help showing his contempt for the private investigation firm saying, "We have the subject of the investigation hiring the firm. That is a conflict. They have a habit of obtaining information on one person and selling it to another person."

Davies promptly imposed a gag order on all concerned in the case of *State of Texas vs. Clara Harris*.

But a gag order can't stop unsealed documents from being filed with the court. On November 19, 2002, Davenport filed a document stating, "It has now come to counsel's attention, and has been verified through independent sources, that persons wholly unconnected to Ms. Bridges, but with direct contact and friendship with the accused Clara Harris, her alleged paramour and Ms. Bridges' ex-husband, Steven Bridges, that said persons posing the threat to Ms. Bridges may have indeed been present at the hotel on the evening of the murder."

The court ignored the document.

Bobbi Bacha was frustrated, terribly frustrated, that she hadn't even seen the tape that her investigator, Lindsey Dubec, had recorded of the murder of David Harris. The tape was the property of Blue Moon, she believed, yet it was being held by the Harris County District Attorney's Office as evidence and she couldn't lay her hands on it. Now it would be sealed in the chambers of the judge.

But there was more that the court didn't get that Bacha claims she developed during the time that she worked for Davenport. The investigator says that much of the Harrises' lavish lifestyle was financed by dope flown in to an airstrip that abutted the backyards of posh homes in the neighborhood.

Both Davenport and Bacha desperately wanted the district attorney's office to investigate the allegations.

After the hearing in which Davies imposed the gag order, a bank of television cameras awaited the aftermath of the events upstairs in the courtroom. When Davenport emerged she was drawn like a moth to a flame as she moved toward the awaiting cameras. A glow came over her face. Valorie Davenport disregarded Davies' gag order and gushed, gushed like the legendary Texas oil well at Spindletop a hundred years before. She publicly challenged Mia Magness and the district attorney's office to look into the matters that Bacha had turned up in her investigation. Again, she said that Gail Bridges might not live past the trial of Clara Harris.

Unbeknownst to Davenport, Judge Carol Davies witnessed the lawyer violating her gag order in front of the cameras as she pulled out of the courthouse parking garage. She eased her automobile to the curb next to the sidewalk news conference and watched as Davenport gushed before the cameras. The lawyer never knew that Davies was there. When Davenport was finished, she walked to her car alone.

Parnham emerged from the courthouse angry, again blasting Blue Moon.

"If these folks were lawyers, they wouldn't be lawyers for very long," he told the reporters.

TWELVE

Judge Carol Davies' gag order and later treatment of the media demonstrated a stunning ignorance at best, and hostility at worst, of the way the press does its business. The order came close on the heels of two other equally draconian gag orders in celebrated cases being tried in courtrooms along the Texas gulf coast. First, Judge Belinda Hill had gagged all concerned in the case against Andrea Yates. Later, Galveston's Judge Susan Criss issued an even more sweeping order in the murder case against cross-dressing New York billionaire Robert Durst, who was subsequently acquitted. She had read of the gag order in the Yates case in the *Houston Chronicle* and decided to get a copy of Hill's work to see if she could apply it to her own upcoming high-profile case. Criss' gag order went far beyond what the Houston judge had done.

This order not only gagged local witnesses in the case, but also prevented members of the Los Angeles police and the LA County DA's Office, from discussing a murder case in California in which Durst was a possible suspect. It even gagged the Westchester County, New York, DA's office from discussing its investigation of the disappearance of Durst's wife years before.

All three judges were former prosecutors, steeped in the take-no-prisoners tradition of maximum penalty tradition of justice in the Lone Star State. Among state's attorneys there is a long-standing tradition that, unlike defense lawyers, representatives of the district attorney's office don't talk to the press. The tradition is so ingrained in prosecutors that it is the assumption that all participants in a case should take the same attitude and try the case in the courtroom rather than in the newspaper or on television.

Reality dictates something else altogether. Gag orders simply don't work. If the press wants a story it will get it. If a witness wants to talk, the witness will talk, given the right circumstances and the skill of the reporter working the case. The same holds true for the much-vaunted secrecy of grand juries. In highly publicized cases, somebody who is privy to the closed-door proceedings will leak the likely outcome of a case. More often than not, the press has a pretty good idea if an indictment is about to come down before it actually does.

Both the Hill and Davies gag orders prohibited interviewing within the Harris County Courthouse. The press skillfully found nooks, crannies, and any other space to do the interviews necessary for their jobs. Within thirty seconds of Davies' ruling from the bench, one reporter covering the case was passing notes to one of its star witnesses, in direct violation of what the judge had just ordered. The witness was writing answers to the queries. The two were in the audience, and the judge was still on the bench, oblivious to what was going on under her nose.

All three judges appeared contemptuous of the history of Texas journalism in the state's courtrooms. It is a history in which reporters have richly respected the dignity of the courts. It is a history replete with generations of unassuming reporters sitting quietly in court taking careful notes of the proceedings happening before them. It is a history in which the corridors of courts are often used for a quiet conversation between a reporter and a news-maker. It is a history replete with judicial respect for the press and its constitutionally protected mandate to report the news.

Yet Davies barely tolerated the journalists who would crowd her courtroom for the Harris trial. The press was instructed to sit silently if they chose to stay in the court-room when the court was in recess. They were not to read newspapers or anything else. They were to sit, period. Eventually, Davies saw the cruelty of the order and re-lented, allowing reporters to quietly read a newspaper when she was not on the bench.

Like Hill in the trial of Andrea Yates, Davies ruled that reporters were not to enter and leave the courtroom once the judge was seated. If a journalist left the courtroom, they were to be barred from the rest of the trial. The edict made it impossible for local beat reporters to cover more proceedings than the Harris case. The twenty-floor build-ing houses multiple district courts that daily produced multiple stories.

Davies barred photos or sketches of jurors. She also barred all photos inside the entire courthouse, and limited interviews to those brave enough to publicly speak to journalists on the sidewalk outside the courthouse. No matter how bad the winter weather was outside, inter-views would not be conducted inside the building.

Davies' rules were inconsistent regarding her admis-sion of cameras in the courtroom. Although she allowed the devices, they were only able to broadcast sound dur-ing opening and closing arguments, and the verdict and sentencing in the event Clara Harris was found guilty. One pool television camera and one pool still camera would silently record the fate of Clara Harris. A pool sketch artist would also be allowed to draw the proceedings before the judge. Yet some witnesses would request that there be no television of their testimony and Davies granted their requests.

Also flying in the face of longtime Texas journalistic tradition, Davies ruled that jurors were not to be questioned after they had reached their verdict.

Strange as it may seem, although one-on-one interviews of participants in the Clara Harris case were forbidden, reporters could conduct interviews on their cell phones. The order read, "With the exception of telephone interviews, no person shall conduct an interview about this case, whether recorded or not, of any person connected with or participating in the proceedings in the case of the *State of Texas v. Clara L. Harris* at any location inside the CJC at 1200 Franklin."

Finally, Davies threatened violators with contempt if they did not follow her orders.

Davies would call a jury pool of 120 to choose the twelve who would decide the fate of Clara Harris. Jury selection would be out of the sight of press and public, carried on closed circuit television into a courtroom down the hall from the large twentieth-floor ceremonial courtroom named for the late Harris County Judge Myron Love. Davies' courtroom was too small to house a trial with this much interest.

As the trial date neared, Parnham and his team concentrated upon the prospective show-and-tell of accident reconstructionist Steve Irwin.

He was a blue chip expert, a civil engineer with a 1985 degree from the University of Texas at Arlington who had spent the early part of his career designing roads. Later,

Irwin formed his own firm, much of his business coming from his testimony as an expert witness. He claims to have studied more than 1,500 automobile accidents, and to have testified in more than 100 jury trials.

The engineer would produce a high-tech computer-generated re-creation of the defense version of the "accidental" death of David Harris. Parnham planned a media assault on the senses of the jurors. In fact, Irwin planned to testify that Clara Harris had hit her husband, carried him for a few feet, and then deposited his body near a bloodstain found on the asphalt by homicide investigators. He would attempt to convince the jurors, despite the testimony of multiple eyewitnesses that she'd only run over David's body once, and then never ran over him again.

In the event that Irwin's video was not admitted into evidence by Davies, who Parnham was aware had a reputation as a jurist with a pro-prosecution bias, the canny defense lawyer had another visual up his sleeve that was almost certain to be admitted: huge, professionally drawn artist renderings of the hotel and its parking lots.

Irwin would produce these maps using the technique of photogrametry, making a map from measurements taken from photographs. The sophisticated artwork was used by high-budget police departments and the armed forces. He would produce the maps using photographs shot by Parnham's private investigator at the scene. Irwin also visited the scene and photographed it.

He and the investigator took pictures of the asphalt, grass, curbs, and even tire marks left on the pavement.

For his trouble, Irwin's firm would be paid between $40,000 and $50,000. The high-tech animation was a costly gamble with Clara Harris' money. It was a gamble that Parnham had to take, because the rest of the defense that he had to work with in the case was so thin.

All of the major television networks requested media credentials for the trial of Clara Harris. The court had allotted only 50 seats for the local, national, and international journalists who would cover the event. Like the arrangements for the trial of Andrea Yates, the press would fill the center section of seats in the courtroom.

Coverage would beam into Latin America as well, and in particular to Colombia, where the fate of the former beauty queen was a national sensation. One television network in the country planned a one-hour special on the case. It would be broadcast four times throughout the trial.

ABC, NBC, CBS, and Fox all reserved multiple seats. Houston's local television stations would cover the trial. Both the Associated Press and Reuters planned to give the case comprehensive coverage. Houston's lone newspaper, the *Houston Chronicle*, would staff the trial for its duration. From time to time, there would be coverage from the *Dallas Morning News,* the *San Antonio Express News, The Los Angeles Times* and *The New York Times* and the *New York Post*.

Inside Edition, as well as the network news magazines planned comprehensive coverage. *People*, would send its veteran Houston bureau chief, Gabrielle Cosgriff, to follow the proceedings. Court TV would staff the trial for its duration, but not broadcast live because of Davies' prohibition of audio.

In November, Parnham had blitzed New York with personal appearances by Clara Harris herself. The dentist was a hot property, with each of the networks vying for "exclusive" interviews. All three would have their time with the beautiful dentist. The networks would put their best talent on parade in interviews with the now famous "Killer Driller" from Texas.

One by one, Clara Harris sat down in a studio with Ann Curry, Dianne Sawyer, and Hanna Storm. Each of the networks had agreed to the ground rules that Parnham laid down. There would be no questions regarding the facts of the case, and there would be no photos of the twins shown during the interviews and subsequent programs that the networks were planning.

The network interviews were taxing, an emotional drain on Clara Harris. Up until the trip to New York, her world had consisted of time at home with the twins, time with Gerald and Millie, time with friends, church, and the frequent conferences with her lawyers and experts to prepare her defense.

Although she cried on all of the network programs, at the end of the last interview, Clara Harris couldn't finish. She broke down, the emotional upheaval she was feeling now overwhelming as she came face to face with the alien world of network television and the empathy the female anchors seemed to show her. And it was network television's mistress of empathy, Dianne Sawyer, who brought Clara Harris to an emotional state of collapse. She left the studio spent. Clara boarded a jet and cried all the way back to Houston.

It was all-important that the potential jury pool be as untainted as possible, or miracle of miracles, even be biased toward Parnham's client. Clara was facing life in prison, and Parnham knew that it would be difficult, if not impossible, for the panel he would face on January 21, 2003, not to have heard of the case. His client had run over her husband in her silver Mercedes, and some media reports had even stated that after driving the luxury car over his body multiple times, she had parked on top of David for good measure.

Early in the case, Parnham had successfully corrected the press on that score—after a rash of stories had said that she had cruelly parked on the body of her husband, the press corrected itself, saying that the reports were a mistake.

But there were still traps to be run before the case went to trial. Parnham's investigators were out in full force, interviewing any and all who would talk to them, as was Milton Ojeman and his crew of sleuths from the DA's office. Parnham was also ever mindful that there was a wild card out as well. Valorie Davenport and Blue Moon seemed to be popping up everywhere, and they appeared to be getting a disproportionate helping of press coverage.

The highly respected *Texas Monthly* magazine assigned one of its most talented journalists to do a quick turnaround story on the Clara Harris murder case. Skip Hollandsworth did a remarkable job, literally overnight, of putting all of the players together in one concise easy read. Contacted by the magazine and aware of the positive appeal the story might generate, Parnham allowed Clara to pose for a photo wearing a dark business suit and white silk shirt. Her hair was re-dyed to its natural dark color. The image as it appeared on a full page of the magazine was of a competent professional. Hopefully some jurors would see and remember Clara Harris this way, rather than the image of the harried distraught woman they saw over and over again on television newsclips.

Hollandsworth began his research for the story sitting on the floor of a fifth-floor corridor of the Galveston

County Courthouse interviewing reporters who had been covering the case. They were waiting outside a closed courtroom in which both press and public were denied access; Judge Susan Baker was hearing the latest chapter in the custody case of *Bridges vs. Bridges*. Immediately upon hearing that his former wife was the other woman involved in the death of Dr. David Harris, Steve Bridges again filed suit to modify the parent–child relationship with his three children from the judge's original custody order rendered three years before.

Gail Bridges had been awarded custody of two of the couple's children at the time of her divorce from her husband. Now, he was asking for joint custody.

He charged that the new order was necessary "because the children's present living environment may endanger the children's physical health or significantly impair the children's emotional development."

In a supporting affidavit, Bridges charged that while one of the children lived permanently with him, two remained with their mother and were with him on visitation periods allotted by the court in its original order. Steve Bridges got the kids during an extended period each summer. But that period was drawing to a close, the school year was approaching, and should he return the children to their mother they would be exposed to emotional harm, stress, and "possible physical harm."

Steve Bridges charged in the affidavit that in the wake of the murder of David Harris, Gail had told him that she believed Clara Harris was initially aiming for her. He further said his former wife was in hiding because the media had staked out her house (which they hadn't done), and were constantly knocking on her door (which happened for a brief period right after the murder).

Bridges alluded to the alleged affair of his wife with

Julie Knight in his affidavit and told the court that he assumed that both women would deny the allegations.

Regardless of the true nature of the relationship between Julie Knight and Gail, I do know this:

A. Julie Knight is staying with my wife right now.

B. Julie Knight has filed an absolutely groundless civil lawsuit against me, State Farm, Mr. Knight and others. A true and correct copy of the lawsuit is attached . . . In her suit, Ms. Knight makes many strange and false allegations. For example, she asserts that the defendants are somehow intercepting and recording her conversations and phone calls now.

C. Julie Knight spends a lot of time around all three of my children and she lives just around the corner from my ex-wife's home. According to my children, Julie Knight has discussed her civil lawsuit that includes me as a defendant with my children.

D. The relationship is a stormy and sometimes violent one. Just a few months ago my . . . daughter had to call 911 to get police to help break up a fight between Julie Knight and Gail at Gail's house, according to my daughter.

Finally, Bridges charged that "Gail is currently very upset and emotional. I am concerned that Gail may not be not [sic] mentally stable at this time. Gail has attempted suicide at least once in the past [In 2000 she took a huge number of pills but then forced herself to throw up]. Gail has threatened to take the children in the past and run away. Julie Knight has a house in Colorado. I am concerned that Gail will leave town with the children."

Bridges asked that his kids not be returned to his former wife until after a court hearing because they "should not be returned to a physically and emotionally injured mother who is besieged by the media clamoring for kinky details of their mother's sex life. My children should not be around Julie Knight at this time . . ."

A closed hearing was held on Steve Bridges' petition, but nothing was changed in the original custody order because Baker determined that Clara Harris was no longer a threat to the children of Gail and Steve Bridges.

The-made-for-media murder case generated a flurry of airline ticket sales as network crews booked reservations for Houston in order to capture a segment for their news magazine programs. Quickly producers learned that there was not just one story, the tale of David Harris' murder by his wife, but multiple stories and players involved in the relationships growing out of South Shore Harbor, Clear Lake, and Friendswood.

ABC and CBS planned segments on *48 Hours* and *Primetime*. George Parnham agreed to give ABC unprecedented access to himself and his client, including access to the Harris team's presentation before a mock jury the defense had hired to test their theories in the meeting room of a local hotel. Parnham also opened the doors to his home, and his quiet cabin in East Texas. Even his wife and paralegal, the usually reserved Mary, gave the network interviews.

More important, ABC had Clara. The crew was invited into the mansion's master bedroom for a glimpse of the accused murderer at home. What they filmed was a weepy woman lost in her grief and still consumed by the hurt and anger that her husband had inflicted upon her.

Parnham discussed his fear of the testimony of Lindsey Harris when she took the witness stand with his associates and the journalists now blanketing him with coverage. The daughter of David Harris was his client's worst nightmare. She had ridden in the front seat of the Mercedes as her stepmother took the life of her father. What she said on the stand could put Clara in prison for life, and this was one witness he couldn't risk destroying upon cross-examination for fear of angering the jury at this victim of his client's rage.

And George Parnham took care of George Parnham. The canny jurist knew that network television was where the reputations of giants in the field of criminal law were made. He knew that because of the Yates case viewers already knew him across the nation. This was his opportunity to become well known—to become one of the larger-than-life figures of American jurisprudence.

Parnham embargoed the ABC program until after the trial. The interview would do nothing for Clara before the jury, but it potentially could do a lot for the reputation of a gray-bearded, quiet-spoken lawyer named George Parnham.

The CBS crew from the beginning targeted the harder, seamier aspects of the case. Eventually, they settled upon the investigator, Bobbi Bacha, and the work that her agency had done working for one player, then another, then another. Bacha was taped in a segment at home. They followed her as she drove around the neighborhood of Clara and David Harris. Bacha was shown in front of an easel on which were placed the photos of herself, the Harrises, the Bridgeses, and the Knights. As the interviewer pointed to Julie and Gail, Bacha confidently proclaimed that the two had not been lovers. CBS neglected to point out that Bacha's most recent client among the players was Valorie Davenport, the lawyer for Julie Knight and Gail Bridges.

* * *

The sight of the bearded George Parnham and his strikingly beautiful client walking into the Harris County Criminal Justice Center was becoming commonplace as the two made their way to Davies' court for a final hearing on pre-trial motions just days before the case was to begin.

There would be no postponements, no reset, and certainly no plea bargain in this case. After all, what did Parnham have to bargain with but a beautiful soft-spoken woman and nothing more? The crime had been caught on video tape. It was an undisputed fact that Clara Harris had killed her husband. No, the trial would begin and there was nothing that the bearded lawyer could do to stop it.

The morning of the hearing Parnham drove to the courthouse from his home in Garden Oaks, an upscale neighborhood ten minutes from downtown. The suburb had been built just after World War II on the GI Bill. The mostly frame homes had weathered the '50s, '60s '70s and '80s. By the '90s they were showing their age, and professionals seeking a way to ease Houston's increasingly difficult commutes from the city's far-flung suburbs dusted off these comfortable old homes and brought them up to date. Garden Oaks and nearby Oak Forest instantly became fashionable among young professionals who worked downtown.

By now, Parnham could live anywhere he wanted in the Bayou City. Highrise condos were becoming the residence of choice for many lawyers who wanted to live near the downtown courthouse. Huge town homes were displacing the longtime residents of the Montrose from their bohemian nests as workers in the city's energy sector gladly spent large chunks of their six- and seven-figure incomes to be five minutes from the office and the trading floor.

But Parnham continued to live among the stately oaks and towering pines of his neighborhood, a quiet island in Houston where some residents continued not to lock their cars at night, where kids raced their bikes down the street without fear, and where there was actual silence at night, the constant whir of the city's freeways nothing more than a far-off rumble.

Parnham left his idyllic neighborhood for the opening salvo of the Clara Harris case, facing a judge who he knew by reputation would almost certainly have pro-prosecution sympathies. As he and Clara Harris entered the last of the pre-trial hearings, he expected little good to come from the appearance. He didn't have long to wait.

As the January 16, 2003 hearing began, Mia Magness wasted little time in getting an explosive statement before the judge, and almost equally important, the media. She told Davies that Lindsey Harris would tell the jury that her stepmother had told her, "I could kill him and get away with it for all he's put me through."

The seventeen-year-old murder witness had cited the statement during a deposition. Now, reporters frantically scribbled the explosive and damning quotation on their pads.

But there was more to come. Magness continued, saying that Lindsey had witnessed Clara Harris saying "I'm going to hit him," immediately before striking her husband with the Mercedes. She told the jurors that David Harris' daughter would testify to that from the witness stand.

Parnham throughout the case had attempted to speak with Lindsey Harris to no avail. Her lawyers fiercely protected the fragile young woman, who had already attempted suicide. Magness protected her star eyewitness as well. Parnham knew about the statements Lindsey had made and had asked Davies to suppress them. Now, the judge had allowed the prosecutor to read them from the deposition in open court even before a jury was seated.

Parnham's usually calm demeanor burst.

"The horse is out of the barn unsaddled," he said. "The jury will have heard them. It is extremely unfair to Clara Harris."

The statements would be allowed, although Magness would not be able to use them in opening arguments.

The judge then made one of the more curious rulings of the case, declaring that Clara Harris' lawyer could not speak in court about the allegations of an alleged lesbian relationship between Gail Bridges and Julie Knight.

Parnham's frustration again burst forth. "It has to do with the relationship of the parties. I don't care how inflammatory."

Parnham knew that his client's anger stemmed not only from the fact that David Harris had been having an affair, but also from the fact that he was having an affair with Gail Bridges, who, Clara believed was known in the community as a bisexual. His client believed that because of Gail's alleged dual sexuality, her husband's lover only wanted his money. Coupled with the public humiliation of David's relationship with Gail, the embarrassment had been overwhelming to her. While he ran the risk of establishing a motive of jealousy for the killing, he believed that the jury would respond to Clara's humiliation brought on by David and Gail Bridges and her reputation in League City. To him, the humiliation factor was worth the risk of the twelve jurors believing that Clara had killed for jealousy.

The investigators from Blue Moon and the district attorney's office weren't the only ones who had been working hard since Clara had hit David in July. Parnham's private investigator, J. J. Gradoni, had felt frustration heaped upon frustration as he investigated the witnesses to the event.

"I've never met so much resistance in a case," he says.

Gradoni felt that resistance not only from witnesses, such as desk clerk Garrett Clark, who wouldn't talk with him, but also from the owners of the Nassau Bay Hilton.

"They told people who worked for them that they would be fired if they talked," he recalled. In fact, Clark, who ultimately did consent to be interviewed, claimed to Gradoni that he had ultimately been fired as an outgrowth of the incident.

He even got resistance from officials such as the Nassau Bay police and EMS.

All investigators, be they private or police, are accustomed to a degree of opposition. However, what they dislike most is the wild card, the event that is totally unexpected.

That was exactly what Gradoni got when he and his boss Parnham learned that the new office that David Harris had so carefully planned had been broken into over the Christmas holidays, little more than a month before the trial. A cleaning crew discovered that burglars had broken into the building, stole a computer and computer games, and the personnel file of Gail Bridges.

Gradoni quickly surmised that the break-in was the work of juveniles, not operatives of the DA's office, nor any of the players involved in the case. He concluded that the missing file had simply been misplaced.

"There wasn't anything in it anyway, a resume and little more," he later said.

But rumors on the street had it much different. Sources said that the file contained brokerage documents that would provide for David Harris' girlfriend's future financial well-being, as well as the promise of a rosy future for her children.

Hogwash, Gradoni says. "Why would you put something like that in a personnel file?"

THIRTEEN

On January 21, 2003, Clara Harris entered the twentieth-story courtroom of Judge Carol Davies wearing a brown print suit with her hair pulled back, with white pearls and earrings. She walked into the room on the arm of her husband's mother, Millie Harris. The trial had now moved to the more spacious ceremonial courtroom on the building's highest floor. Outside, the Houston weather was cloudy and cold.

The week before, George Parnham had come down with a bad cold, one which he would later describe as the worst in his life. But now he was feeling better, his body filled with the remedies that flew off store counters in Houston during the wet mid-winter months along the Texas coast.

Just down the hallway, nineteen journalists sat in Project Courtroom #2 watching the proceedings on closed circuit television. What they saw were the now-familiar figures of Mia Magness and Dan Rizzo for the prosecution. At the adjacent defense table, his closest companion and law partner, Wendell Odom, and jury consultant Robert Hirschhorn, joined George Parnham.

Voir dire, or jury selection, had begun in the case of *State of Texas vs. Clara Harris*. It was the first of potentially three phases of trial in the state. Next would come the guilt or innocence phase in which lawyers present witnesses, then argue their cases before the panel. In the case of a guilty verdict, an additional phase would be played out in which both defense and prosecution could present witnesses to help the jury to determine or mitigate the now-convicted defendant's punishment. In the end, after all of the lawyers' shouting was over, the woman on the bench would pronounce the jury's sentence.

Davies dripped with Southern charm and sincerity as she greeted the jurors and began her standard judicial oration on the merits of jury service. It is a lecture that every judge delivers at the beginning of a trial. It is a tradition that every juror must endure in agonizing silence. The judge introduced the defendant and lawyers to the jury. Parnham nodded in acknowledgment, while the prosecutors both gave a strong "Good morning" greeting to the people they would try to woo with their considerable skills for the next few weeks.

At the end of voir dire, twelve jurors and two alternates would be chosen to decide the fate of the Friendswood dentist. At 10:45 a.m., Davies read the indictment before her. Clara Harris would stand trial for "striking the complainant with a vehicle and did then and there eventually cause bodily injury to David Harris and did intentionally cause the death of David Harris by striking him with a motor vehicle."

Davies then looked at the jury and explained that, should they find Clara Harris guilty, she faced a sentence of from five years to 99 years to life in prison. The judge continued, explaining that probation became an option if the sentence were 10 years or less. By 10:57 a.m., Davies had moved on to explain the possibility of lesser included offenses to the jury. At 11:04 a.m., the judge told the jury that accidental killing is not a criminal offense; however, recklessly causing the death is a lesser offense than the murder with which Clara was charged.

Davies asked the jury panel if any of them knew any of the players that would be participating in the trial. She also asked if any had other reasons that they believed might preclude them from passing judgment upon the defendant.

One member of the panel stood and told the judge that she had met Clara Harris. Another said that she worked in the dental field.

Clara Harris now sat at the defense table surrounded by her team of lawyers. Parnham was joined by the boyish-looking Dee McWilliams and a six-months-pregnant Emily Munoz Detoto, who had once interviewed with Parnham, but turned down his offer and went to work for another firm. The famed defense lawyer had so liked her work, however, that he had gone outside his own firm and hired her to work on the Harris defense team.

The night before had been so wonderful, Clara thought. The mansion had been filled to overflowing because most of the congregation of Shadycrest Baptist Church had come over to offer their love and support. They had gathered around David's grand piano and had sung the beloved old hymn, "Amazing Grace."

Clara knew that she would not be alone as she endured her trial. She was serene, her faith buttressing her. She had placed her fate in the hands of her creator. Nothing could go wrong, she told a member of the defense team, "when this many people are praying for me."

And the support had followed her to the courthouse as the people of Shadycrest stood by their fellow congregant. Millie Harris had even brought cookies, candy, and snacks to the courthouse.

Voir Dire is the most boring of all court proceedings, and the reporters covering the case, veterans all of this phase of justice, sat in their isolated location as jury selection droned on. Some read newspapers, while others worked crossword puzzles. Enforcement of Davies' order not to read in the courtroom was lax in the room reserved for the press during jury selection. Others simply stared at the big-screen television monitor that was now broadcasting the ponderous closed-circuit proceedings from the pool camera stationed in the larger room.

By the following morning, after a full day of elimination of prospective jurors, there were seventy-three left. Clara again faced them, wearing a pale blue double-breasted suit with a white blouse reminiscent of the Victorian era. Finally, it was time for the lawyers to speak to what was left of the original panel from which the twelve jurors and two alternates would be chosen. At 10:53 a.m., Mia Magness rose and walked to the lectern, the first time that the panel would hear her strong and persuasive voice.

Magness didn't stay behind the lectern for long. Wearing a lavaliere microphone, she paced around the courtroom, her speech clipped. Magness pronounced her Rs hard, in the accent of the Texas coast, vastly different from the slightly Southern, slightly Western speech of the rest of the state. She had grown up in the affluent town of Conroe, just north of Houston.

Magness spoke with a direct quality in the way she addressed the jury. There was nothing obtuse or veiled, no verbal sophistry was exercised. Instead, she spoke in plain English, keeping her words simple and understandable. Her words were unmistakable in their meaning.

"This case is about murder," she said.

Across the room, Clara Harris watched, her elbows placed on the oak counsel table as Magness explained the law to the jury and explained why she believed Clara should spend a huge portion of the rest of her life behind prison walls.

The state had been allotted up to an hour-and-a-half for its presentation. She began asking the potential jurors questions about their feelings on issues such as adultery that were likely to be introduced in the case.

"One of your questionnaires stated, 'He deserved it, he had it coming.'" She asked the panel if others felt that way.

"If you are unfaithful, you deserve the consequences of your actions," she said. "Does anybody feel that way?"

A handful of hands went up. Magness made a mental note of the identity of the jurors, while Rizzo wrote down their names at the defense table. Both prosecution and defense would challenge, and eliminate, some of the panel when it came time to pick the jury based upon their response to the questions now being asked.

Two jurors told Magness that they could not sit in judgment of another person. Yet another told the prosecutor that she favored the defense.

Magness was finished quickly, yielding to the defense a bare thirty minutes after she had begun.

George Parnham arose, his snow-white hair shining bright in the subdued lighting of the courtroom, his voice velvety soft as he began to address the jury.

"How many of you believe that Clara Harris is guilty of something?" he asked. "That's okay."

A juror raised his hand and answered the famed defense lawyer.

"I feel like she's here because she did something," he said.

About twenty others agreed with Parnham. He asked for a show of hands of those who concurred with the statements.

Next he asked, "Considering what you have heard at this point is there any member of the jury panel that favors the prosecution?"

None raised their hands.

Parnham now spoke to the potential jurors earnestly when he asked, "The issue will be, did she accidentally hit her husband, or did she intentionally hit her husband with a car?"

Parnham became more and more animated in his questioning as he continued to ask a series of questions developed over thirty years of legal practice and through sitting with Hirschhorn, his jury consultant.

Parnham and the consultant now used what they had learned from the mock jury they had hired in phrasing their questions. The lawyers had presented their case and tried out their theories. The paid jurors had given the team their "honest" opinion of their case. But now it was time for the real thing as he faced the panel that in a few days would hold the fate of Clara Harris in their hands.

"How many of you think that she is guilty of something?"

This time seventeen hands were raised.

"How many of you believe that Clara Harris is guilty of murder?"

Now, only six hands went into the air.

Then the lawyer began to talk about the legal principle of finding a person guilty beyond a reasonable doubt. He explained that a jury must acquit, he told them passionately, if they have a reasonable doubt.

"Do you have the courage to stand up and say it?" he implored. "I want this jury to look at Clara and say to her, 'Clara, I will not give you a fair trial.'"

George Parnham was finished ninety-three minutes after he had begun.

After a brief recess, Davies unceremoniously re-entered the courtroom tripping on her robe. A court coordinator whispered to the press, "She does that a lot."

Clara Harris instinctively jumped from her seat at the counsel table and went to the judge's side, her medical training at the ready. Quickly, it became evident that the judge was not suffering from a medical emergency and the defendant returned to the counsel table.

Finally, Davies seated the panel that would decide Clara Harris' fate. The jury would consist of nine women, three men, and two female alternates. As the jury was seated, Parnham walked over and briefly placed his hand on the well dressed shoulder of his client.

Parnham had secured a hole card in the jurors

Only four of the jurors were ethnic. Three of the jurors were Black, one was Hispanic and the remainder Anglo.

At the end of the day after the courtroom had emptied, Clara Harris walked outside into the mild Houston winter day with the parents of the man she had killed. Gerald Harris told the waiting reporters that their daughter-in-law was family, and he and his wife Millie would support her because they wanted Clara to be with the children.

On the third morning of her trial, Clara wore a dark suit boasting wide lapels similar to those of a tuxedo, while her blouse was rust colored. Her dark hair was down, hanging above her shoulders as she entered the courtroom through the corridor doors. The room was packed, filled with friends and family.

Gerald and Millie Harris sat on the front row near his brother Dr. Lowell Harris, a recently retired country doctor from Hope, Arkansas.

The large courtroom boasted waist-high burled wood panels around the walls, cream-colored burlap wall cov-

ering with swaths of blue, a barrel-vault ceiling, oak
benches, and gray carpet. It was a much more pleasant
and serviceable setting than the location of Houston's last
trial of national interest, that of Andrea Yates. In that
courtroom, the operable word was dark—dark wood,
dark lighting, dark everything. To make matters worse,
the courtroom was located in the old criminal courts
building. Decades of air had blown through the building's
ventilation system, which had accumulated dust and par-
ticulate matter that was never cleaned. In short, the Yates
courtroom suffered from what is called by air quality experts "sick building syndrome." All those who suffered
with allergies and sat through the trial got sick. The Harris case would be tried in much cleaner surroundings.

Outside the courtroom, George Parnham looked into
the mirror of the men's room, checking his appearance
once more before beginning the trial.

"Good morning," an acquaintance said to the lawyer.

"It is not a good morning," Parnham answered, feeling
the stress of the trial's beginning and the ravages of the
cold upon his ailing body.

Judge Carol Davies entered the courtroom and took
her seat at the bench. She looked out upon the throng. In
the center, the press from across the nation and beyond
filled almost every seat of the large center section.
Friends and family of the well-heeled and now famous
defendant were seated on either side, wanting to show
support for Clara. A smattering of the curious took up the
remaining seats. One member, not chosen, of the original
120 on the Harris jury panel was there because she had
now become fascinated by the case and her brief proxim-
ity to its outcome.

Davies recognized Gerald and Mildred Harris and ordered the two to be sworn in as witnesses if they were to

testify. After the oath, the elderly couple was asked to leave the courtroom in keeping with the long-standing legal tradition of not allowing potential witnesses to view proceedings simply known as "the rule."

A distressed look came over Clara Harris' face as the parents of her husband left the courtroom. Up until now, Gerald had been with her at all of the proceedings, showing his daughter-in-law unwavering support. Now she began to grasp the reality of court. It was the judge who would now control her life and the lives of those around her.

On the bench was a portly woman. She was Everywoman—the kindly aunt, the doting grandmother, the loving mother. In fact, Clara Harris was to face a judge with scant sympathy for the defense, whom she would find to be anything but kind.

Again, she stood before the bench as the indictment was read to her yet another time. When she was asked how she pleaded, Clara Harris answered in a strong voice without a trace of her native Colombian accent, "Not guilty, your honor."

Now seated, Clara Harris was still, her head held high, her prominent jaw revealing a proud profile as she sat waiting for the jury. At 1:39 p.m., the panel walked into the room and took their seats in the box. They were a mystery of sorts, their identities were so carefully guarded by the judge. Later, after the trial was over, staff members in Parnham's office could not reconstruct any of their professions, much less their names.

For the second time, Mia Magness stood before the jury to address them.

"This is what I expect the evidence to show," she began. "On July 24th, 2002, David Harris was forty-four years old, smart, successful, well liked, a generous person. He was the father of three children. The evidence will show that he was a good person, a loving person."

Magness spoke softly, matter-of-factly, not displaying the emotional fireworks that were sure to come as the trial progressed.

"He became involved with a person who was not his wife," she stated, adding that he had even revealed his indiscretions in a family meeting with his parents seven days before he was killed.

Methodically, in slow, simple sentences, the prosecutor wove her account to the jury, leading up to David's death, saying that the day before she killed him, Clara Harris had hired a private detective firm to "dig up dirt on Gail Bridges."

Magness methodically recounted the brawl that had happened in the lobby of the Nassau Bay Hilton when Clara caught her husband with his lover as they emerged from an elevator and were eventually escorted from the hotel to the parking lot.

"The defendant got mad," the prosecutor continued. "She drove to the back parking lot."

Finally, Magness used the line that would thematically set the tone of her case for the entire trial.

"She turned her seventy-thousand-dollar luxury Mercedes into a four-thousand pound killing machine," she said.

In conclusion, Mia Magness looked at her jury, looked them in the eye as she stood before them, saying, "It will come down to this: Clara Harris got mad. She intentionally hit David Harris. He died. That is murder."

George Parnham watched his opponent with respect as she practiced the lawyer's craft with skill. You don't work as a criminal defense lawyer in Houston, Texas, and not respect the people who, day after day, work in the environment of prosecution created by Johnny Holmes and later, Chuck Rosenthal. Defense lawyers as a matter of course put themselves through the meat grinder opposing that office in court, and come out battered, bruised and bloodied.

Part of the problem for the defense bar was the law. Over the years, loopholes were closed that had previously given criminal defense lawyers a fighting chance. The people of Texas hate criminals. They hate them to the point that even candidates for state attorney general, a largely civil post, run their campaigns as rigid law-and-order candidates. Candidates for judicial offices tout their tough-on-crime stances when in reality they largely act as a referee during trial and rule on matters of law as judges.

George Parnham looked at Mia Magness as she finished her opening argument knowing that this trial would be one of the most difficult of his career.

Next to him sat a woman who had run over her husband, probably multiple times, and killed him. Next to him sat a woman whose words would likely damn her before the jury when Lindsey Harris told her story of the hot July night in the parking lot of the Hilton. But also seated next to him was the beloved Dr. Clara, the church-going mother of twins whose friends now filled the courtroom to overflowing. If he could only convince the jury of the warmth of his client, he might, just might, have a chance to save her from prison.

Privately George Parnham had been honest with the journalists he had come to know well during the trial of Andrea Yates. Months before in the federal courthouse across downtown from the courtroom where he now sat, he had accidentally and casually met with a gaggle of reporters there covering the trial of the accounting firm,

Arthur Anderson, LLP. In a moment of levity, the lawyer acknowledged the uphill battle many of the journalists would witness him fighting in a few months. The case was one that he quite likely would not win.

Now he rose to face the jury. Before him were nine women. One was an acquaintance, while another was a person who "related" to the actions of his client at the hotel that night. Was it a made-for-Clara jury now seated before him? Parnham didn't know, but he did know that it was unlikely that he could have secured a more favorable demographic to sit in judgment of his client. Nine women would judge whether killing was an acceptable answer to adultery. A verdict of innocent was even possible if a single juror believed that way. Jury nullification was a possibility.

The courtroom was silent as the bearded lawyer began.

"July 24, 2002, started out as the best day in the last eight in the life of Clara Harris," he said quietly, his voice matter-of-fact. "She took care of the kids she had given birth to. She kissed David goodbye."

Parnham looked at the jury as he spoke words he said had come from David Harris' mouth.

"Tonight will be the termination of my involvement, my sexual involvement, with my receptionist," Parnham droned.

The lawyer related how the day turned routine.

"David left, and Clara went to a tanning salon," he continued. "She knew that night that she would bring her husband home. She told Maria, [the governess], 'I have a mission to accomplish. I'm going to bring my husband home.'"

Parnham now flashed the jury back to the previous day, beginning his effort to target a culprit other than his client in the killing.

"She hires Blue Moon to eavesdrop," he continued.

"Blue Moon makes a phone call and says they are not at Perry's Steak House. They are at the fourth or sixth floor of the Hilton Hotel."

Parnham continued, now jumping the story to the arrival of Clara and Lindsey Harris at the hotel.

"She pulls the car in the parking lot," he said. "Lindsey spent the summer with David and Clara, who she calls Mama."

"[In the lot] They find Gail's Navigator. They break the windshield," he continued. "She looks around and can't find David's truck.

"She checks to see if David is registered," Parnham continued, spinning out the framework of his defense. "Lindsey calls her dad on the cell phone. To Clara's absolute relief, David answers and says 'I'm on the way. I'm at Pappadeaux, [restaurant], and I'm on my way.' "

Quietly now, Parnham intones, "Her husband was coming home."

He paused.

"The elevator door opens and there is her husband," he continued, his voice now rising. "Clara loses it and throws Gail to the floor."

Parnham then threw out a tidbit for the jury to chew, but didn't expound on it—just a fact for them to think about, to store in the back of their minds.

"David was a martial arts aficionado." He would return to the fact later in his defense of Clara Harris. The attorney wanted to place the seed of a thought in the panel's minds— that David Harris knew how to beat someone up, even a woman, and perhaps a wife. The tidbit that the jury would chew promised the possibility of things to come in the trial, including family violence between husband and wife.

Parnham continued, saying, "David escorts Clara to the Mercedes."

Parnham now spoke quietly to the jury again, saying, "I want you to observe what happened in that parking lot."

The lawyer next began to paint a picture of an idyllic marriage.

"On February fourteenth, 1992, this woman and her husband were married at the yacht club at that hotel," he said. "They were young dentists. She went through infertility treatment again and again, and it didn't work. Finally, she conceived and gave birth to those two boys."

Parnham's presentation began to get disorganized as he jumped to yet another subject.

"Eight days before the twenty-fourth, Diana Sherrill talked to Clara about David's affair for the first time," he continued. "The affair [Clara believed] was nothing more than talk. Clara calls the office to tell them that 'I can't practice dentistry anymore.' "

"That morning, [July 17th], Lindsey tells her, 'Everybody knows, the patients know.' "

"Upstairs, David throws her to the floor," Parnham told the jury, now animated. "He says, 'I'm out of here.' "

Parnham sat down at the counsel table. His opening argument to the jury had been a disjointed rambling mess. His cold was again getting worse.

FOURTEEN

Greek immigrant Evangelos Smiros took the stand as the first witness in the state's case against Clara Harris. The handsome and urbane food and beverage manager of the Nassau Bay Hilton was sworn in at 10:10 a.m.

Magness didn't waste any time in getting to what the hotel executive had heard during a commotion happening on his watch. Parnham and Clara Harris watched as the man told an articulate and compelling story, narrating in exquisite and chilling detail the murder of David Harris.

Parnham knew that Smiros would be only the first in a parade of eyewitnesses who would tie Clara to the death of her husband, and ultimately end with the almost certainly damning testimony of Lindsey Harris.

Smiros described how he and three hotel employees, Jose Miranda, Garrett Clark, and Blake Doran, had intervened in the fight between the two women. He told how Clara had heard her husband screaming, "It's over, it's over, it's over." He described her face as, "very mad, if looks could kill" when she lunged toward David Harris. The witness' Greek accent added an exotic flavor to what he was describing.

Smiros related how, outside the hotel, Clara had walked with him to her Mercedes, started it with her step-daughter in the front seat beside her, and then peeled out across the parking lot heading for a group of bystanders. He described his terror at the thought of the woman hitting the people in her way, and told how he screamed at her to stop as they scattered, escaping with their lives.

Damning for Clara Harris was the testimony of this first witness that she was unemotional. The woman Smiros had watched was not hysterical as she took the wheel of the car, he said. She was not crying. She was not out of control. What he had seen instead was a coldly calculating, angry woman hell-bent on doing damage to the rival who had taken her husband away from her, and probably doing damage to her husband himself.

Smiros was the first witness, Parnham knew, who would describe the impact of the Mercedes upon the body of David Harris.

"Oh my God!" Smiros said that he'd screamed as he saw Clara hit her husband the first time.

As the wily defense lawyer watched Smiros weave his deadly tale, Parnham knew that this first impression from a witness would stay with the jurors throughout the trial and deliberations. Some would take the Greek's words home with them that first night of testimony and mentally chew upon them until the following morning.

At the counsel table, Clara Harris watched as Smiros told the jury that what he saw was as clear as could be. There were no visual impairments, he said. "There was plenty of light." Her attention was riveted upon the man as he continued to weave his tale of murder. She leaned forward and rested her hand upon her finely chiseled chin, her elbows upon the surface of the table. Finally, she listened as Smiros told of the screams of Lindsey Harris as she shouted, "Stop, you are killing my dad!"

Smiros described how the teenager was attempting to get out of the car as the driver continued to circle.

Clara Harris sat impassively in the courtroom as Evangelos Smiros concluded his direct examination by Mia Magness.

It had been a powerful start.

Parnham rose to cross-examine the witness. Smiros had set the scene in the jury's mind. He had been a good witness for Magness, a good opener. It was the chore of the defense to try to direct the assault away from the client. The mild-mannered Parnham introduced himself, then asked about something he had said during Magness' direct examination.

"You testified that 'If looks could kill . . .' "

"Yes," Smiros answered.

"Nevertheless, you allowed Clara Harris to get behind the wheel of a car," Parnham continued. It was a good start for the defense lawyer, but his cross-examination was cut short when he was interrupted by the judge ordering a break in the proceedings. The rhythm of the moment was lost almost as soon as it had started.

After the jury had passed out of the courtroom, and Davies had left the bench, Clara Harris looked relaxed as she chatted with family and friends. Her lawyer was now in charge. He would hammer the prosecution with his defense of her. Clara Harris had faith in George Parnham. The two had worked together for months crafting the defense he would present—the best defense her money could buy.

Clara Harris looked relaxed, but the look was deceptive. The finely crafted jaw was working overtime as she furiously chewed gum.

When the jury returned to the courtroom, Parnham again went on the attack. Smiros had testified that Clara Harris had stopped the Mercedes at the end of a deadly set of circles he had described the car making, then backed it up, and then run over her husband again. The defense lawyer questioned the executive as to how he could be so sure of what he'd seen from the vantage point of where he was standing when the incident occurred.

Smiros had made it to the end of the long wall that separates the two parking lots, and slightly beyond it when the car made impact. Using the elaborate and expensive charts prepared by the defense team accident reconstructionist, Steve Irwin, for the first time Parnham demonstrated that from his vantage point, the events resulting in the death of David Harris were some distance away across an expanse of parking lot.

Finally, Parnham asked Smiros when he had given the cops his statement. The hotel manager answered that he hadn't given his statement to police until the next day. Parnham hoped that he had planted a seed of doubt regarding the recall of the witness in the minds of the jury. It was a small seed, but seeds grow.

The parade of prosecution witnesses had begun. Magness would stay with the tried-and-true formula that had put so many behind bars in Harris County. She would present eyewitnesses, forensics experts, and cops. All were believable. All were upstanding members of the community. All were people with whom an honest and unbiased juror would have a hard time finding fault.

Young, twenty-two-year-old Blake Doran fit the bill when he took the stand next for the state. Doran was just starting out, working his way up through the ranks at the resort hotel. He had been there a year and was now a bell captain. Like Smiros, he told the same story of hearing screaming, and witnessing the tall desk clerk Garrett Clark jumping over the front desk to break up a fight in the lobby.

Doran's testimony was brief, but it did have one telling line that would stay with the jury, Magness hoped.

The bell captain described what had happened to him when he saw the body of David Harris lying on the asphalt of the parking lot.

"I walked away," he said. "I got kind of sick."

Parnham took Doran on cross-examination, gently questioning him, trying to elicit something favorable to Clara Harris. He soon hit pay dirt when he got the hotel employee to describe the scene he had witnessed immediately after the car came to a halt and the two women got out.

"She was lying on top of him, she was telling him how much she loved him," Doran told the court. 'You're breathing, you're breathing,' she gasped."

Garrett Clark was a key witness for the prosecution, the first to have seen the fracas in the lobby of the hotel as it unfolded when Clara Harris began her assault upon Gail Bridges, and the last to have seen David Harris before he was hit by her Mercedes. He had worked at the hotel for about six months, but had been fired. He was now working as an auto mechanic in League City, a job far removed from the clean, air-conditioned job at the Nassau Bay Hilton.

Magness worked Clark through his testimony about the events of July 24 during the 3–11 p.m. shift at the hotel. Clark testified how he had checked the couple into a room but did not record the transaction because he had tricked the computer into showing the check-in as a same day, in/out event. For the first time, jurors learned that the two had been given the key to room 604. The couple had gone to the room briefly, and then returned to the lobby before getting in the elevator to go back up to the room.

Magness skillfully walked Clark through details of the fight in the lobby. For the first time in the trial, the prosecution allowed a witness to describe David Harris in a negative light. The desk clerk testified that David had not intervened when his wife had attacked Gail.

Before the jury, the tall desk clerk described a frightened Gail Bridges during and after the assault. "Her blouse was off. She was scared for her life. She was shaking. She was frantic."

She had had good reason to be frightened, she quickly found out when Clark escorted her to the hotel parking lot and was standing beside her as she was getting into the Navigator.

"I saw the accused driving very fast around the corner, accelerating toward me," Clark told the jury as he testified that the Mercedes had grazed his hip as he stood by the door of the SUV helping Bridges get in.

"I looked at his face. I saw bulging eyes, a terrified look in his eyes."

The horror and fear of David's last moments would be imbedded in the jury's mind, Magness hoped. Now she wanted to make sure that the horror of broken bones and torn tissue was implanted indelibly as she had the closest eyewitness yet to the murder describe how Clara Harris had run over her husband three times, then put the car in reverse and run over him again for good measure.

But Magness wasn't finished with Clark yet. He described the terror and fear of Lindsey Harris as well, telling the jury that he had seen Clara run over her husband two more times after her stepdaughter pleaded with her to stop.

Finally, Clark described how the car had come to a stop and Clara Harris had run to the body of her husband shouting, "David, David, David."

Angered, he told the jury, he grabbed the woman by the wrist and "put her on the ground.

"I didn't want her to cause any more altercations," he said.

Unlike Smiros, Garrett Clark had given his statement to Nassau Bay police officers one hour after the murder assault on David Harris. Magness knew that Parnham would have difficulty challenging this witness on how fresh his recollection of the event was.

Magness had a little housekeeping to do in order to blunt a likely defense attempt at destroying the witness. Savvy lawyers know that it is best to get your witness' own dirty linen on the table yourself, rather than letting the opponent do the work for you discrediting otherwise solid testimony.

Garrett Clark admitted to the assistant district attorney that he had been busted for marijuana possession since leaving the Hilton. He had paid a fine.

Then she had one more shot to fire before the jury with this witness. She asked Clark what he had heard as Clara Harris drove the last two feet into her husband's body the first time.

"She was cackling or laughing," he said. "She drove over David Harris while she continued to scream and laugh."

Clark told the court that Clara Harris had run over the body of her husband a total of five times, three times forward, one time backing up over David, then rolling forward over his body again.

Parnham didn't seriously challenge Garrett Clark. It was best that the witness get off the bench.

Hilton night manager Jose Miranda had only been at the hotel since March when David Harris was killed during his shift. Again, Magness walked the witness through the now familiar details of the fight in the lobby, the escort of the two women from the hotel to the waiting Mercedes, and the assault by auto on the body of Dr. David Harris.

When it was time for cross-examination of the witness, Parnham could contain himself no longer. He would use this witness to advance his theory that the car driven by Clara Harris had only struck her husband once. It was time to plant this seed in the minds of the jury in preparation of the testimony of defense witness Steve Irwin. After the prosecution had rested, Parnham planned to present a sophisticated show-and-tell of his theory of how the "incident" happened. The seed could grow, he knew.

It didn't really matter how Miranda answered his questions. It was the questions themselves that Parnham wanted the jury to hear as he began his cross-examination.

At 5:08 p.m., Parnham struck his first serious blow at the testimony of the parade of eyewitnesses who were coming before the jury.

"Is it possible that as you saw the Mercedes going around in circles, is it possible that the body was inside that circle?" Parnham asked.

"With my eyes, I saw the car running over the body," the manager answered, not giving the defense lawyer the answer he wanted.

"Was it possible that the body of David Harris was in the middle of that circle and was never touched?" Parnham continued, disregarding Miranda's answer.

"I saw the car go over the body," the man repeated emphatically.

Parnham's questions had planted another seed of doubt. Miranda's answer mattered little.

* * *

Next Keller William Real Estate agent Heidi Hendrick took the stand for the prosecution, testifying that when she'd heard a commotion in the hotel lobby, she at first believed that a purse-snatching was taking place. She and another agent, Norma Ramos, were carrying balloons to their cars after a conference at the hotel on business promotion.

"They were yelling and screaming at each other and calling each other vulgar names," she said. "She was red in the face. Her hair was all messed up. She had been in a fist fight. She was angry."

Now Parnham took the witness on cross-examination.

Hendrick testified that she had heard Lindsey Harris yell, "I hate you. Daddy, I hate you!"

At the counsel table, Clara Harris began to weep as a flood of memories of the night of July 24 now swept over her.

Parnham continued, getting nowhere with the witness, and buttressing the case of the prosecution, if anything, as the woman continued to tell how the young girl had collapsed on the sidewalk outside the front door of the hotel sobbing.

She then said that Clara Harris grabbed her stepdaughter by the wrist, saying, "Let's go."

Parnham had no further questions.

Norma Ramos told much the same story to the jury as Magness continued her relentless parade of people who had seen the behavior of Clara Harris the evening of July 24.

When it was Parnham's turn to question the woman, he returned to the matter of Clara Harris' abrupt order of "Let's go" to a sobbing Lindsey Harris sitting on the hotel sidewalk.

Instead of her grabbing the girl's wrist, Parnham now spoke with the witness of how Clara Harris had "helped" her stepdaughter up from the ground, attempting to put a gentle spin on Clara's behavior.

For her part, Clara Harris had now recovered her composure. Her quiet weeping had stopped. But she was unable to raise her head from her hands. She cradled her eyes at the table as her lawyer continued.

"Did David look at Lindsey?" Parnham asked.

"He looked down. He looked up. He looked at Mrs. Harris. He walked away. His head was down."

Again, Clara Harris began to weep, this time briefly drawing the attention of the jury, then again looking at Ramos.

Parnham did not cross-examine the realtor, seeing little to be gained from her, and choosing his targets carefully.

With the exception of Garrett Clark, all of the previous witnesses had been minor, simply players in a game where they were supporting the stars, whose testimony Magness knew would have a profound impact on the jury. The prosecutor knew that the graphic testimony the jury would hear next would stay with them. Some would dream about it. Some would even suffer from nightmares, because what Julie Creger would say to them was the stuff that guilty verdicts are made of in a brutal murder case like the one that was playing out before them.

The Conroe, Texas, homemaker had been the first person on the scene of the assault to actually touch the body of David Harris. She was the first to feel the broken bones inside the skin that was little more than a pliable sack holding the crushed parts that had once run, swum, walked, sat, and made love to the woman sobbing above them.

Julie Creger was the kind of woman whom most, if not all, on the jury would want as a neighbor—solid, kind, thoughtful. She was a loving mother to her two children, a throwback to the days when moms stayed at home to raise the kids. Although she was single, Creger was engaged, about to cement the long-term relationship that she had enjoyed for years with marriage to Robert Williams, the man with whom she lived.

Julie Creger had been profoundly, emotionally touched by the death of David Harris. After her initial interviews with Magness, the tough assistant district attorney says that she became emotional herself just listening to the tapes of the potential witness as she described the events of the night of July 24. Magness knew that she would be a great witness for the prosecution if Creger could keep her deep feelings under control.

When the jury heard from Creger, she would convey to them that she'd known what she was doing when she touched the body of David Harris. That she had participated in some significant anatomical first aid and life-guard training and would speak with authority about what she had seen and felt with her hands.

Creger's testimony was damning to Clara Harris not only because of the vivid verbal picture that she offered of the man's injuries, but because of her recitation of the words of Clara Harris as she'd knelt by the body of her husband. The words would stay with the jury, their power the kind of thing they would chew on as individuals again and again as they worked their way through the trial.

"David, look what you made me do," Creger testified that she'd heard Clara say.

The words were an acknowledgement that David Harris had driven Clara to kill and both Magness and Parnham knew it.

Creger's testimony about the fluids that were pouring from David Harris' body was telling as well. It was vivid, chilling. "There was something coming from his mouth and nose. His eyes were closed. I looked down to see if there was blood coming from his ears. He didn't have any ears. I reached my hand in his mouth. His jaw was tightly clenched. There was a loose tooth that came out. I put it on the ground."

Then Creger described the breathing of David Harris. The jury watched attentively as she demonstrated the "labored" and "wet" breathing of the dying man. Creger gasped. There wasn't a person on the jury who didn't relate to what they were witnessing from the woman sitting before them.

Clara Harris put her hands to her face and began to weep.

"At this point, I knew that there was nothing I could do," Creger continued as the defendant's shoulders began to move up and down in sobs.

"He was dying, there was nothing more that I could do," Creger said, describing what she believed were the last moments of David Harris' life.

The words were not lost on Clara Harris as she relived the painful and gruesome death of her husband.

Creger next described her first notice of Lindsey Harris, saying "I heard a young girl crying."

Julie Creger is a take-charge kind of woman, accustomed to ordering her own children around in a kind but firm manner. She told the jury how she'd ordered Lindsey Harris to "Shut up."

Creger had quickly surmised that the man lying upon the ground was the father of the crying teenager.

"She was looking at her dad," she told the jury. "She asked me if he was dead."

She said that although she knew that David Harris was

dying, there would be no useful purpose in telling his daughter so.

Creger began to cry from the stand as she continued, her testimony the most powerful the jury had heard thus far.

"Whatever I was going to tell her was not going to help her in any way."

The power of Creger's testimony was evident as Clara Harris sat at the counsel table, her head resting on her hands. On one of the fingers, she still wore a wedding band.

"Who did this?" Creger said that she'd asked the girl.

"My mom, I mean my stepmom," she said Lindsey had answered.

"Did she mean to do this?" Creger asked.

"Yes," Creger testified that the girl had said at the scene.

Clara's hand continued to cover her eyes, her elbows now on the table in what was becoming a characteristic pose. The emotion of what she was hearing overcame her and she began to cry.

Again, Parnham would not touch the witness with his questions.

Retired diesel mechanic Robert Williams followed his fiancée to the stand. The man looked straight out of central casting, perhaps an extra who had liked his clothes and continued to wear them long after shooting had stopped on a period western. Williams' long hair was pulled back. Outdoors it usually was under the cowboy hat that was now held in his hand in deference to the decorum of the courtroom. He wore a long dark frock coat as he took purposeful strides toward the witness stand. His pants were held up by a belt attached to a large silver-and-gold buckle, similar to the trophy buckles that winning bull riders wear at rodeos.

To all of the Texas natives in the room, a succinct description of the man before them came to mind when Williams opened his mouth to answer Magness' customary greeting to witnesses of "Good morning."

All knew that before them was what natives and would-be natives of the state knew as a good ole boy. His deep, slow voice and slow manner of speech was characteristic of what most in the rest of the country thought a Texan should sound like. Williams' speech pattern perfectly fit the way he was dressed.

Williams' testimony paralleled that of his fiancée in many ways. Now he spat out seven words that buttressed what she and the other witnesses had already said.

"Now you see what I can do," the tall man in archaic Western garb related that he heard Clara Harris say.

Mia Magness liked her witness—had liked the man from the start, and she would like him even more as time went by, because after he left the stand, Robert Williams called her every day during the trial to bolster her and wish her well.

She liked his mind. Williams, she believed, was one of those blue-collar people whose mental capacity more than compensated for a lack of formal education. He was smart, she believed, as smart as she was in his own way.

Williams too had touched the body of David Harris, had heard the "wet" breathing and had stuck his hand on the man's chest only to find that there was no chest where the tires of the Mercedes had crushed him.

The defendant's hands remained over her eyes as she heard the tall man's testimony telling the nine women and three men of the jury about how he'd pleaded with David Harris to try to live until help came.

"I said, 'David, your daughter's watching. Breathe!' "

"Did he respond to you?" Magness asked.

"Yes," Williams answered.

"Keep breathing, you can't die here in front of your daughter," he recalled saying to the dying man.

"Pass the witness," Magness said, satisfied that Robert Williams had done enough damage to the defendant she was trying to imprison.

George Parnham didn't like Robert Williams. He saw in the witness his first opportunity for a robust cross-examination. Now the jury would see a side of the defense lawyer far removed from the soft-spoken, kindly graybeard who had thus far appeared before them. They would see a Parnham at once disbelieving, incredulous, angry, hostile, abrupt, rude, loud, and disdainful of the witness. Parnham would reveal to the jury that it was his duty to extract the truth from the cowboy who sat smugly on the witness stand answering the prosecution's softball questions lobbed at him with a slow pitch. Parnham would perform.

Immediately, the defense lawyer pounced.

"There is nothing in the police reports written down about what you said at the scene?" he asked, hostility immediately evident in his voice even at the beginning of his cross-examination.

"Did you talk with your fiancée about the events of the twenty-fourth?," Parnham asked, acid dripping from his voice.

"Basically not," Williams answered as Parnham arched an eyebrow.

"You live with Julie Creger, don't you?" he said for the benefit of those on the jury moral enough to care that the couple lived together but were not wed. "You live with her, but you didn't talk about it?" Parnham asked incredulously.

Now, the lawyer questioned Williams about what he saw of Clara at the scene.

"She appeared to be angry?" Parnham asked.

"I really wasn't focused on her," Williams answered.

"Did you hear her say, 'I'm sorry, breathe, breathe?'" the lawyer prompted, attempting to lead the witness to agree that Harris was being compassionate toward the man she had hit.

"No," Williams answered.

Parnham was getting nowhere, so he returned to the lack of communication between Williams and Creger regarding the events that they had witnessed on July 24.

"You never told your fiancée?" Parnham asked.

"No, sir, I didn't," the witness answered emphatically.

Finally, Davies looked down from the bench and reproached Parnham, warning the defense lawyer not to continue to be argumentative.

"I pass the witness," Parnham said, frustrated.

Off the stand and in the corridor outside the courtroom, Williams grabbed Dan Rizzo, Magness' boss. During cross-examination, he had told Parnham that he had not been drinking. Now, he wanted to correct the record. Williams remembered that he had ordered a bourbon and Coke at poolside, where he and Creger had been swimming with the kids. He didn't think of it until the break because he had only drunk a small portion in the two hours before the events he had just described on the stand.

Back on the stand, an appreciative Magness quickly allowed her witness to correct the record, lest Parnham know that the witness had been drinking, albeit very little.

More important, the prosecutor elicited an answer from the witness regarding why he and his fiancé had not discussed the events that they had witnessed. It was an answer Magness would have difficulty dealing with because it appeared so unlikely.

"We made a decision not to talk about the events and to

turn off the TV when the story came on," he said. "We knew that we would be called as witnesses."

On re-cross, Parnham believed that he had found an opening, a chink in the armor of Robert Williams, a way to discredit at least one prosecution witness before the jury that was trying Clara Harris.

"Then you were drinking," the lawyer, who enjoys a good cocktail himself, said ominously.

"It wasn't strong," Williams answered, knowing that he was under attack and that it was his own fault. "It tasted more cold than anything else."

Parnham moved to another front, feeling that he was getting a small victory before the judge and jury.

In his earlier testimony, Williams denied knowing Mia Magness. Parnham now asked him to look at the subpoena he had carried to court with Magness' name on it.

The witness acknowledged that it was Magness' name on the paper. For a defense lawyer in Harris County, Texas, even a small victory was a triumph because there are so few moments like that in the courts there. Parnham savored his little moment of victory.

FIFTEEN

Seating in the courtroom was tightly controlled. The press was seated in the center section with each media spot designated by a neatly typed white label that court administrators had stuck to the top of the bench's oak back. To the right side of the aisle, the first two rows were reserved for the defense. Family members of both David and Clara Harris occupied the benches each day as they sat showing their support for the defendant.

On the left side, guests of the prosecution sat, more fluid in their coming and going than the friends and family who occupied the spots reserved for the defense.

The front row was divided as well. The left side was filled with friends of Magness and Rizzo. The right end was occupied by the staff of the three defense lawyers. Immediately behind Parnham, his wife sat in that row with team member Mark White to do the bidding of the lawyers if the two were needed to fetch a document or witness who may have wandered off when called. Mary Parnham was the behind-the-scenes coordinator, the go-to "guy." It was Mary who brought even more warmth and compassion to clients of her husband. If Clara Harris suffered defeat in the courtroom, it was into her caring arms that she would ultimately come.

Now, the audience watched as Parnham brought Creger back to the stand for a second time.

Parnham began questioning the woman about what she'd said to the police, attempting to find an inconsistency in what she had uttered the night of the murder, and what she was now saying to the jury, hoping that something would touch one of its members.

"I don't remember what I said on the tape," Creger said, blunting Parnham's effort to sow confusion.

"You told the detective that Clara's intermittent crying stopped when they put the cuffs on," Parnham said.

"I believe that her emotion was feigned," Creger snapped back, the question backfiring on Parnham.

The second cross-examination of Julie Creger ended quickly.

Mia Magness did not have an army behind her as she did her solo act in the courtroom of Judge Carol Davies. A handful of staff was responsible for getting witnesses to the courthouse on time to testify. "I always got the feeling that I was in charge of a pen of cats," she would say later.

Nothing was under the tight control that it appeared to be to those who sat in the courtroom day after day. Evangelos Smiros had been called as the first prosecution witness for no reason other than that he was expected to turn in a strong performance on the witness stand, and could get to the courthouse more quickly than any other witness, and was ready to testify at a moment's notice. If any one of a score of others could have made it there as rapidly, Magness would have been just as happy starting with them. There was no grand plan for who went on the stand other than following the DA's tried-and-true formula of eyewitness, medical examiner, cops, and wrap-up witness, hopefully a family member victimized by the death of a loved one. Who went first, second, or in the middle didn't matter. They would all go on the stand.

Thus it was that John Turman was called next to the witness stand. The League City private investigator had been in the practice of spying upon his fellow man for twenty-one years. Turman and Associates primary mission was investigating insurance fraud.

Turman's purpose on the stand was simple. It was to demonstrate that Clara Harris was relentless in her quest to find out about the hidden life of her husband David. The public knew only about the woman's involvement with the Bachas' Blue Moon Investigations. In reality, the firm had been Clara's second choice, Turman related.

At 9 a.m. on the morning of July 22, 2002, Clara Harris had dialed the number of the small League City office. The call rolled over to Turman's home number.

"She was speaking to me continuously," Turman began. "I was told that her husband was an orthodontist and she felt that he was having an affair with an employee and that it was still going on. She said that she had fired the employee."

"What did she want you to do?" Magness prompted the man.

"She told us that she wanted us to tape a conversation at Perry's restaurant," Turman answered. "I told her it was illegal to even get close enough to tape in that case," he continued. The investigator said that he'd declined to take Clara's case on the telephone and set an appointment for the following Thursday.

"I wanted to let her calm down," he said.

Quickly, Magness passed the witness to the defense.

Parnham began with a series of questions regarding
Texas law and its application to third-party taping. The
bottom line, it's illegal. A third party can't tape a conversation between two or more others without their knowledge. Parnham's questioning had Turman going over old
ground, ground he had already covered with Magness in
her brief direct examination. The lawyer was getting
nowhere fast.

The defense lawyer finished with the witness quickly,
knowing that he would gain little with a protracted cross-
examination. Yet he had one tiny morsel of information
that he wanted to get before the jury from Turman. Early
in her career, Bobbi Bacha had worked for his firm as a
novice investigator. The sleuth was vague as he spoke of
his largest competitor and its thirty-eight investigators,
saying that he didn't know much about her business.

"Who is your next witness?" Davies asked Magness
from the bench.

"Lindsey Dubec," the prosecutor answered.

Davies interrupted, saying, "The next witness has
asked that she not be photographed, and therefore we will
not have video of her testimony." Joe Vargas, the free-
lance camera operator hired for the duration of the trial,
reached up and turned off his equipment.

The tall statuesque, young blond woman walked into
the courtroom and down the left aisle between the press
and prosecution seating. She was wearing tight clothes as
she stood behind the bar and was sworn in as a witness.
Lindsey Dubec walked tentatively to the stand.

Her fear was evident. Clearly, here was a witness who,
despite her profession, had never been in a courtroom.
She was intimidated by her surroundings, even though
her bosses at Blue Moon had prepped her for what she

was about to say. They had given her woman guidelines for proper conduct in court. Their attorney had met with her as well, reassuring her that all she had to do was tell the truth.

"Why did you become an investigator?" Magness began.

"I always wanted to try," Dubec answered, her voice so quiet and tentative that the judge asked her to speak directly into the microphone placed before her.

"What was your training?" Magness continued, knowing the answer already.

The woman hesitated, as if she couldn't remember how she'd learned to investigate.

"We had to come in for a half day on Saturdays for three weeks in a row," she answered. "On the last Saturday, I went out with the chief investigator for some training."

"That was it?" Magness prompted, making the point with her voice that the training was scant indeed for such delicate work.

"Yes," Dubec answered.

"There was no further training?" the prosecutor asked again, driving home the point that educational standards for Blue Moon investigators were abysmally low. Moreover, Dubec said that she didn't recall ever being given any rules or standards to follow by the firm.

Dubec said that when she went out on an investigation, her bosses at Blue Moon generally gave her a description of the subject—find people with whom they might be in contact with, their addresses, a description of their vehicle, and the address of where they might be going. This was what she expected to be given when she got a call from Blue Moon the afternoon of July 24, 2003. The woman from the office had asked Dubec if she was free to work that night.

Although Blue Moon investigators such as Dubec

worked on a one job at a time basis, and were paid an hourly rate, she was around the office enough to know others who worked there, particularly the receptionist/investigator who had given her the assignment. But Dubec's testimony before the jury began to falter when she couldn't remember Claudine Phillips' name. It was she who gave Dubec her orders.

"When you got to the office, what were you told to do?" Magness prompted.

"I was told to follow him from work to Perry's," she answered.

"Were you given anything?"

"I was given a video camera and told to wait because someone was bringing in the man's license plate number."

Dubec said that she waited in the office until Clara Harris showed up. She was shocked when she was called in to meet the dentist.

"I've never met any of my clients," she testified.

Dubec testified that Clara gave her a photograph of a smiling David Harris, wearing a light jacket and sweater.

Magness introduced the photo as evidence and it was placed on the screen of a large television monitor on the left side of the courtroom adjacent to the jury box. The picture was of a casual and relaxed David Harris, looking as if he had just gotten in from a fishing trip or a sail on Galveston Bay.

Dubec said she had left the office and driven to the strip mall where the Space Center Orthodontics office was located, and waited in the parking lot.

"The subject came out," she said, using cop language. "He went to the Bank of America, and then got into his car. He drove to the Hilton and parked at 6:18 p.m.. And then he went inside."

"What did you do then?" Magness asked.

"I circled the parking lot," she said.

Dubec had quickly found Gail Bridges' Navigator. She had previously been given its license tag number. The investigator said that she'd picked up the video camera and shot pictures of the SUV in the still-bright sunlight, as well as tape of David's Suburban.

"At 6:57 I saw David Harris walk out with Gail Bridges to the Navigator," she said. "She stayed in the Navigator about twenty minutes."

Dubec's friend, Andrea Thompson, had come to the hotel parking lot to meet her. After David and Clara went back into the hotel, the two young women talked about playing hooky, getting away from the surveillance for a few minutes to break the monotony. Perhaps they could drive to Perry's restaurant, "so that it would look natural" to Lindsey's bosses if the two were spotted. After all, the eatery was on the list of likely spots where the cheating couple might be observed.

Instead, the two decided that Andrea would take a peek inside the hotel to see what the couple was doing. The young woman went through the rear door and saw David and Gail register at the front desk, then walk to the restaurant briefly, and then back to the elevators.

Clara Harris sat at the counsel table listening to the investigator tell what she had seen as she had spied on David and the other woman. With her eyes closed, the accused began to weep again at the thought of her husband going up to a hotel room with Gail. The memories of the dreadful night were again engulfing her.

Lindsey Dubec told the jury that she and Thompson had sat in her car waiting.

"What did you see next?" Magness said.

"I saw them walking to the Navigator," she said.

"Where were you sitting?" the prosecutor asked.

"I was behind the wheel," Dubec answered.

Lindsey Dubec then looked at her watch and noted the time as 8:50 p.m. for the report she would have to write up for the agency.

"What did you do next?" Magness probed.

"I turned on the camera, and then I turned it off," Dubec answered, saying that she'd laid the camera on the car seat at her side.

"I saw a car coming at a high rate of speed and driving crazy," she continued.

"And then what?" Magness asked.

Dubec hadn't captured the initial impact of the Mercedes hitting David Harris because she was picking the camera up off the seat where it had lain, and had raised it to her eye. It took her ten seconds, she estimated, from the initial impact until the tape in the camera began to roll.

"I picked the camera back up and the car went past and I saw it go inside. It then drove past the left side of the Navigator. It had hit the Navigator on the side."

"What did you see?" Magness continued probing as the young woman reconstructed the nightmare she had witnessed.

"I was looking through the viewfinder," she said. "I didn't see the car hit David Harris or run him over. It was blurry."

"What did you do after the car had stopped?" Magness asked.

"I got out to go see with my eyes so that I could see what was really happening. I walked up to him, and then I walked away."

"What did you do then?" Magness asked.

"I called Blue Moon and spoke with a receptionist," Dubec answered.

"What did you say?" Magness continued.

"I told her that the subject, Clara Harris ran over her husband. She [Natalia, the investigator on duty] told me to cooperate."

"What did you do next?" the prosecutor asked.

"I drove next door," Dubec said. "I had to get her, [Andrea Thompson] under control. She was screaming. I had to straighten her out. I called Mr. Bacha, but there was no answer. Five minutes later I went back because I was a witness. The cops came one minute after I got back."

"Did you speak with them?" Magness said.

"I spoke with a female officer," Dubec answered.

Clara Harris buried her head in her hand as Lindsey Dubec continued to tell of the murder of her husband.

"How did you feel?" Magness asked.

"I was in complete shock," Dubec answered.

Clara Harris broke down. George Parnham laid his hand on her shoulder as he approached the bench. The defendant cried more and Emily Munoz Detoto consoled her as she sat at the table, her hands over her face and her body quaking.

Davies called the lawyers to the bench for the first of several stern warnings that she would give to Parnham about getting control of his emotional client.

After the bench conference, Magness passed the witness.

Parnham's question for the woman who had shot the video of his client murdering her husband was lame, provoking smirks from the press who were becoming increasingly critical among themselves of his performance.

"Was there any concern that the person who went to the lobby of the hotel to observe them was not a licensed investigator?" he asked before passing the witness.

* * *

As tentative, frightened and unsure of herself as Lindsey Dubec's performance on the stand had appeared, the woman who had given her her marching orders on July 24 was a picture of competence, professionalism, and poise. Dressed in a black suit, white blouse, and wearing no makeup, Claudine Phillips, 32, took the stand. The woman whose name the young investigator couldn't remember had once worked at the agency three days a week as she went to the University of Houston. But at the time of the death of David Harris, she had been a full-time employee of Blue Moon.

Like all first-time clients, Clara Harris had asked the standard questions when she first appeared at the office the day before killing David Harris and wanting to hire an investigator.

"They want to know what the agency does, exactly," Phillips said.

Phillips answered Clara, and then told her that she could pay for the services of an investigator by cash, check, or credit card.

"Where did she sit?" Magness asked.

"She sat in the reception area," Phillips answered. "She told of his affair. She then said that he was scheduled to meet with the woman."

"Where?" Magness asked.

"At the restaurant or the Hilton," she answered. "She was very professional. She was very straightforward in what she wanted us to do. She felt that her husband was being deceived by this female and that she was trying to get his money."

"What did she say about her relationship with him?" Magness prompted.

"You could tell that she really loved her husband," Phillips answered. "She said that he was a good man but he was falling into a trap. She said that she felt like she had neglected him. She had paid more attention to her children. She said that she had opened the door of her home for her [Gail Bridges] to come in and steal her husband."

"How long did the two of you meet?" Magness asked.

"Forty-five minutes," Phillips answered.

"Did she give you pictures?" the prosecutor probed.

"She provided pictures of David, but no pictures of Gail," Phillips answered.

"What other information did she give you?" Magness said.

"She gave us the type of car that Gail drives, and the number of Gail's kids," Phillips answered.

"What did you ask next?" Magness asked.

"What does Gail look like?" Phillips answered.

"What did she say?" Magness said.

"She was so angry that she couldn't describe Gail," the woman answered. Seeing the anger of the prospective client before her, Phillips testified that she'd outlined the Blue Moon policies to her.

"We are allowed to wait until the following day to give an update to the client. We are very clear that it is for the client's protection, for our protection, and for the subject's protection."

Phillips said that the policy is spelled out, in writing.

"All clients must read that and understand that we will call off the surveillance if they show up."

"And then what did she do?" Magness continued.

"She wrote a check for $1,547."

Phillips told the court that Harris had then left. She would bring back more photos the following day.

"On the twenty-third, she had a calm demeanor," the woman continued. "When Clara Harris came back, Lindsey Harris was with her. She [Clara] was briefly tearful, and then she composed herself."

"What did she say to you?"

"She said that we were her best friends," Phillips said. "I reached for some tissues, but by the time I had them, she composed herself."

"And what about Lindsey?" Magness asked. "What was she doing?"

"She was kind of in awe that she was in an investigative agency," Phillips answered. "She said, 'You are going to follow my dad?' She thought that was cool."

Magness relinquished the witness to the defense. She had what she'd wanted.

Parnham then returned to the record of what the woman had said under direct examination, introducing a 22-page transcription of her testimony.

"She devoted time to her twin boys, and as a result, she hadn't attended as much to David's needs as she should have," he read, using the investigator's words to portray his Clara as a loving mother, but a neglectful wife.

He targeted Clara's motive for hiring Blue Moon, reading to Phillips from the transcript.

"She wanted Blue Moon to document this so she could show her husband that he was falling into a trap."

Parnham attacked the witness' testimony that Harris seemed to be in control of her emotions during her visit to the detective agency.

"She started to cry, you testified, and then she stopped crying," he paused. "Like that?"

"Yes," Phillips answered.

"She was very emotional on the phone," Parnham read, "when she told me she would have to come to the office to bring the photograph."

"I don't mean she was crying. She was never crying," Phillips countered regarding the initial telephone conversation between herself and Clara Harris.

Then Parnham struck, hammering the witness in an attempt to get Phillips to open up a door, even if it was a back door that had been closed to the defense by the judge.

"She said that there would be no reason to surveillance her if she was with her children, right?" he asked.

"Yes," Phillips answered.

"She said these two women were engaged in a lesbian relationship. She needed to show that her husband was falling into this trap. She mentioned that several people had told her that."

Magness objected and the judge sustained the objection, but Parnham had a possible opening. At the very least, the jury had heard the dreaded word lesbian to describe Gail Bridges, Clara's rival for the affection of her husband.

"Blue Moon is presently representing Gail Bridges?" he asked. "Do you know if Blue Moon has been hired by a lawyer named Valorie Davenport who represents Gail Thompson Bridges?"

"I do not," Phillips answered.

Parnham now questioned Phillips regarding her grand jury testimony. Again he found an opening to get the allegations of a lesbian relationship before the jury.

"She was told of a lesbian relationship by several people?" he questioned the woman.

Parnham didn't get an answer to his question before Magness objected and Davies sustained the objection. He didn't care because he had again gotten the word lesbian before the jury.

"Did she mention a trip out of the country?" Parnham asked next.

"Yes," Phillips answered.

"Did she say it gave her [Gail] time to seduce her [Clara's] husband?" he continued.

"She did mention this, yes," Phillips said.

"Pass the witness," the lawyer said, his back already to the woman on the stand as he walked to the table where Clara Harris sat.

Another tiny seed was now planted for the jury to perhaps cultivate and grow.

A large woman in a dark full-bodied dress stood in the aisle between the press section and the benches reserved for guests of the prosecution.

"Bobbi Bacha," the bailiff called.

The woman from Blue Moon Investigations advanced toward the bar, which separates the spectators from lawyers, judge, and jury.

Bacha wouldn't have to stand for long. Suddenly, the judge called a recess. When the allotted fifteen minutes was over, Bacha was nowhere to be seen, and was never called. A new witness was about to be sworn in. It was the only appearance of the owner of Blue Moon Investigations at the trial of Clara Harris. Even that appearance was curious, considering that Bacha had never met Clara Harris face to face, and had only talked to the dentist briefly when she'd asked for a refund.

Kimberly Maldinado, Nassau Bay, Texas, public safety dispatcher would begin the prosecution's parade of police witnesses. The woman was comfortable on the stand, telling how she had sent officers Reyna and Staudt to the Hilton believing that they were there to quell a routine disturbance.

She said she quickly knew that the call was out of the

ordinary when the cops soon called in asking for a wrecker and the EMS.

Maldinado was accustomed to the quiet of the communities surrounding Clear Lake. Up the highway, Houston was where the action was. In towns like Nassau Bay, the norm was for the police to be called to a rare domestic disturbance at one of the tiny village's upscale residences. As often as not, police found themselves dealing with high or drunken teenagers. Murder was the most unusual of crimes in the rarefied atmosphere of Nassau Bay.

Magness finished with Maldinado as she described the radio traffic between herself and the police as they reported that David Harris, the "complaintant" in police jargon, was being transported to the St. John Hospital.

SIXTEEN

Magness' parade of public safety officials continued as each walked through the double doors of the courtroom, down the left aisle, through the bar, and on to the witness stand to take the seat to the right of Judge Carol Davies.

The judge presided at the bench dressed in her black robe. Yet something was different from other female judges who wore the judicial garment with the mysterious braid down the back. Davies made a slight concession to her feminine side each day by adorning it with large elaborate silk scarves draped around her neck. Knowledgeable women in the courtroom said that they looked expensive and likely came from Hermes of Paris, the pricey shop in the fashionable Galleria district.

The judge could easily afford such a scarf, longtime acquaintances in the courthouse said. Davies is fiercely protective of her privacy. Her scant official biography contains no information regarding the first forty years of the woman's life.

In Texas, state district judges stand for election every four years just like other state officeholders such as the Governor, Lieutenant Governor, State Treasurer, and State Comptroller. In recent years Democrats and Republicans alike have supported transparency in government and have made their lives an open book. Not so Carol

Davies. Yet voters have returned her to the bench, despite their scant knowledge of her life.

Parnham made little headway with the next two witnesses, former Nassau Bay Patrolman Mike Reyna and Detective Teresa Relken. Magness continued her assault upon the freedom of Clara Harris as the two cops dispassionately related the events of the night of July 24.

The jury sat quietly, again hearing the increasingly familiar story of how the Mercedes had rounded the wall at a high rate of speed, turned, struck the Navigator, and then struck David Harris, propelling him across the parking lot.

But their interest became more attentive as Relken's testimony told them of the condition of the corpse of David Harris as she photographed it at the hospital.

"The ear was shredded off," she said. "There was a bloody tube in the mouth. There was bruising on the shoulders and legs. He lay on a back board. Blood came from the back of the head."

"Were you alone with the body as you photographed it?" Magness asked.

"No, an elderly woman was there, his mother I think."

Clara Harris' head slumped, her cheeks resting on clenched fists as she listened to the detective.

"I continued to photograph the body," the woman added.

Clara now buried her face in her hands and began to sob quietly.

"What did you do next?" Magness probed.

The defendant continued to cry as she heard Relken describe the autopsy of her husband.

On cross, George Parnham now had pictures to show on the large courtroom television monitor. The photo was of Clara Harris, and the person shown had little resemblance to the elegant woman dressed in a suit sitting at the counsel table. In fact, she looked absolutely terrible in the police photo taken early in the morning she was booked into the Harris County Jail.

Clara Harris, who had spent the previous evening in a mansion with her husband, appeared in the photo as a puffy-faced wretch, dressed in a blue turquoise blouse with a gaping neckline and blue jeans.

The woman had a laceration on the right arm. Parnham was giving the jury a taste of things to come. He wanted to show that, before she'd killed her husband, Clara Harris had been physically abused.

Now, the defense brought the timid Blue Moon investigator Lindsey Dubec back to the stand in another attempt to get at the alleged alternative lifestyle of the girlfriend of David Harris.

As the lawyer mentioned Gail Bridges, Magness began shouting objections. Parnham then tried the back door approach.

"Do you remember Valorie Davenport?" he asked.

"She was not there," Dubec said.

"Were any interviews conducted when that woman was present in this case?" he said. Parnham was getting nowhere.

Next, he tried his luck again with detective, Relken, now back on the stand.

"Where was David Harris' cell phone?

"It was retrieved from the Navigator," she answered.

"How was it retrieved?" Parnham asked.

"Julie Knight handed Officer Carpenter the phone, she answered.

"Do you know who Julie Knight is?" Parnham continued.

"An acquaintance of Gail Bridges," she answered.

At last, the attorney had what he wanted. The name of Gail Bridges' alleged lover was now in the record as Davies adjourned court for the day. Now it would be up to Parnham to make something of this minor victory.

Clara Harris looked particularly fetching when she entered the courtroom on the morning of January 28, 2003. Wearing a black suit and black turtleneck, her light brown hair was down, in contrast to the way she most frequently wore it, with a large bow tied at the back.

Magness called Detective Julio Rincones of the Webster Police Department. The father of four said that he had been awakened to come to the scene, hearing from the dispatcher that "A guy in a car went nuts. He ran over somebody."

When he arrived, he was surprised at how large the crime scene was.

It was his job that night to escort the Mercedes back to his department, just down NASA Road 1 from Nassau Bay. Because of their size, police departments in the small towns scattered around the lake cooperated in working major crimes. Webster would do the detail work on both Clara Harris' Mercedes, and Gail Bridges' Lincoln Navigator.

When he arrived at the scene, the barely alive body of David Harris had already been transported to St. John Hospital, and Clara had been taken to jail.

Rincones pointed to the front of the Mercedes being shown to the jury on the courtroom screen.

The photograph clearly showed black stains on the

front of the hood where fingerprint powder had captured David Harris last desperate act to save himself, as he held his hand out against the oncoming Mercedes.

"How many prints did you take from the front of the car?" Magness asked.

"Six," the detective answered.

Now, Magness placed another photograph on the screen. It showed the undercarriage of the luxury car. On the steel there was a large stain.

"What did you find under the car?" Magness asked.

"I collected blood and hair from under the Mercedes on the driver's side door," Rincones answered.

The horror of David's body being ground against the asphalt by the automobile with its six-inch clearance from the ground came home to Clara Harris as she involuntarily moved her left hand to her face, then her eyes.

She briefly looked up at the photograph on the screen, the bloodstain evident on the underside of the Mercedes. Again her hands covered her eyes.

In an act of unusual self-control, Clara looked at the picture again, then stared off into space for a moment. Finally she looked at Rincones.

"What is the clearance from the bottom of the Mercedes to the ground?" Magness asked.

"Six inches," Rincones answered, driving home the grisly nature of the murder.

When George Parnham faced the detective on cross-examination, he had an opening, albeit a tiny one, to cast doubt upon the efficiency of the Webster Police Department's forensic unit.

The police had secured the Mercedes in custody for months in preparation for the trial. However, in a moment of unusually sloppy police work, the investigators had neglected to seize evidence left in the automobile.

Parnham questioned the detective about the items, getting him to acknowledge each—the personal checkbook of Clara Harris, a torn check, pictures of David and Clara, and most important, a note.

The lawyer returned to the photo of the blood on the underside of the car.

Clara again placed her face in her hands in what was now becoming a typical pose when she was confronted with unpleasant evidence associated with her act.

Parnham began an attempt to get the detective to bolster the defense theory that Harris' body had only been hit once by the Mercedes, and then only accidentally.

"Were you able to analyze frame by frame how fast the car was going?" he asked regarding the Blue Moon video now in police custody.

"Were the circles getting tighter and tighter?" Parnham asked, knowing that he wouldn't get an answer, but getting the theory before the jury simply by asking the question.

He led the detective through a series of questions regarding the placement of the body of David Harris, finally getting him to acknowledge where the head was lying in an attempt to bolster the defense theory that the car driven by his wife had come to a stop next to the body of her husband.

Parnham continued questioning Rincones about the prints he had taken, attempting to show that the placement of the hands on the very front of the Mercedes' hood was consistent with David Harris being carried for a small distance by the car, as the defense would later contend.

When the defense attorney passed the witness back to Magness, she pounced, unwilling to give the defense anything of value.

"Did you see anything in that photo album the defense mentioned that was pertinent to whether the defendant killed her husband?" she asked, attempting to blunt any damage the department's sloppy police work had done to her case.

"No," Rincones answered.

"You sat behind the wheel of the Mercedes?"

"Yes," the detective answered.

"When you sat behind the wheel, could you have seen a six-foot man in front of you?" Magness continued.

"Yes," he answered.

Now, the two lawyers passed the witness back and forth in a series of brief questions, each scoring minor points. Parnham was next.

"You made a determination that the wedding album was not important?" he asked.

"I don't even know that it was a wedding album," the detective answered.

"Do you know who that belongs to?" Parnham asked.

"No," Rincones answered.

Davies had enough, chiding Parnham, "That is a non-issue."

"Pass the witness," he told the judge.

"Gail Bridges' name was inside that checkbook found in Clara's car. It was on the cover, with her phone number?" Magness now asked, demonstrating that the accused was possibly calling the other woman at best, and probably stalking her at worst. Now the prosecutor passed the witness back to Parnham.

Parnham went through the checkbook, check by check,

citing entries to a hair salon, a spa, and a check to the Shadycrest Baptist Church building fund, laying a foundation for the defense contention that Clara Harris was desperately making herself into a new woman.

Next, Parnham reached entries that showed how Clara Harris had attempted to transform herself from the dowdy wife of ten years into a sexy lover for her husband.

He noted checks written to Victoria's Secret and Cashet.

Clara held her head in her hands, wiped tears from her eyes and her red nose.

Finally, Parnham drew carbons of two large checks in the book, each made out to Bank of America. The checks were for the purchase of cashier's checks in the amount of $5,000 and $310. Each was written on July 24, 2003. The cashier's checks were made out to Clear Lake cosmetic surgeon Dr. Thomas Wiener.

Throughout the testimony, Davies' impatience with Parnham was beginning to show as she frequently chided the defense lawyer to stop rambling and get to the point in his questioning. Parnham, for his part, showed his customary deference to the increasingly obdurate judge and sat down.

A new group of witnesses were called into the courtroom by the judge. They stood on the left aisle as they raised their hands to be sworn in. Among them was a tall, bearded professorial-looking man who stood out from the crowd. He was Dr. Dwayne A. Wolf, MD. His resume carried a curious e-mail address, perhaps a reflection of his occupation. Online, he was neurobone@aol.com. It was to the state's pathologist that Magness now turned to to continue to cement the fate of Clara Harris for the murder of her husband.

On the stand, it was evident that the man had testified

many times before juries like the one he would now address. His demeanor was confident, self-assured, and even cocky. Before them was an overachiever who had excelled throughout his life and had become bored with those who were not at his level of intellect or accomplishment. Magness began to question Wolf on her steady march down the list of wounds inflicted on the body of David Harris. It was through the pathologist's testimony that she would show the jury precisely how the orthodontist had died.

Parnham was hedging his bets. Sitting on the front row, with special permission from the judge, sat the man whose job it was to counter the testimony of the state's pathologist. Dr. Paul Radelat, MD, JD, was known as the darling of defense circles, a personable witness whose service to the defense team went well beyond the testimony he would render. He would watch Wolf as the prosecution's pathologist went through the autopsy results with Magness in agonizing detail.

But it would not be easy. Wolf, who averages between one and two autopsies per day as assistant Harris County Medical Examiner, had performed more than 1,500 autopsies, including hundreds of homicides. And while his own medical record is unblemished, Radelat had spent only one year as a government pathologist.

Magness quickly established Wolf's credentials for the jury, laying the groundwork for what was to come, and effectively blunting the expertise of Radelat when his time came to testify.

Next it was time for show-and-tell as Magness introduced thirty autopsy photos into evidence as Clara Harris again buried her face in her hands, took a breath, then looked up to stare at the courtroom ceiling.

The screen of the television monitor was filled with the

body of the dead David Harris, lying on his side in the morgue, the collar on his neck, a tube still in his throat, a defibrillation pad and EKG sensors attached to his skin. His eyes were closed.

Clara Harris again summoned her strength and looked at the photo of the man she had killed, then turned her head and began sobbing, holding her face in her hands. Ignoring her, Magness continued to show close-ups of the body as well as David's clothing, including his shoes, as the physician testified.

The prosecutor zoomed in for a close-up of the face of David Harris. The jaw was clearly broken and there were lacerations. The ear, or where the ear should have been, was a bloody mess.

"It's hard to recognize as an ear, considering the injury," Wolf testified.

Now, Clara Harris would have nothing to do with looking at the dead body of her husband.

The judge and jurors were totally attentive as they looked at the photo. The head, usually covered with a hair piece, was completely shaved bald, except for a patch of hair about three inches around.

Wolf testified regarding the differences between injuries produced by an automobile striking a victim, and an automobile rolling over and crushing a victim. He was like a professor instructing a freshman class.

"How would you characterize these injuries?" Magness questioned.

"Rolled over by the car," Wolf testified.

Next she zeroed in on the leg.

"This injury is consistent with the side of the tire scraping against the leg," Wolf said, using a pointer to indicate the injury.

"Consistent with the car rolling over him?" Magness responded.

"Correct," the ME answered.

Next, Wolf told the jury how all of David Harris' ribs were fractured.

Clara Harris' fragile emotions broke. Forty-five minutes into the vivid description of her husband's autopsy, she collapsed onto the counsel table. Her sobs were audible for the first time in the trial as Davies looked sharply in her direction.

"There will be no outbursts during testimony," the judge told the defendant harshly, showing no sympathy toward the widow. "It will have to be controlled."

Davies called for a recess as Mary Parnham rushed to the side of the crying woman whose sobs became louder, her shoulders quaking. Davies, still on the bench looked down at Clara.

"I cannot permit this display," the judge continued. "You may leave the courtroom and we will continue the trial without you."

When the jury returned, Clara had composed herself at least to the point that she was not loudly sobbing in the courtroom. Yet her face was red as it was buried in her hands, the woman's eyes tightly narrowed into a squint.

During the recess, Magness had rolled in a model of a hanging skeleton such as might be seen in the office of a physician. Now, she bade the witness get up from the chair and walk to the model to point out the breaks David Harris' bones had suffered. Slowly, without emotion, Wolf described the "crushing" injuries that his body had endured.

Again, the shoulders of Clara Harris began to shake as Wolf said, "the lungs collapsed into the chest cavity when the ribs punctured them."

"If someone described that there was wetness to the breath, what would that mean, Dr. Wolf?" Magness asked.

"That would be caused by bleeding into the lungs," he answered as the woman who had caused the injury he described sobbed.

The jury disregarded the outburst, concentrating on what the physician had to say. Parnham was concerned for his client, holding her hand and looking at her as Wolf continued his grisly narrative.

"The lungs show a huge puncture, and the vena cava was torn from the heart. That is the vein that brings blood back to the body," he said.

Finally, Parnham had had enough of the relentless detail of Wolf's testimony as he stood to address the court.

"The defense stipulates that the cause of death was that the victim was hit and run over by an automobile," he told the judge, who ordered the jury again removed from the courtroom as Clara Harris sobbed loudly at the table.

When the door closed behind the jury, Davies looked at the defendant, then at her lawyer.

"The defendant has been weeping audibly for several minutes," Davies said. "The jury can hear it. I've seen several of them look over. In trial, if a defendant can't sit quietly, I will remove the defendant from the courtroom.

"Which is it going to be?" the judge asked Parnham and his client. "We are not going to have a big show going on."

Clara Harris tried to talk, tried to speak with the judge who was treating her so harshly, but she was cut off by her lawyer.

"This is not a show," Parnham said, himself showing emotion.

"It means sit there and be still," Davies countered sternly. "And that means you will not add to the display in the courtroom by getting up and leaving the court-room."

Magness chimed in as well, not content to let Parnham suffer the indignity of being browbeaten by the judge without a little help from the prosecution.

"It's unfair to the state when we try to present evidence and the jurors aren't even listening."

When the jury returned, Wolf continued the graphic testimony, minutely describing the broken, crushed, and torn body of David Harris.

Yet another photo was placed on the screen of the television monitor as the pathologist told how the man's bladder was torn from the rest of his body, and how the joint connecting the pelvis to the backbone was broken. The lower pelvis was broken as well, he said.

"There are two separate compressive injuries," he said. Earlier, the pathologist had explained to the jury that a compressive injury simply meant that the bone had been crushed.

Finally, at 4:56 p.m., Dr. Dwayne Wolf began the summation of his conclusions regarding the death of Dr. David Harris. Initially the bumper of the car had hit the left leg, he said. There had been impact to the back of the head, then, face down, the car had run across the back, breaking the jaw as the tire rolled down the body diagonally, then crushed the pelvis.

David Harris had been "run over at least twice, and maybe more," the pathologist told the jury.

Again, Clara Harris broke out sobbing loudly in the

courtroom, this time shouting to the judge as Davies prepared to admonish her again.

"This is the first time I heard what happened," she cried loudly, her emotions overcoming her fear of the judge.

SEVENTEEN

For the first time in the trial a defense attorney other than Parnham took the witness on cross-examination. It was late in the day, 5:05 p.m. Other courts in the building were shutting down. Jurors were tired, exhausted from the complex testimony of Dr. Dwayne Wolf. Yet Davies, impatient to move the trial along, had not called a recess as Dee McWilliams approached the podium and began to address the witness in a quiet, barely audible voice. Davies was determined that the jury would work a long day, but the business of the court would not progress at a rapid pace. After one question, McWilliams asked the court for a five minute recess to confer with the defense forensic expert, Dr. Paul Radelat.

McWilliams, a former assistant district attorney, had prepped himself for this witness in order to spell Parnham from cross-examination on complex medical testimony so that he could concentrate on other witnesses who could be more productive for the defense. It was the young lawyer's first trial representing the defense.

When questioning resumed, McWilliams targeted Wolf's testimony regarding blunt force trauma, attempting to catch the pathologist in an inconsistency. But the forensic scientist, his disgust with the line of questioning evident, shook his head as McWilliams continued. Using the same charts and photos that Magness had used in her direct examination, the young lawyer attempted to get the by-now weary physician to acknowledge that the car could have run over David Harris' body going from bottom to top, instead of from top to bottom as he had testified. The skills of the defense lawyer weren't working though, as McWilliams dipped into his bag of tricks and extracted smoke and mirrors for the jury. He challenged Wolf's basic conclusion wanting him to agree that it was at least possible that Clara Harris had only run over her husband one time.

Wolf wasn't buying it.

As the day grew even later, McWilliams went on in excruciatingly boring detail, finally getting the pathologist to admit that the injury that had broken David Harris' back was likely not the same one that broke his hip.

"You still say that he was run over at least twice," McWilliams asked, hoping that he would get a different answer than the one he got.

"With reasonable certainty," Wolf answered.

"If you had scientific evidence that David Harris was struck, rolled over, and then run over, would it change your opinion?" McWilliams probed.

"If that is what the autopsy had indicated," Wolf answered back. "I don't see the kind of injury fitting the kind of injury you are describing. My opinions are based on the autopsy."

"Did you review the police report?" McWilliams continued.

"The police were at the autopsy," Wolf snapped.

"Then you were told what happened," McWilliams responded for the benefit of the jury.

Now Wolf was smiling, clearly liking the pull and tug of the adversarial relationship between defense lawyer and government pathologist. Across the room from him, Clara Harris sat between Munoz Detoto and Parnham, her face still in her hands covering her eyes.

At 5:44 p.m., even Davies had had enough. She recessed the trial until the next morning, and let the jury go home.

The following morning, when the jury had been led into the box and taken their seats, one of its members raised her hand and said that she hadn't been able to hear McWilliams questions. In fact, the young lawyer had questioned Wolf in a soft, almost feminine voice, so quiet that it was barely audible in the cavernous courtroom.

Now, Clara's young lawyer began his questioning of Wolf anew in a more robust voice, returning to his attempt to get the pathologist to change his conclusion that the dentist had been run over "at least twice and maybe more." McWilliams questioned him regarding whether the body was face up, bent, or face down.

"I've considered every option that I could think of," Wolf answered him, now refreshed after a good night's sleep.

"You have considered every conceivable option?" McWilliams asked again, this time emphasizing the word conceivable.

"Did you go to the scene to look at residual evidence such as bloodstains?"

"I've done hundreds of other motor vehicle crashes," the doctor answered, unwilling for his expertise to be challenged.

"I'm asking you about this case," the lawyer continued sharply as Clara Harris looked on, now composed again after sleeping at the mansion.

Finally, McWilliams gave up, passing the witness back

to the prosecution. Magness finished the forensic portion of her prosecution of Clara Harris with minor housekeeping details, then allowed Wolf to return to his lab and the macabre but necessary work he performed each day. She had gotten what she'd wanted from the doctor. Now she would put on a series of lesser state's witnesses, one of whom testified that lab tests showed that neither the orthodontist nor his wife was doing drugs at the time of his death and her arrest.

There were no surprises.

EIGHTEEN

At noon, January 29, 2003, the bailiff called the witness who would put the Widow Harris in the penitentiary. Lindsey Harris came back to Houston with steely determination to imprison forever the woman who had killed her father. Now 17, poised and articulate, the scars on her wrists healed, she would be a difficult witness for Parnham.

The defense lawyer was frightened by Lindsey. First, she was likable. Second, she was credible. And third, she was the eyewitness who could, with certainty, come closest to telling the jury about Clara Harris' actions and motive in the days, hours, and minutes leading up to the murder of Dr. David Harris.

To her credit, Davies ordered the courtroom's camera turned off. There would be no feed to the networks and local stations during the testimony of the case's most important and tragic witness. The judge then ordered the trial into a brief recess. After lunch, the corridor outside the courtroom was packed with the press in anticipation of what they expected Lindsey to say. At one end where the witness area was located, a large picture window faced east looking out on I-10 as it headed into deep East Texas from the state's largest city. The space, off limits to the press, was filled with people, many of them family members, who could not get into the courtroom because they had been sworn in as witnesses. Chief among them were Gerald and Millie Harris. The couple would not see their granddaughter testify. She was now estranged from them because of Lindsey's civil suit and their unwavering support of Clara Harris.

Clara walked from the witness area to the courtroom wearing a bright green suit. She greeted friends from Shadycrest Baptist Church as she walked down the right aisle. They were there as usual, there to show solidarity with the sister whom they all loved. Two of Clara's Colombian cousins sat against the wall. They had been in court daily in a show of support for her. Gerald Harris' brother, the steadfast retired physician from Arkansas, sat in the front row to hear the testimony of his great niece.

At 1:28 p.m., Lindsey Harris took the stand on this, the second most eventful day of her life.

Clara looked at the stepdaughter she hadn't seen since July and smiled. The girl didn't smile back, and the defendant looked down, knowing that the next hours would be the hardest of her life.

"Bring the jury in," Davies told the bailiff.

Lindsey sat on the witness stand, weeping slightly, her straight hair parted in the middle, falling halfway down her chest, her oval face pretty. The well-washed Ohio cheerleader was the all-American girl, the daughter anyone in the courtroom would have been proud to have. In the audience, Debra and Jim Shank watched as the young woman they had so carefully protected these past months prepared to testify.

Magness began quietly.

"How old were you when your parents got divorced?" she asked.

"I was four," Lindsey answered.

"And how did your dad get along with the new woman that he married?" Magness continued.

"They loved each other. They told each other that they loved each other all the time," Lindsey answered. "They got along very well."

Composed now, Lindsey settled into her testimony more comfortably as she answered Magness' questions, her speech clipped.

"And what about after the twins were born?"

"They became a little apart because Clara was playing with the twins a lot," the girl answered. "We got along fairly well. I felt like I was a part of the family before the twins. After they were born, there were no pictures of me, but there were pictures of the twins all over the house."

"You worked in your father's office quite a bit?" Magness said.

"Yes, I came in late June," Lindsey answered.

"And what about Gail Bridges?" Magness continued to probe.

"I thought she was really nice and really pretty," Lindsey continued. "She was pretty bubbly. Her hair was perfectly in place all the time, and her nails were always done."

"What was the first thing you saw that was out of the ordinary?" Magness asked.

"I saw him put his hand on her leg," the girl answered. "At the time, I didn't think anything of it. Later, I was really confused, he wasn't like that."

"And how did Gail treat him?"

"Gail was the aggressor," Lindsey answered without emotion.

"What happened the night of July sixteenth, 2002?" Magness asked.

"We were at home in the music room. He had his piano

and drums there. It was pretty late. It was around ten and we were getting worried. Clara came home and she and Dad went upstairs. I stayed down'stairs on the computer. I heard them talking."

"And the following morning?" Magness probed.

"I was on the computer," Lindsey began. "I heard yelling upstairs. Clara, I could hear her. At first I was really scared. They never yelled. They were in the bathroom."

Magness now went to a large blackboard that was set up in the courtroom and began to walk the witness through the events, charting the things that Lindsey Harris had observed between July 16, 2002, and the fatal night at the Hilton.

"What did she say to you after the fight?" Magness asked.

" 'I have to tell you something, he is having an affair,' " Lindsey answered matter-of-factly.

The girl had been shaken by what her stepmother was saying, despite the things that she had witnessed in the office between her father and his receptionist.

"He just wouldn't do anything like that," she continued. "He went to church. He loved Clara. I felt really bad for her."

Suddenly, there was a bond between the girl and her stepmother that wasn't there before, Lindsey testified.

"We became very close," she said. "We went shopping. She told me everything. It made me feel important."

Later alone with her father, Lindsey confronted him about his relationship with Gail Bridges.

"He told me that I didn't understand, I did not live there," the girl told the court.

After the three of them had dressed, they all got into David's Suburban for the trip to his Clear Lake office. Clara didn't want her husband out of her sight.

"On the way in, Clara said that she was going to fire Gail, but he said, 'No, no, we need her today.'"

When they arrived, Lindsey had headed for the front desk.

"Lindsey, are you okay?" Gail Bridges asked the girl after she had come through the front door of the office. "What's the matter?"

"'Yes, there's something wrong,'" Lindsey said that she'd answered. "I had been crying.

"I was really upset, I was lashing out at Gail."

Clara came in next with David.

"She was very angry, crying," the girl continued, describing Clara's confrontation with her rival. "She was red in the face. She was ready to fire her. Clara grabbed Gail by the arm and led her to the office. She was very mad, but she was also very professional."

Lindsey said that after the firing Clara and David had left to attend a previously scheduled luncheon meeting. That evening she saw Clara at home at the mansion. Her father and stepmother stayed up late talking "about things." Later she learned that he had told her stepmother where he and Gail had met. The next morning, Clara Harris told Lindsey that her father had confessed to her that he'd had a sexual relationship with his girlfriend.

Later in the day, Clara and David went to the home of Gerald and Millie Harris and Lindsey was sent by her stepmother to Baybrook Mall to purchase self-help books.

"When they got back home, I got the impression that things were going to work out."

When she'd learned of her husband's infidelity, Clara Harris immediately went on a crash diet to lose weight. Lindsey had watched as her stepmother now concentrated on the new woman she would become. She went shopping with the girl at upscale women's shops purchasing a new and sexier wardrobe.

"He told her he loved her for the way she looked already," Lindsey said. "The whole family got in the pool that evening. I felt that he was going to give Gail up. I asked him and he said, 'Yes,' and I was happy."

That Sunday, the family went to Galveston beach. On Monday, Lindsey learned of the meeting David planned to have with Gail at Perry's restaurant on Wednesday to break off the affair.

"Clara was kind of nervous about it and had doubts," Lindsey told the court. "She kept doing her hair and shopping. She was nervous. I assured her that everything would be okay."

But things weren't okay. David Harris had told his wife that he missed Gail Bridges.

The following day, Lindsey Harris shadowed her stepmother, now her new best friend.

"We went to the Hilton to see a room and see where they went," she said. "Clara went to the front desk and asked to see a room. She was calm. When we got up to the room, she said, 'Well, I guess this is where they spend their time.' "

The following morning, July 24, 2002, Lindsey Harris continued her close friendship with Clara.

"I told her it was wrong, but I still loved him," Lindsey said.

Throughout the day, Lindsey Harris drove Clara's Mercedes as they made the rounds looking at the places where the lovers had met. Finally, they ended up at an atrium office building on Bay Area Boulevard, the surreally decorated space of Blue Moon Investigations. Lindsey had not been there before.

"She was nervous, angry, confused," the girl said of Clara. "But when we got to Blue Moon, she was calm, and then she started to cry. I didn't know why we were there."

But when she figured out that the two were asking the people at the office to spy on her father, Lindsey had negative thoughts.

"I felt that was invading his privacy," she told the jury, strongly countering the testimony of Claudine Phillips, who had said that the teenager was excited to be at the offices of a private investigation firm.

When the two got home, she learned that Blue Moon investigators were not the only ones spying on her father. The phone rang and Clara picked it up and spoke with the manager of their companies, Susan Hanson.

"Susan gave Clara directions to Gail's house," she said. "She had followed my dad there after work."

"She was upset and crying," Lindsey said. "At 6 p.m., we got back into the car and went to Perry's. They were not there. We then went to Gail's, and Clara got out, went through the back gate, and looked in the garage for David's car. It wasn't there. She was on a mission to find out where he was. She was crying."

"Where did you go next?" Magness asked.

"We went to Tommy's Patio Café," she said. "They weren't there either."

They drove to the Nassau Bay Hilton, but saw no sign of Clara and David. They drove around the lake and across the tall bridge to the Kemah. They stopped at the Aquarium restaurant, but the two were not there either.

"We were going to forget about it and go shopping," Lindsey said. "But things changed. A man called and said he knew where my dad was and he couldn't tell her until the next day. He did anyway."

Lindsey told the jury how her stepmother had called the governess, Maria Gonzalez, and told her loudly to pack her husband's things and put them in the garage of the mansion.

"She then said, 'Go back to the Hilton,'" Lindsey said. "I said, 'I'll go there.'"

"Why?" Magness probed.

"To comfort her," the girl answered.

Lindsey again drove the Mercedes west down NASA Road 1 to the hotel and parked near the front door, she said.

The girl described how the two of them entered the front door of the hotel and walked to the front desk and asked if David was registered at the hotel, Clara telling desk clerk Garrett Clark that her son was sick and she needed to find her husband.

The attention of the people in the courtroom was riveted as the girl on the witness stand began to tell her version of what happened next.

"We went outside and found Gail's Navigator," she said. "On the trailer hitch part, there was a heart. She broke it. Clara looked angry. She then bent the wipers and keyed the car."

At the counsel table, Clara Harris, dressed in a green double-breasted suit, her hair once again back in the trademark black bow, lowered her head, took a deep breath, and looked up at Lindsey Harris as the girl testified. Her gaze moved down to the table again as she listened.

"We then went inside the hotel and called him," Lindsey said.

"He answered and I said, 'You need to come home.'"

Two minutes later, Lindsey testified, Clara Harris dialed the same number. The girl heard her say to her father, "You need to come home, Bradley's sick."

"He didn't come down immediately," Lindsey told the court.

"I next got her outside the hotel by the back doors so that if there was a fight, it wouldn't happen inside," she continued. "We looked through the glass door of the hotel and into the lobby."

Suddenly the two saw David Harris and Gail Bridges emerge from the elevators to their right as they looked through the glass of the door.

"She ran inside," Lindsey said. "She was ready to go inside and fight. She began hitting Gail. She tore her shirt off. It was a big fight."

Now the tension of the courtroom became electric as the young girl continued to tell of the violence between the two women, looking directly at Clara Harris, and her stepmother looking back at her. Finally, Clara lowered her head and listened.

"Outside, she told me that she could kill my father and get away with it for how he's been acting," A gasp emerged from the spectators as they heard the words that would begin to seal the fate of Clara Harris.

"When did she say that?" Magness probed.

"Thirty minutes before the fight."

"What did you do when all this was going on?" Magness asked.

"I was standing back and asking people to help," she answered. "I was really scared. I had never seen anything like this before."

Next the girl described to the jury how she had gone outside the hotel and sat down outside the front door and cried.

"She came out and she was really mad," she continued. "She said, 'Come on, let's go.' She helped me up and we went to the car."

Now, looking directly across the courtroom at her stepmother, Lindsey broke down.

"He said, 'It's over,' " she told the court, suddenly crying very hard.

Clara lowered her head and covered her eyes. When Lindsey recovered her composure, she continued.

"Did you see where your father or Gail Bridges went?" Magness asked.

"No," Lindsey answered. "She got the keys and we got into the car. She was driving."

"What happened next?" the prosecutor said.

"She backed out," Lindsey said. "She wasn't saying anything. I knew that she was mad. She was red, and she had this evil look on her face."

"And what happened next?" Magness continued, probing.

"She sped up and a Hilton employee dodged to get out of the way," Lindsey answered. "He would have been hit if he didn't get out of the way. I was hoping that we were going home, but when she passed the exit, I shouted, 'Stop, go the other way!' "

Clara Harris's face was now in her hands as she prepared herself to hear what she knew was certainly coming next in the girl's testimony.

Lindsey described how the car had sped around the long wall at the end of the hotel, and how she'd seen her father and Gail Bridges standing next to the Navigator.

"Gail was closest to the door," she continued. "Dad pushed her out of the way."

"Was there anybody else standing by the Navigator?" Magness probed, reminding the jury of the testimony of Garrett Clark, who had also been there at the time of impact.

"No," Lindsey said, apparently not remembering the image of the desk clerk standing nearby.

"What happened next?" Magness asked.

"Dad pushed Gail Bridges out of the way," she said.

Clara buried her face deeper into her hands when she heard what Lindsey said next. " 'I'm going to hit him,' " Lindsey said she heard her stepmother say.

"How did she say it?" Mia Magness asked gently probing.

"Like it was going to happen.' I said, " 'No,' " Lindsey answered. "She stepped on the accelerator and went straight for him. He pushed Gail out of the way. When she stepped on the accelerator, it threw me back in the seat."

"What did your dad look like?" Magness asked.

"He was really scared because he was trying to get away and he couldn't," Lindsey said, describing her father's panic. "She circled around and ran over him. She had no expression on her face."

"And then what?" Magness asked.

"I felt the bump," Lindsey said. "I knew it was him. I said, 'You're killing him.' The bump over the median was different from when she was going over my dad."

"What did you do?" Magness probed.

"I opened the door, so that I could help my dad," Lindsey answered. "But she ran over him again after I told her to stop."

Across the room, Clara Harris continued to hold her face in her hands as she heard the girl who had only recently started calling her "Mom" describe the murder.

"How many times did she run over him?" Magness asked.

"Three times," Lindsey answered.

"Did you ever hear a problem with the car?" the prosecutor asked anticipating a contention by the defense that the steering wheel and accelerator had locked.

"No," Lindsey answered.

"What did you do when the car came to a stop?" Magness said.

"I went around and I hit her," Lindsey Harris answered. "She then got out and kneeled down and said, 'I'm so sorry, I'm so sorry. It was an accident.' She wasn't sorry. She had killed him."

Lindsey testified that she was hysterical and ran to Gail Bridges. She noticed people coming from everywhere.

"I heard someone say, 'he's not going to make it,' " she continued. "I knew she had killed him."

"Did she try to comfort you?" Magness asked.

"No," Lindsey answered.

Magness had one final question for Lindsey Harris before relinquishing the witness to Parnham.

"Did you have any more contact with her?"

"She called two days later when I was at my grandparents," the girl said. "She said she was so sorry. She said she wanted me to be an orthodontist and be a part of the business."

NINETEEN

There is nothing that a lawyer fears more than the unknown. That is what George Parnham faced as Mia Magness passed the witness to him. Immediately after the killing of David Harris, the newly hired lawyer had attempted to speak with Lindsey Harris but her stepfather, Jim Shank, stepped between the two of them at a meeting of the entire family at his office. Now Parnham was to cross-examine her without having had any prior contact with the girl. He had not been able to establish rapport with Lindsey, and that was one of Parnham's strong suits.

People liked him. Again and again throughout the trial, as with the trial of Andrea Yates before, the journalists who were assigned to cover the two cases would comment among themselves that Parnham was not that great in the courtroom, that he stumbled and sometimes even fell, but he sure was likable. He was just such a nice guy, such a warm human being.

But Lindsey Harris didn't know that, had no way of knowing that because she had been blocked from having any contact with the man who represented the woman who had killed her father.

Moreover, Lindsey Harris was suing Clara and the estate of her father. That complicated matters for the lawyer. The lawsuit, even though he wasn't representing her stepmother on the civil matter, complicated things for Parnham in his attempts to speak with the girl.

Throughout the case, he had made attempts to meet the girl, but had been thwarted. When he stood to cross-examine Lindsey in the courtroom she smiled at him.

"We met briefly in my office," Parnham began after introducing the defense team sitting with Clara in the courtroom.

"Yes," the girl acknowledged, remembering the bearded lawyer with the nice office and a beautiful view of Houston.

"That day, when we all met, you hugged Clara Harris?" Parnham asked.

"Yes," she answered.

"And after the civil suit was filed, you moved out of your grandparents' house, didn't you?"

"Yes," she said.

Now Parnham began to work, trying to get something, anything, positive out of the girl regarding Clara.

"I get the impression that you and Clara got particularly close the week after she found out about your dad's relationship," he probed.

"Yes," Lindsey answered in the simplest form possible, not giving the lawyer anything more than an acknowledgement of the question.

"You had a shared relationship with your dad?" he asked.

"Yes," she answered. "I called her 'Mom.' We got along very well."

Parnham had his breakthrough, small though it was. He now talked to the girl about family vacations, her own room in the mansion and how it had been especially designed for her.

Next he got Lindsey to admit that Clara Harris had once traveled to Ohio to speak to her class about dentistry. Across the room, the defendant was now smiling at the memories her lawyer was bringing back about those happy days.

"And your brothers," Parnham continued. "You love your brothers."

At the mention of the twins, Clara, who had contained herself during Lindsey's testimony about the fight in the hotel lobby and the subsequent murder, now broke down crying in the courtroom.

Davies exploded.

"It will not be tolerated," the judge roared. "It is not going to happen in this courtroom."

"I'll do my best," Parnham stuttered, walking over to the sobbing Clara.

"My instructions are going to your client," the judge shouted above the woman's sobs.

"She's wailing and sobbing in front of the jury," Magness chimed in, ever ready to twist the knife in the side of the defense. "She is fine when the jury is out of the courtroom."

Clara again took control of herself as she buried her eyes in her hands. Parnham continued, this time asking about the office decorum of Gail Bridges.

"Did you see her put her butt up in your dad's face?" he asked indelicately.

"Yes," Lindsey answered.

"Was your dad disgusted?" Parnham asked.

"I figured he'd be, but he didn't do anything, no."

Next, Parnham got the girl to confirm that on July 16, 2002, she had talked to Susan Hanson and Diana Sherrill about how the two acted in the office and the women had confirmed that her father was having an affair with Gail.

That evening, Parnham said, there was an argument in her father's closet.

"You heard a commotion, didn't you?" he asked. "What did you tell her?"

" 'I know. Everybody in the office knows,' " Lindsey answered.

"Do you remember seeing your father grab Clara Harris' arm and put her on the floor of the closet? Do you remember telling him, 'Dad, she just found out.' "

"I don't remember," came back the answer.

Next, Parnham moved to the firing of Gail Bridges, attempting to show that David was more interested in business than in saving his marriage.

"What did you hear him say?" the lawyer asked.

" 'We can't fire her. We've got eighty-five patients today,' " the girl answered.

"And what did Clara say?" Parnham continued.

" 'She's going,' " Lindsey answered.

Parnham moved to questions regarding Clara's self-help regimen, discussing the diet she was on, and the diet used by her father to lose thirty-two pounds between Christmas and the summer of his death. But he quickly returned to David and his lover.

"Were the intimate details of your dad's relationship with Gail Thompson Bridges told to your stepmother by your father?" Parnham asked.

"Yes," Lindsey answered.

"Do you know if your dad dictated a list of things that Clara Harris needed to do to measure up to Gail?" Parnham continued, laying the groundwork for likely testimony by Clara herself.

"No," the girl answered.

"Do you know if Clara planned liposuction and breast augmentation?" the attorney continued.

Lindsey didn't answer.

Her stepmother sat with her face covered by her hands, her elbows on the hard oak table, as the girl testified that Clara had called her rival a "devil" and "so fake."

Lindsey said under questioning that she'd warned her father that if he divorced Clara, there would be consequences that he wouldn't like.

"I told him, 'You are not going to see your babies very much if she leaves,'" Lindsey said.

Again, Clara Harris began to cry at the mention of the twins—a tissue now in her hand.

"Would you say that everybody was very proud of Dr. Clara?" Parnham asked, using his favorite endearing term for the defendant.

"Yes," the girl answered.

Now Parnham moved to the events of the 24th.

"They were holding hands when they got out of the elevator?" Parnham questioned, bringing the visual image of the couple back to the jury.

"Yes," the girl answered.

"When Clara Harris said that she could kill David Harris and get away with it, she didn't believe she would really do it?" Parnham asked, not getting an answer.

Now, Parnham had stumbled. Lindsey Harris had the lawyer on turf where she was in control of the testimony. He had allowed her to relate again how, immediately before the impact, she had shouted "stop" and Clara had accelerated.

"I was saying it very loudly," Lindsey said as Parnham looked on helplessly. "She knew there was a man standing in front of the car."

After the defense lawyer finished with the witness, Magness asked a few brief questions, on cleanup. Then she uttered the magic words that ended her portion of the case.

"The state rests," she said.

The prosecution's case had not gone well for Parnham. It seldom does for a defense lawyer practicing before a

Harris County jury. Magness had presented a nearly perfect case. Now it was time for Parnham to work his magic before the panel and the judge who sat high on the bench in the ceremonial courtroom.

But things had gone even worse than usual for Parnham in this case. He had stumbled more than usual. He had rambled more than usual. He had seemed lost at times and everybody in the room had known it. George Parnham was off, way off, and there were rumbles among the observers that he was sick, really sick.

Yet the attorney continued onward as if nothing was wrong. When asked, members of the defense team acknowledged that Parnham had been ill, but was getting better.

Parnham had one chance of saving Clara Harris, and he knew it. All he had to do was put enough doubt into the head of just one juror and the case could be won. Only one juror had to question beyond a reasonable doubt that Clara Harris had meant to kill her husband. Even if he lost on guilt, he could still win a victory of sorts during the punishment phase of the trial if but one juror could force the rest to vote to convict for the lesser-included offense of manslaughter. If Parnham could get one of them to believe strongly that Clara had killed with sudden passion, then the doors of probation without prison time opened before her. The option belonged to the jury. The heavy lifting belonged to Parnham, now suffering from the worst cold of his lifetime, which had relapsed.

Clara Harris' hopes ran high as Steve Irwin took the stand on January 31, 2003 in an evidentiary hearing on the admissibility of the video animation of the defense version of what happened. While not Disney quality, the tape was good, very good. It would show a far different version of events the night of July 24 than the state had thus far depicted. Irwin, a Dallas-based expert witness, would swear under oath that he believed that Clara Harris had not run over her husband again and again.

The video had cost a bundle. Such testimony does not come cheap. Irwin's firm had been paid $50,000 to come to its conclusion that the Mercedes had hit David only once. The reconstruction expert would say David Harris had rolled off the hood of the car, which, had then run over him once and then again. Irwin would testify that the car had traveled at a speed of between 15 and 20 miles per hour.

The defense also asked the judge if it could present an enhanced (lightened) version of the video taken at the scene by Lindsey Dubec.

In a bizarre move, Davies briefly barred the press and public from the fifty-three-minute hearing, in which lawyers argued the merits of the admission of Irwin's tape. Finally, they were readmitted, and the reconstructionist was still on the stand. The court ruled that the enhanced version of the Blue Moon video could be used. However, the animation upon which Parnham and the defense had placed such high hopes was barred.

Davies' ruling was a crushing blow to the defense, and it showed. Until the judge made her decision, the defendant had appeared confident with what she heard Irwin say from the witness stand. Now her body language and that of her lawyers underwent a transformation. Where it had been upbeat, even buoyant that finally she was being able to present her case to the jury, the defense was now troubled and it was evident.

Fox news reporter Sue Speck passed a note to a colleague saying, "George is so utterly defeated, disappointed, angry and frustrated, he is in no condition to be asking questions now." Her fellow journalist concurred. Parnham was now being hammered by illness to the point that what came out of his mouth was largely disjointed.

Yet he had to go on. Parnham would have to present the most important witness in his case with his hands tied, able to use only a portion of the sophisticated show he planned for the jury. Worse still, he felt so bad he could barely speak.

Now in front of the jury, Irwin was poised and confident as he reeled off his qualifications, saying that his company had been in business for fifteen years, that he had a degree in civil engineering and that he was, by profession, a road designer.

The man was an engaging witness, and likable. Visions of crash-test dummies could have danced through the jury's heads as Irwin described the activities of his professional association, the obscure Texas Association of Accident Reconstruction Specialists.

Like many experts who had been in the field of providing paid testimony for defense lawyers, Irwin danced a dance of numbers. He testified that he had studied 1,400 automobile accidents, had testified 100 times for both the defense and the prosecution and had made 1,500 measurements at the scene of the "accident" at the Hilton. The measurements, he said, were made for the purpose of photogrametry, the process of making maps from measurements taken from photographs. Irwin was doing fine until he lost all credibility in one unbelievable answer. The jury had seen photograph after photograph of the blood and hair deposited on the underside of Clara Harris' car when it had crushed her husband under its six-inch clearance from the asphalt as it rolled over him.

Under Parnham's questioning, Irwin said that when he raised the car on a lift, he'd found no blood.

Parnham knowing the testimony was potentially costly, quickly returned his witness to the numbers Irwin said that he had taken 200 measurements from the area of a red plastic [tail light], lens that he said had been found where the Navigator had been parked.

He spoke with authority as he looked directly at the jury and told them about the turning radius that a model such as Clara's Mercedes could make. "A forty-foot circle is the minimum turn . . ."

Irwin said he based his work on the markings made at the scene of physical evidence such as tire marks. Yet neither he, nor any of the prosecution witnesses had testified that the black tire marks he'd used had been made by Clara Harris' car the night of the assault. For all the jury knew, the marks could have been six months old. Yet Irwin was paid to present the defense theory. To him, the tire marks were made by Clara Harris and they proved that she could not have hit and run over her husband more than one time.

"Where did you get your information on the turning radius of this model?" Parnham asked.

"I base this on published data, and I have driven one," Irwin answered.

Next, Parnham moved to numbers of a different sort, getting the expert to testify regarding the height of Gail Bridges' Lincoln Navigator.

"It is seventy-five inches tall, or six feet three inches tall," Irwin testified.

"When she rounded the end of that wall, could she see

people on the other side of the Navigator?" Parnham asked.

"No," Irwin answered confidently.

Now, Parnham moved to the testimony that he hoped the jury would believe from the warm, handsome and smart witness before them.

"In your interpretation of the Blue Moon video, how many times does the Mercedes run over David Harris?" he asked Irwin.

"It hits him once and runs over him once," the man answered.

Until now, Clara Harris had appeared bored by the sometimes dreary recitation of numbers that seemed to drone on for hours as Parnham laboriously presented his witness in agonizingly slow detail. Yet now, it was show-and-tell time as the defense lawyer began to play the new enhanced Blue Moon video. At critical moments, the attorney would stop the action and seek comment from Irwin. Clara moved her eyes from the big screen to the jury and back again, apparently fascinated by the engineer's testimony.

"The circle gets tighter and tighter as she goes around?" Parnham asked.

"Yes," Irwin answered as the two held a large chart up directly in front of the jury.

By 3:08 p.m., fatigue began to show in the face of the defendant. She held her eyes with her thumb and forefinger pinched on the top of her nose. Involuntarily, she sighed as the testimony returned to tire marks and photogrametry. Meanwhile, Magness stood in a corner of the courtroom watching, taking notes.

Yet even the dry testimony of Steve Irwin was too much for the fragile emotions of Clara Harris.

"When the car turns, does it pass over the blood stain?" Parnham asked.

"No," Irwin answered.

At 3:53 p.m., the Clara Harris broke again, sobbing, she turned from the defense table attempting to show only her back to the judge as she buried her face in her hands to compose herself. Regaining control after the brief outburst, she turned back to the table, her face again in her hands as the judge stared at her.

Finally, Parnham reached the point that he'd wanted to with the witness before he would pass Irwin to Magness.

"Bodies do not bounce off of cars, right?" he asked Irwin.

"Generally not," the engineer answered.

"Was there any evidence of any blood marks on the car?" he continued.

"I saw no evidence," Irwin answered.

"Was there any evidence of dragging?" Parnham continued.

"No," the expert answered.

"Was there any evidence of run-overs here?"

"I said no," Irwin answered.

"Pass the witness," Parnham said, having fired his best shot of the entire case, weak as it was.

Mia Magness was nice to Steve Irwin. She clearly liked the man whose theories she planned to destroy. Yet destroy them she must, and the destruction would be easy, so far-fetched was what he wanted the jury to believe.

Irwin had mentioned as he was establishing his credentials before the jury during his testimony that he had helped author a book on accident investigations. Now, he had to admit in front of the jury that he was one of a host of authors of the book.

Next she pounced on his statement that bodies don't bounce when hit by cars.

"Where did you get your training on how a body reacts when hit by a car?" she asked. "Have you ever looked at a body in an auto pedestrian accident?"

"I have never been in a morgue," he answered. "I have never been to an autopsy."

"Have you spoken to any of the eyewitnesses in this case?" she asked. "Do you recognize the name Paul Garrett Clark?"

"No," Irwin answered.

"Do you recognize the name Evangelos Smiros?" Magness continued.

"No," the man answered, smiling.

"How about Jose Miranda?" Magness continued.

"No," he answered.

"They testified that he had been run over three times," she continued. "What about three more eyewitnesses?"

"No, ma'am," he answered.

"Four more?" she pushed.

"No, ma'am." Irwin answered.

"Ten more?" Magness said, her voice now raised in disgust.

"Are you married to your opinion no matter how many eyewitnesses come forward?" she said.

"Yes, ma'am." Irwin answered.

"You didn't talk to the passenger of the vehicle," she continued. "Is there any of the witnesses that would change your opinion?"

"I have a videotape," Irwin answered meekly.

The withering cross-examination continued as Magness continued to hammer Irwin relentlessly. Next she moved to his assertion that the Blue Moon investigator had been parked in a corner of the parking lot. Much of his opinion was based upon this assertion.

"If you were wrong about where Lindsey Dubec was parked, then you were wrong about everything, right?" Magness asked.

"It would mean that I was wrong about everything, everything," Irwin answered.

"Did you ever talk to Lindsey Dubec?" he asked.

"No," Irwin answered.

"You can't tell then that she ran over the body again because you do not know where the body was positioned?" Magness asked.

"Fair enough," Irwin answered, seeming to smile at the skill with which his testimony was being methodically destroyed. Magness was a worthy intellectual opponent.

"You testified that it was impossible for her to stop," Magness continued in regard to Irwin's testimony about how fast the Mercedes was traveling before it hit David Harris.

"Yes," Irwin answered.

"If she accelerated, it would be even more impossible for her to stop?" Magness asked.

"Yes," the engineer answered as the audience gasped, his testimony in a shambles.

Across the room, anguish now showed on the face of Clara Harris as the reality that she might actually face prison began to come home to her. All of the money she had spent was not working on the jury, and she knew it. She had hoped and had expected more from her defense lawyer. Her star witness, the expert whose showbiz presentation before the jury was to save her, had just crashed in flames before her eyes. She sighed uncontrollably and looked down at the counsel table.

Clara Harris had paid Irwin to convince the jury that the killing was an accident, although she and everybody else in the courtroom knew that it was homicide. The prosecutor was methodically destroying whatever thin plausibility his theory contained, and the defendant knew it.

But Magness wasn't finished with Irwin.

"You said that you have testified more than one hundred times before a jury for both the defense and the prosecution, right?" Magness inquired.

"Yes," he answered, knowing the next question before it was even asked.

"When and where was the last time you testified for the state?" Magness probed, driving a dagger into the testimony of the paid defense witness.

"It was in 1995 in Fort Worth," he answered. "I also testified once for the attorney general's office."

"And what are you paid?" she asked.

"Generally $195 per hour," Irwin answered.

"And how much to you expect to bill in this case?" she asked.

"Between $40,000 and $50,000," he answered.

Irwin's testimony was the last before Davies recessed court for the weekend. On the morning of February 1, 2003, the space shuttle Columbia was lost with its crew. When court resumed the following Monday, Davies opened the proceedings with everyone standing and reciting the Pledge of Allegiance, albeit out of the presence of the jury. When the jurors were brought in, the judge asked if any had seen anything about the trial during the intense media coverage of the tragedy. One admitted that she had seen "a snippet."

When testimony resumed, Irwin was still on the stand as Parnham attempted to repair the damage Magness had done to his expert.

He homed in on the missing seconds of the Blue Moon video during which Lindsey Dubec had not been able to tape a portion of the murder.

"Five seconds were missing," the lawyer said. "Then there were an additional five seconds for her to get the video up and running."

At the adjacent table, Mia Magness was ready to pounce, her visage catlike, eager to continue the near-nuclear destruction of Irwin. When Parnham passed the witness after an unproductive and brief series of questions, she was ready.

At the counsel table, Clara Harris sat, her eyes only slightly open, looking at the table.

"Mr. Irwin, I'm going to ask you for only yes or no answers," she began. "You don't know how fast she was coming around that corner?

"No," Irwin answered.

"She could do it a lot slower?" Magness continued.

"Yes," he answered.

"If it were slower, it would give her more time to perceive what was in front of her?" Magness probed.

"Yes," Irwin answered.

"She could have said, 'I'm going to hit him,' and then blow on through that parking lot?" Magness hammered with devastating effectiveness.

"Yes," he answered.

"At a slower speed, she has more time to correct or make an adjustment?" the prosecutor continued.

"No question about it," he answered.

"Now, regarding the missing time on the video," she continued. "Do you know how much of the evening on July 24th was not captured?"

"No ma'am," she answered.

"Do you think that if you are paid $50,000 you are going to come here and say she did it?" Magness finished.

"I spent more time working than I have testifying," Irwin said weakly.

TWENTY

Occasionally, a defense attorney puts a witness on the stand for a minor purpose and the testimony suddenly becomes important—important to the other side. Such was the case with former Nassau Bay emergency medical technician Robert Hebert, and such was the case with George Parnham. The lawyer called the EMT to the stand for one purpose, to establish where the body was lying when the ambulance had arrived, hopefully to place the body next to the pool of blood to try to show that after the initial impact, the Mercedes had never touched the body of David Harris again.

It was important for Parnham to convince the jury that Clara had run over her husband only one time. That could be explained as an accident, while more than one time would go to the heart of what Magness was trying to prove—intent. If he could convince the jury that Clara hadn't intended to run over David, she might be found innocent. It was a long shot, but Parnham had to try.

Hebert told the defense lawyer that "David Harris was on his back with his left cheek to the ground, his head facing north, his feet facing south. His right leg was lying over his left leg, and twisted. His head was in a pool of blood."

That said, Parnham passed the witness, apparently ignorant of what the bloodthirsty prosecutor would do with someone on the stand who could describe, one more time for the jury, the gory spectacle that had become the body of David Harris.

"What did he look like?" she asked the witness, as if finding out for the first time that David was a mess when the ambulance had arrived.

"He was bleeding from the head, the clothes were torn," Hebert answered. "But just looking, there wasn't much obvious."

Magness walked to the video monitor, and Clara Harris looked away, knowing what was coming next. She placed her hands over her eyes.

"What did he feel like?" Magness asked.

"There was no real texture to his facial area," he said. "And he was real soft in the chest area."

Clara Harris' head now shook, her hands again completely covering her face. Then she looked up.

"He was gasping," the man continued. "There was blood in his mouth."

Magness withdrew the bloody shirt David Harris had worn the night he was killed from an evidence bag, and held it up for the witness to identify.

Clara's head now fell into her hands as her shoulders began to shake through her sobs.

Parnham began a parade of character witnesses who would tell the jury one by one about the good side of the woman on trial for murder.

Maria Vivina Perkins was a fellow Colombian who had lived in the United States for thirty-two years. She'd known Clara Harris for ten years professionally and socially, and had designed the mansion. Perkins, like many of these witnesses, described the relationship that Clara

Harris had enjoyed with David's daughter. The architect and interior designer said that she had designed one room of the mansion for the girl, at Clara's request, describing it as "a very special room."

Parnham also played another card in his strategy to put David on trial instead of the woman who had killed him. He would show the jury that Clara Harris had endured injury at the hands of her husband, introducing photos of bruising on her arms.

Clara had told her attorney that she had suffered years of physical abuse at the hands of David Harris. However, she wouldn't allow Parnham to bring this before the jury. Moreover, she had told the team representing her that her husband had sometimes forced sex upon her. This too she made her lawyers suppress.

However, Parnham now had no choice but to show the jury a little of the evidence of abuse that was revealed in the photographs he had taken immediately after he took over her defense.

"They show the woman horribly bruised after three days," he said as he prepared to put the pictures on the screen.

But Magness objected, saying that the photos were not relevant, and for the time being, Davies agreed with her. In frustration, Parnham threw up his hands.

"These are the facts and I think the jury needs to see what went on," he said, anger and frustration in his voice.

"You are not going to do it by asking the witness about hearsay," Davies shouted back. Perkins had not taken the pictures, therefore, under the law, she could not testify to their accuracy.

But Perkins was allowed to testify to the bruises verbally, saying that Clara had them on her arms, face, under her chin, her thighs and elbows.

Savoring his brief victory by at least getting the witness to describe Clara's injuries, he passed Perkins to Magness.

"Are you familiar with the term catfight?" the prosecutor asked, knowing that every juror would understand the negative connotations the term would evoke.

"No," Perkins said, in her strong Spanish accent. "This is the first time."

"Have you ever watched TV where you have seen people fight?" Magness asked.

"Yes," the woman answered.

"It's a violent situation, it is likely to hurt?" the prosecutor asked.

"Correct," Perkins answered.

"Someone rolling on the floor might actually bump themselves," Magness said, not caring what the answer would be, but hoping that the jury would remember Clara's violent attack on Gail Bridges in the hotel lobby.

Parnham's moment of success was brief. Magness had again blunted his witness' testimony and turned it against his client.

Diana Sherrill now came to the witness stand, dressed in a blue pin-striped suit, well groomed, and by her own testimony so well liked in the Lake Jackson area that the Harrises had chosen her to handle public relations for the Brazoria County office. It was her job to keep the customers happy, and handle advertising and the media.

"Everybody refers to them as Dr. David and Dr. Clara, right?" Parnham prompted, now knowing that he could use the warm fuzzy term for the two dentists with abandon.

"Yes," the woman answered.

Sherrill described how David Harris had changed, and stayed in the back office during the one to two days each week that he came to practice with Clara in Lake Jackson.

The woman told how she had come to know about the affair of David and Gail, and how she didn't think that the conduct was appropriate.

And Sherrill said she had discussed the woman with her friend Susan Hanson. She also related how others in the office "were nice to her but were physically ill when they left work after seeing what was going on."

As Diana testified, Clara's courtroom demeanor changed. She smiled at the well-dressed woman on the stand as her employee went on to tell of the good times that the office staff had enjoyed with Dr. David and Dr. Clara. Diana Sherrill spoke of the pool parties at the mansion for the kids. There was a surreal quality to the testimony as she continued to refer to her bosses by the affectionate nicknames used around the dental offices. It was as if she were not speaking of adult professionals in the serious atmosphere of a courtroom, but instead, was speaking of them to children in an attempt to secure their trust. For her, the two would forever be Dr. David and Dr. Clara.

Diana Sherrill said she was the first to tell Clara Harris that her marriage to David was in trouble. Surely, Parnham reasoned, the jury would begin to understand Clara's anger.

"Did she believe you?" he asked.

"No, not at first," Sherrill answered.

When Magness took over on cross-examination, she pulled no punches with the woman, and her questioning was brief.

"Do you think that the fact that he was having an affair justified his death?" she asked.

"Objection," Parnham shouted. But the damage had been done. The jury was reminded that in the eyes of the State of Texas and its petite prosecutor, Dr. Clara had murdered Dr. David.

* * *

Next, Susan Hanson was called to the witness stand. Blond, with a fair complexion, and a bit overweight, the woman was as impeccably dressed as she had been when she appeared at the side of Clara Harris for most of her court appearances. Hanson had spent her time outside the courtroom since the trial began because Davies had invoked "the rule," which prohibits potential witnesses in a case from hearing the testimony of other witnesses.

Parnham smiled at the mother of three, the head of Space Center Management, the Harrises umbrella company under which all of their other business entities were controlled. Hanson was the business person in the group, hard nosed and ice cold when she believed it was to her or her boss's benefit.

Despite her good looks, she was not likable on the witness stand.

"Tell the jury what you do." Parnham asked the woman.

"I make sure we are meeting our goals day to day so that we have a good month," she answered. "I also handle hires and terminations."

Hanson would not have described the practice thusly, but it was easy for the jury to draw the conclusion from her testimony that Clara was an active player in the money mill that the ever-growing practice had become. And although Parnham would not ask the woman on the stand about it, rumors circled the lake from time to time that David Harris put braces on kids who maybe didn't need them.

"She was always on the lookout for potential orthodontic cases for David," Hanson said.

Hanson told the jury the oft-repeated story of the affair of David Harris and Gail Bridges. Again the panel heard the timeline of how Clara had learned of the affair on July

16, and then gone through a week of self-help to recapture the attention of her straying husband.

"She stuffed her bra one day to make her breasts appear to be larger," Hanson said, as Clara shook her head at the table and smiled in embarrassment.

"Did David ever discuss or compare the physical attributes of Gail Bridges and Clara Harris?" Parnham asked.

"Objection," Magness interrupted.

"Did David ever discuss or compare the breasts of Gail Bridges and Clara Harris?" Parnham tried, using a slightly different question.

"Objection," Magness again cried to the judge.

Finally, Parnham gave up, knowing that continuing the line of questioning would only bring another scolding from Davies.

"Did you consider what he was doing with Gail wrong?" he asked the woman.

"Yes, very wrong," she answered. "They were having an affair. He had a very high moral standard and he was breaking his own code."

"Did you try to talk to Clara about it?" Parnham asked.

"I tried, but it had to come from David to tell his wife," Hanson answered.

It was Mia Magness' turn with the witness, and it was clear that the two women had met before and did not like each other. However, Magness began gently, targeting both women's disdain for Gail Bridges.

"She was a little bit uppity?" Magness began.

"You can say that," Hanson answered.

"What she's responsible for is being a pain in the rear in the office and having an affair with David Harris?" the prosecutor continued.

"He was having an affair," the blond woman answered.

Magness then moved in, beginning with a series of questions which included Hanson acknowledging that she had traveled with the Harrises on vacations and business trips—that working for the couple was a 24/7 experience. Ultimately, she got to the question that would surely anger some jurors if they objected to employees spying on their bosses, no matter how noble the motivation.

"Was it work when you followed David Harris to Gail Bridges' house?" Magness asked, venomously.

"Yes," Hanson answered.

"You did follow him?" Magness continued.

"Until I lost him," she answered. "I actually lost him at a red light. We all knew that David was supposed to have dinner with Gail that night and they were going to Perry's Steak House."

"David told her about that meeting?" Magness pressed.

"David told me he was staying with Clara," Hanson answered elusively.

Magness erupted because the witness was being evasive and not answering her questions directly.

Davies cautioned the witness to answer the questions, but Magness had achieved the impression that she'd wished for in front of the jury—Hanson had come across as if she were covering up something, hiding something, or at least not being cooperative with the prosecution. Magness still had one more shot to fire at the woman.

"Two weeks ago, you said you didn't want to talk to my investigator, because you told him, 'I don't want to hurt Clara's case,' didn't you?"

"Yes," Hanson answered.

"Then why don't you want to talk to me?" Magness asked, as she passed the witness back to Parnham.

The defense was pleased with Hanson. The witness had done her job, not giving the prosecution much. More important, she had given Clara Harris the one thing she needed most right now. She had given her friendship, and after all, Clara was spending her birthday in a Houston courtroom.

The following morning, Maria Gonzalez, the beautiful governess hired by the Harris family to care for the twins at the mansion, was sworn in. For the first time, Clara Harris, dressed in a blue suit, looked directly at the media as Detoto began questioning the young woman in English through a Spanish interpreter. Gonzalez, in her mid 20s, had immigrated to Wharton, Texas, from her native state of Jalisco, Mexico five years ago, had found work with the family, and had been with them ever since.

Clara smiled at the woman, and Gonzalez smiled back as Munoz gently led her through a recitation of the daily life of the family, speaking of the children, and referring to the defendant as Señora Clarita.

Next, Munoz Detoto led the governess through a description of how David had begun to change when Clara had made a trip to Colombia—how he had suddenly started dressing impeccably and had lost weight. Maria had noticed changes in his wife, she said, but much later. In July 2002, Clara had lost weight as well. She changed her makeup and hair, Gonzalez noticed.

The translator then struggled as he attempted to tell the jury what the witness was saying. Finally he said, "I need help." Struggling, the man finally came up with an adequate translation of Gonzalez' words as the courtroom erupted in laughter. Blushing, he cupped both hands over his chest in a non-verbal translation revealing that Clara wanted larger breasts and had told her Mexican governess so.

In minute detail, Parnham led the live-in babysitter

through the trauma of the breakup of the marriage, finally saying that she had received an angry call from Clara to pack up David's clothes and put them in the garage on the afternoon of the 24th.

Parnham moved in to extract the testimony from Maria Gonzalez that he wanted to leave the jury with.

"Why was she looking for David that evening?" he asked.

"She told me that she was on a mission to bring her husband back to save her family," Gonzalez answered through the interpreter.

After Gonzalez was released, another group of witnesses was marched up the left aisle of the courtroom to be sworn in. Among them was a large woman with dull blond hair who protested that she was being forced to take the oath.

"I am here in representation of a witness," Valorie Davenport told the judge as she protested to being sworn in. Davies didn't mention the lawyer's antics in front of the media in violation of her gag order. But Davenport was now in the hands of Davies no matter what. She was now a sworn witness and bound to tell the truth if she was called to the stand for any reason.

As soon as the oath was administered and the witnesses had left the courtroom, Davies called for the next witness.

"Gail Bridges," Magness answered.

Then Davies performed one of the most incomprehensible acts of the entire trial. She ordered that the television cameras be turned off and that there be no still pictures taken of the lover of David Harris during her court appearance. Gail Bridges was indirectly responsible for events leading to his death, yet unlike most of the other witnesses, would be given the gift of anonymity by the judge. Members of the press were stunned. They had been waiting for visuals of the mystery woman. Now they would have to be content with chasing her when she left the courthouse.

When Gail Bridges entered the courtroom, she looked older than many had expected. Perhaps she had aged during the hard years since she had left Steve Bridges, allegedly for Julie Knight. Perhaps she had aged because of the marathon court battles the two women had waged against their former husbands. Perhaps she had aged because of her grief for the loss of David Harris, who, she'd told friends, had planned to marry her.

She was small, with straight dark hair swept to one side to reveal a finely chiseled face.

But the lines of age softened as Bridges walked to the stand, wearing a black suit and a gray turtleneck. As she sat down, she now looked pretty, her lipstick bright red and her dark hair falling down perfectly.

Across the room another woman looked down, not acknowledging the presence of Gail Bridges with as much as a look.

The woman spoke in a soft, low, sexy voice as Emily Munoz Detoto began her questioning of the hostile witness for the defense.

"You knew he was married, the father of twins, did you?" the lawyer began.

"It was explained to me by David that she had an affair in the past," Bridges answered.

"What is meant by an open marriage?" Munoz continued.

"It is understood you are dating other people," Bridges answered.

"How much were you paid?" the attorney continued regarding Gail's compensation as the office receptionist at Space Center Orthodontics.

"Eighteen hundred per month, and then it was upped to two-thousand per month," Gail answered, her voice still low and almost inaudible.

"You were the only front office worker who was included in the bonus program?" Munoz Detoto asked. "Is that correct?"

"Yes," Bridges answered.

Clara Harris finally looked up from the counsel table, but not at her rival on the witness stand. Instead, she looked across the room at the jury, then at the press.

"You flirted in the dental office," Munoz continued. "You bent over and put your butt in his face."

"I did not do that," Bridges answered, showing a brief flash of anger, a witness hostile to both sides in the trial.

"You got closer and closer with Dr. David!" Munoz said.

"Yes."

"You said, 'I have nothing to lose so I'm game, babe,' " Munoz said, repeating a phrase that the prosecution had heard that Gail had said when she was approached for a relationship by David. There was no response from her, and Munoz moved on.

"On May 4, 2002, you went shopping at the Galleria," the attorney said. The Galleria is Houston's premier shopping destination, a three story-shopping mecca built with an ice-skating rink at its core, surrounded with posh and trendy retail shops. The Westin Oaks Hotel is its centerpiece

"You checked in to the Westin Oaks Hotel at 6 p.m.. You made love."

"Yes," Gail Bridges answered.

As Munoz continued her probe of the woman, George Parnham sat at the table next to his client. For the first time in the trial, he looked at the jury, studying them, looking at their eyes as they watched and listened to the witness who was now on the stand, her skin a soft hue in the subdued light of the courtroom.

"Everybody in the office knew about us," she continued.

"As your relationship intensified, your salary increased," Munoz asked.

"Yes," Bridges agreed.

Clara Harris studied her jurors as Gail told how she had stolen the man they both had loved from her. As Clara tried to read the jury's thoughts, Gail related how she and David had made plans together. Munoz next wanted to talk about plans of another sort.

"David and Clara had made plans together for their new office," she said. "They had made plans for their future together. It was their dream."

Gail made no answer, as the defense lawyer moved her questions to a party that Gail and Clara had both attended.

"You spent time with Clara Harris, didn't you?" Munoz said.

"Yes," Gail answered.

"Did you think you should tell Clara?" the attorney pressed.

"I don't know that I should have," Gail answered. "I was under the impression that she knew pretty much, yes."

She then said that she was surprised when she had been fired.

"During the firing, she asked me about kissing and touching," she told the jury. "I told her she needed to ask her husband. I admitted I had lunch with her husband. It was a situation at the time I didn't want to be in. The situation made me frightened."

"I said, 'why don't I just leave,' " she said. "Clara told

me I was fired. David told me I was not. I was never really clear on that."

"You filed a complaint with the EEOC, didn't you?" Munoz asked venomously. "You wanted vacation pay, overtime, and severance pay. You didn't consider your dates with David overtime, did you?"

Now Munoz moved to the fatal day, July 24, 2002, as she began to probe what Gail had done.

"I had a bad headache," the woman began. "I went to lunch with Julie Knight and to the mall with Julie Knight."

"She is a friend of yours?" Munoz asked, smelling an opportunity to open up the witness to questions about an alternative lifestyle with her friend.

"Yes, ma'am," Bridges answered.

"Did you have several conversations with Julie Knight on July twenty-fourth, 2002?" Munoz asked.

"Yes," Gail said.

"When you met David at the Hilton, where did you meet?"

"We sat by a window in the restaurant," she said. "David had a Corona, and I had a Bloody Mary."

It was Gail Bridges herself, not a hotel employee or other witness to her behavior, who was telling the jury of what had happened in the Hilton lobby and parking lot. Munoz led her through testimony of how she and David had left the restaurant and walked to the parking lot, how she had gotten into her Navigator, and he stood outside in the hot Texas sun.

"Did you and David make a decision to rent a hotel room?" Munoz asked.

"Yes," the woman answered.

"Did it appear that your relationship was going to end?" the attorney asked, gentle now.

"No, ma'am," came back the answer.

"You guys were going to have a future together," Munoz continued.

"Yes, ma'am." Bridges answered.

Now Munoz was on all-too-familiar ground as she probed Bridges about the phone call from Lindsey Harris regarding a sick child, and the call from Clara herself shortly thereafter.

"He said, 'I'm going home,'" Bridges told the jury.

"When you left that hotel room, was that the end of your relationship?" Munoz asked. "When you were holding hands with Clara's husband, were you happy, were you smiling, were you thinking about your future together?" Munoz demanded.

"Yes, ma'am," Gail Bridges answered as she collapsed in tears on the witness stand.

When the woman recovered, she briefly described the fight she had with Clara in the lobby of the Hilton.

"She hit David first, and then she hit me," she said, crying again and looking down.

"Do you blame her?" Munoz probed.

"No, ma'am. I do not," Bridges answered. "I understand. She attacked me."

"All of that physical violence that was directed at you, she was crying with you," Munoz probed.

"Yes ma'am," Bridges answered.

Bridges said that during the fight, she'd seen David Harris trying to pull his wife off her, but the only thing she could think of was getting out of the hotel. When she finally did walk to the Navigator, she had no idea that David had followed her.

"I was trying to leave," she said.

Bridges said that after the assault, she was taken to the hospital suffering from contusions, a concussion, and post-traumatic stress disorder.

"I was pretty much in a fog for several days," she told the jury.

Munoz now returned the woman to the events that had immediately led to the death of David Harris.

"Where were you?" she asked.

"I was standing inside the door between the door and the seat," she said. "The door wasn't fully open. David was somewhere behind me. I don't know exactly where David was standing. I saw Clara come around in her vehicle. I don't remember Clara hitting the back of the Navigator."

"Did you see the impact, did you see her circling?" Munoz asked.

"No, ma'am, I did not," answered the person who the defense believed was the closest eyewitness to the death of David Harris as she again broke into tears.

"Lindsey came," she continued. "I called David's parents."

"Did you identify yourself as the mistress of David Harris when you gave them the bad news?" Munoz asked contemptuously.

"Oh, no, ma'am," Gail Bridges testified.

Mia Magness did not choose to cross-examine Gail Bridges. She believed that the woman had done enough damage to the defense on her own.

TWENTY-ONE

For practical purposes, George Parnham had presented his case to the jury. Yet there was one witness who demanded to be heard in the murder of Dr. David Harris. It was a troublesome witness, a witness whom the savvy old lawyer didn't want anywhere near the stand. Clara Harris, frustrated by the apparent failure of her defense, now demanded to testify.

Parnham presented all of the pitfalls to her. In a murder trial, a defendant taking the witness stand can be decisive. It can seal the fate of the defendant, resulting in a heavy sentence. Sometimes, a defense attorney will actually beg a client not to take the stand. Such was the case with Parnham.

If the testimony is compelling and the defendant is likable, a defendant's testimony can result in astonishing results in the hands of the right lawyer. Parnham knew that with the luck of the draw, the jury he had cut could have members whose compassion would work to the favor of Clara Harris—if they were willing to forgive. With some jurors, the admission that "I did it, but I'm sorry" would be enough to provoke a much lighter sentence, a hung jury, or even an acquittal.

Clara Harris wanted to testify. Again and again throughout the course of Parnham's case, she had seen witnesses favorable to her cut off by objections from the prosecution and had seen those objections sustained by the bench. The rules of courtroom procedure were a constant frustration to her, and sometimes she showed it at the counsel table when a witness was prevented from telling what she believed to be her side of the story.

Moreover, she had seen the testimony of Steve Irwin crash and burn before her eyes. She and so many around her had had such high hopes for him. Clara had come to believe that if there were to be any hope for her, it was likely to come from the likable and articulate former traffic engineer to whom she had paid a small fortune.

Yet all of that was for naught as Magness had destroyed his theory with almost surgical precision.

No, it would be up to Clara Harris to save herself, and the former beauty queen knew the power of her charm.

And it was no small power that she would wield. Clara Harris is likable. A courtroom full of spectators, friends from Shadycrest, daily gave mute but striking testimony that her support ran deep in her community. The woman was clearly loved by her friends and family.

Patients had come to court as well. Clara Harris' charm was widely known and deeply appreciated by those whose teeth she had cared for over the years. She and David had not built their empire of multiple dental practices by being wallflowers. They had been a lovely couple at the dance, and in some sectors, Clara was the belle of the ball, a prom queen so lovely and personable that her friends were willing to stand by her no matter what, even if she were accused of a brutal murder.

Parnham droned on in his presentation of character witnesses after the drama of the testimony of Gail Bridges. A neighbor, Holly Podlewski, told the jury that on July 22, 2002, she and her husband Curtis had seen

Clara dressed out of character and that she had seen bruises on her arms.

She also testified that during the time she and her husband had known the couple, they had appeared to be in love.

The following morning, before the jury was brought into the courtroom, Parnham stood to make a complaint to the judge.

"There was a news conference in front of the courthouse and various inflammatory statements were made on various news outlets," Parnham complained.

"I'm getting reports of that nature," Davies answered.

The defense lawyer was speaking of Valorie Davenport, the attorney for Gail Bridges and Julie Knight, who had again spoken before the press.

There was another witness who was becoming impatient to take the stand. At 10:32 a.m., the lawyer quietly called his next witness.

"Clara Harris," he said as all eyes in the courtroom shifted to the woman on trial for murder.

Clara walked across the room, passed the end of the jury box, and then moved easily to the stand. When she was seated, she adjusted the microphone to a position directly in front of her mouth so that there would be no strain to hear her testimony. She then smiled. Clara had been coached by the jury consultants, made to go over her testimony, tone of voice, and even body language again and again in the event that she would take the stand. Now all of the coaching had to pay off.

For weeks, the jury had watched the woman as she had cried her way through the state's case and much of her own. Now, the figure before them was anything but a wilting, weeping creature bemoaning the details of her husband's demise. Instead, before them, dressed in a brown suit and white Victorian blouse, was a woman who exuded confidence, a woman who knew her place in the world and had a story to tell.

Clara's hair was pulled back into her trademark large black bow. Her voice was soft, almost lilting in the South American accent so different from the Tex-Mex accent the people of Houston were accustomed to hearing.

She smiled as she told the jury of meeting her future husband three months after joining a large dental practice in the city and later marrying him. Clara said that four months after the two were married in a fairy-tale wedding at the yacht club next to the Hilton, she had left Castle Dental Center to form her own practice, while David stayed.

Clara Harris smiled and laughed as Parnham carried her through a series of softball questions about her life with David Harris, ultimately leading up to testimony regarding the couple's frustrating attempt to have children.

"I went to a fertility clinic in Dickinson. I still couldn't conceive," she said. "It took us five years."

The warm, fuzzy questions were grating to Mia Magness as she sat listening at the prosecution table. She began to object frequently.

Clara said that she and her husband had spent much of their social life with David's parents, Gerald and Millie, weaving a fabric of testimony regarding the couple's home life that was prosaic, commonplace, and simple.

Five minutes into the testimony, journalists in the center section of the courtroom surreptitiously passed notes among themselves saying things such as, "a very compelling witness," and "likable," and "Clara Harris has a very nice smile."

Other reporters in the section were busy, their thumbs on the tiny hand held keyboards of BlackBerrys, as they filed instant e-mail dispatches to their desks in Houston, New York and Los Angeles. Despite the fact that Davies had ordered a closed courtroom, viewers across the nation would know what Clara Harris was saying on the stand almost as soon as she said it. The reporters never had to get up out of their seats, the technology was so efficient.

Clara told the jury, "We were best friends, and very much in love. We had much in common. We were a team."

Now Parnham moved the woman gently to the terrible days between July 16, 2002, and July 24, 2002.

"During the week of July sixteenth, what was he like?" Parnham asked.

"I perceived a change in my husband," she said. "He was more stressed, more intolerant of the boys. He got upset with me a few times. I had co-signed for a vehicle for an employee who had defaulted. We paid the note, and he was upset."

Clara now described how she had traveled to Colombia with her twin son Brian to be maid of honor in a cousin's wedding. The other twin stayed at home with his father and the couple's Mexican governess because neither parent wanted to risk an attack of the child's chronic asthma while traveling.

"He didn't want me to leave the construction site," she said. "He was not happy because I wasn't bringing in the money because I was away while they were building the new building."

Now Parnham asked Clara to describe what life at home had been like with her husband before the marriage began to fall apart.

"He used to spend a lot of time at night playing with the boys," she said. "He stopped doing that. He wanted to be in his room."

Magness was now objecting to almost every question and every answer. Clara Harris frowned in frustration.

"He was talking constantly on the cell phone as well," she continued. "And he put the boys in time-out more frequently. He was stressed."

"What happened on July sixteenth?" Parnham asked.

"Diana Sherrill came to me after I had my hair done. We were at dinner," Clara said. "I was feeling there was something different with my husband and I thought that Diana was mature and I could talk to her. She made me aware that there was something that I needed to find out. I demanded it of her."

"And then what?" Parnham probed gently.

"I took about forty-five minutes to get home," Clara said. "I called my mother-in-law on the cell phone. I talked to her for forty-five minutes. After the conversation with her, I didn't believe that there was any truth to Diana Sherrill's allegations."

"What did you do when you got home?" the lawyer asked.

"I said, 'Do you love me?'" Clara Harris answered sadly. "He hesitated. He looked at me with a question mark in his face. He wasn't sure. That was the first time ever."

Parnham questioned his client about her confrontation with her husband the following morning.

"He came into the bathroom," she said. "I asked him what went wrong. It took him a long time to answer. We sat at the edge of the bathtub. 'Is it that difficult to say?' I asked. Finally, he said, 'I think you have to know that there is somebody else.'"

"What did you say next?" Parnham probed.

"I asked him, 'who?' " Clara answered.

"What did he answer?" the lawyer continued.

" 'Gail,' " Clara answered, then said that she'd asked her husband, "Do you love her?"

"I don't know," she said that he'd answered her.

"Do you love me?" she asked him.

" 'I don't know,' " he answered again. "I started to cry and shake. I cried and he tried to hold me, but I didn't want him to touch me."

"What did you say then?" Parnham asked.

" 'I'm going to help you,' " Clara testified.

" 'What are you going to do?' " David had asked.

" 'I'm going to get an attorney,' " she'd said. "He grabbed my arms and said, 'I'll do anything not to get a divorce.' "

Parnham probed his client about her downstairs conversation with Lindsey Harris, who'd told her " 'I already know. Everybody in the office knows.' "

"And what happened next?" Parnham continued.

"I ran upstairs and slapped him in the face," she said. " 'You said that you only had lunch. You said that it was only a kiss on the hand.' "

Now Clara said that her husband had told her that there had been no intimacy between him and Gail, that he had initially lied to her.

"He had been lonely," he had told her. "She [Gail] had grown up in the area. They had things in common. They talked about snow skiing. She wanted to teach him how to ski. They had all these things in common."

"Did you do physical exercise?" Parnham asked.

"No," Clara answered. "I knew that I had to lose weight. I called the office and canceled all of my appointments."

"What did you want to do?" Parnham probed.

"I wanted to fire her, okay?" Clara said. "I wanted to be there, okay? I wanted to have marriage counseling, okay?

From Lindsey, I had learned that there was more than one lunch."

"And then what happened?" Parnham asked, now moving into an area of the defense that he had only briefly alluded to in his questioning of the neighbor, Holly Podlewski. "What did David do?" he asked.

"He grabbed my arm, and grabbed my hair and threw me down," Clara told the jury. "Lindsey came in and yelled, 'What are you doing to her Dad? She just found out. What are you doing?'"

"Did David know martial arts?" Parnham asked.

"David knew jujitsu," Clara answered.

"And then what?" the lawyer asked.

"He said, 'You two are perfect. I am leaving and you will never see me again.'"

Now Parnham walked Clara Harris through the by-now familiar trip to David's dental office in his Suburban and the firing, but there was a grain of new material in her testimony.

"He said that he was going to have to find an apartment that evening," Clara said. "And Lindsey was lecturing him."

Clara also told the jury that at this point, even though she was on her way to the Clear Lake office of her husband to fire his lover, she didn't yet know that he and Gail Bridges had been intimate.

She next related her version of the firing.

"She was looking at them, [through the French doors] and I turned her around," she said.

"And then what did you say?" Parnham asked.

"'What kind of relationship do you have with my husband?'" Clara answered.

Then Clara Harris turned on the charm before the jury, using her little girl voice.

"'I don't know why you ask me these questions,'" she

said, mimicking the voice of Gail Bridges, "you know how she talks," her accent now charming. Many in the courtroom laughed. Davies and Magness maintained a stern visage until the courtroom calmed down.

Clara Harris continued to mimic her rival from the stand, ridiculing the woman when she described how Gail reacted when she asked for the key to the office.

"She said to David, 'What did I do?' You know how she whines," Clara continued, hoping for the same reaction as before.

There was none, and she settled into a more serious mode before the jury, relating how Gail had left, and then describing the office atmosphere in the wake of the firing.

"I was crying," she said. "I went back to the office where I had fired Gail. Susan came in and was crying, Lindsey was crying, and David kept coming in and out. He was trying to keep up with the patients."

Now, Clara described her desperate attempts to save the marriage, and how she had sent Lindsey out to buy self-help books, *Getting It Together*, by Betty Jones, and *Relationship Rescue* by television's abrasive Dr. Phillip C. McGraw, "Dr. Phil."

Early in the trial, Parnham had attempted to introduce the two books, but the judge blocked their admission as evidence. Now Clara described how she had read and underlined portions of the McGraw book.

If there were ever a chance to save herself, Clara Harris' next testimony would be it. What she said had the possibility of making the jury angry at David, so much that they would acquit her of murder if she got lucky. If not an outright acquittal, the jury might find that she had acted with sudden passion, thereby opening up the possibility of a lighter sentence under the lesser charge of manslaughter, should she be found guilty.

On July 18, 2002, David and Clara Harris needed to talk. The day before, they had met with his parents and he had told the elderly couple that his marriage would withstand the test it was now undergoing. However, later at home that night, Clara would suffer the biggest blow yet to her relationship. David told her that he and Gail Bridges had been intimate, and he told her of the intimacy in detail.

Now, she described how the two had driven from the mansion looking for a bar.

"I wanted to go to a romantic piano bar," she said. "I wanted to talk to him away from Maria, [the governess] and the boys. Neither of us knew where a piano bar was and he got tired of driving."

The two had pulled into the parking lot of a Marriott Hotel near Houston's Hobby Airport. The only bar available was a sports bar in the property.

Parnham interrupted his client's testimony to introduce two fragile pieces of evidence that had been found in her Mercedes by police the night of the murder. In his hand, Parnham held up two cocktail napkins and walked toward the witness chair, asking Clara to identify the notes she had taken as David had compared the attributes of his wife and her rival.

The lawyer had increasingly been stumbling through the questioning of Clara Harris. He was off, and he knew it. The cold had become worse, and Parnham's performance would have been much more noticeable had he been questioning a lesser witness. But the woman he had in front of him was at her best as she did the heavy-lifting on the stand, occasionally smiling, occasionally frowning, and carrying the interrogation largely on her own.

Parnham went to the blackboard, and wrote down two headings, each prefaced with the word, "*general.*"

Under *General Clara*, on the left, and *General Gail*, on

the right, he began to chart the comparison David Harris had made for his wife that night as she took notes on two cocktail napkins in the Houston bar.

Increasingly clumsy now in his direct examination, Parnham stumbled through his words as he questioned Clara. Finally, he asked the judge if the court could recess, but Davies refused. Eventually she relented for lunch.

Earlier in the day, Parnham had told a reporter in the men's room, away from the view of the ever-vigilant bailiff, that he was indeed ill. He was fearful that he would be caught violating Davies' order not to speak with the press. "This wears you to a frazzle. I've been sucking on B12 tablets almost constantly since this trial started. I have stopped working out."

But the B12 tablets didn't help as the courtroom cleared, George Parnham finally collapsed into the arms of Gerald Harris' brother, Dr. Lowell Harris, the longtime family doctor from Hope, Arkansas.

Clara Harris knelt by her lawyer as he lay on the floor of the courthouse trying to help, but a deputy told her to leave.

"I can't," she said.

"Then I will make you," she was told harshly.

Later, after lunch, Davies recessed the court when Parnham was taken to Houston's St. Luke's Hospital. Television crews captured their lead item for the evening newscast as the lawyer was being rolled from the courtroom on a gurney, an oxygen mask over his face. But Parnham gave the thumbs up sign from his stretcher. Later, he would admit that the collapse had frightened him tremendously.

On the sidewalk outside, Parnham's longtime partner and friend Wendell Odom said, "George has been sick. He's got the flu, and in combination of flu and stress he had a sinking spell. We are certainly not going to lose this jury. A trial lawyer has to try cases when he gets sick. Sometimes we push it too far."

Odom was ready to step in and finish the case for his friend.

When George Parnham returned to the courtroom after his release from a night in the hospital, and after a weekend of rest, Clara Harris had again changed her appearance for the jury. This time she wore a black Edwardian coat with no blouse, her hair pulled back in a French roll. At 9:33 a.m., February 7, she resumed her spot on the witness stand. Parnham was now much stronger, much more alert, his time in the hospital obviously well spent.

Now, the blackboard before the jury filled as he and Clara related the contents of the napkin item by item. It was increasingly evident that David Harris had had a cruel streak in him, a very cruel streak indeed, as his wife read the sometimes embarrassing writing on the napkins—for Gail, the words "big boobs," and for herself, "will be big boobs."

More and more, David had attempted to humiliate his wife that night as he compared her to his mistress. Clara had written beside her column, "fat," and under Gail's, "no fat, perfect body."

Now Parnham extracted testimony that showed the desperation Clara Harris felt that night when he probed her innermost thoughts about what she had written regarding her weight.

"I thought I could lose weight with fitness training," she told the jury. "I thought I could do that."

Despite the painful and humiliating list, Clara Harris continued to be a compelling witness on the stand, charming and likable, still smiling often at the jury.

She described seeing Gail Bridges with her children at

the party of another employee. She had good things to say about the woman. "I thought those kids were so precious, so well behaved. Those kids were so beautiful."

She spoke of her relationship with the twin boys and her spending habits. David had scolded her. "I bought too many toys for the boys and too many decorations for the house."

Clara told the jury of the humiliation and loss she'd felt when David had described sleeping all through the night in an embrace with Gail. "We had never slept like that, never," she said.

And she related another humiliation before the jury, a slight that every parent who sat there was certain to feel. "On Father's Day, he told me that he went to the lake house with Gail and spent Friday night." David had chosen to be with the other woman rather than spend the holiday devoted to the traditional head of the household that other families celebrated across America.

Clara said that on the way home from the Marriott she'd asked her husband to send the children to bed early so that the two could talk.

The following morning, the couple had gone to David's office where the staff was assembled. "We had a meeting," she said. Clara announced her retirement from the practice so that she could spend more time with David and the family.

"I had so looked forward to working in that building. But I wanted to be home to take care of my family."

Clara marched her testimony through the week leading up to the killing, telling the jury that she and her husband had had "a pretty good day on Saturday. He was happy."

" 'You know, you are going to have to make closure with Gail,' " she'd told David, believing that the marriage was on its way to being saved. "I suggested that 'if you want to talk to her on the phone, that's fine with me.' "

"And what then?" Parnham asked the woman, still charming on the stand.

"I suggested that they meet at a restaurant so I could sit outside in the car and watch them. He understood. David talked to Gail on the cell phone and set up a meeting at Perry's."

On Sunday, the family had gone to Shadycrest for church. Clara Harris told the jury that she was incredibly in love with her husband and told him so in a superbly romantic line.

"I have custom-made this summer for you David," she said, smiling at the jury.

But on Monday, Clara's distrust of her husband had become evident when she looked up the phone number of an investigator in the Clear Lake Yellow Pages. David had gone to the Lake Jackson office as usual, and Clara had called her trusted employee, Diana Sherrill, to tell her that she wanted her to watch over him.

"I wanted to make sure Gail didn't meet him for lunch," she told the jury. "That morning, before he left the house, I told him I wanted him to be here one hundred percent."

On the day before the murder, Clara Harris had read from her Dr. Phil book, underlining passages, gone to a tanning salon, had her hair done yet again, and visited a fitness center to sign up. She had also gone to Blue Moon and hired the private investigators to tail her husband for four days, telling the firm to follow Gail if she didn't have her children with her.

"Why did you want them to follow your husband?" Parnham asked.

"I wanted to show David that he was falling into a trap," Clara answered.

Now Parnham moved again toward introducing the allegations that Gail Bridges was bisexual and had only pursued David Harris for his money, not for a physical attraction to him.

"Was another motivation to show your husband the lifestyle of Gail Bridges, to show that he was falling into a financial trap?" Parnham asked.

"Yes, it was," Clara answered. "I was absolutely sure that she didn't love him," Clara continued. "I wanted Blue Moon to show David documentation of my belief that Gail Bridges was a lesbian."

Now that Parnham had established Clara's motive for hiring Blue Moon, he moved his witness forward to her first trip to the Hilton with Lindsey Harris, the lunch the two had eaten, and the trip up to a room similar to the one her husband had shared with his lover.

"When you got into the room, what did you do?" Parnham asked.

"I looked through the window and down at the yacht club where we got married," Clara answered, beginning to cry. "I told her I couldn't believe it."

That night, Clara testified that she had made love to her husband until 6 a.m..

"Did he go to work?" Parnham asked.

"He was exhausted," Clara answered. "He was in the closet, and I was still in the bed. He told me, 'I still love you and I am never going to leave you and the kids.' "

Later, the two had had lunch together and talked about the future.

"What did he say to you?" Parnham probed.

"We talked about how I really wanted to go back to work in the new office," she answered. "We held hands in the restaurant."

Now Parnham walked Clara Harris through the rest of the day for the jury, giving her side to the story that they had heard so may times before.

"You looked in Gail Bridges' garage?" Parnham probed.

"I was embarrassed," she answered.

"You drove to Perry's. How did you know what kind of car Gail drove?" he continued.

"I knew it was a Navigator," she answered. "But there was no car. I thought that they had gone to another restaurant. We went to the Hilton and there was no car, then we went to Kemah. I felt anxiety as we drove from restaurant to restaurant. We talked about going to a family restaurant, and we talked about going to Tony's."

"And then what happened?" Parnham asked.

"I got a call from a man," Clara answered. "He said, 'We are the people you hired to follow your husband. They are at the Nassau Bay Hilton.' "

" 'They are in the restaurant?' " Clara Harris said that she'd asked the man.

" 'No, they are on the fourth or sixth floor. They have been there about two hours,' " she said the man had replied.

The judge and jury watched Clara Harris intently as her attorney gently moved her testimony to its climax.

She reiterated how she had parked, gone into the hotel, and asked the desk clerk if they were registered, and had been told no. The jury listened as she spoke of finding the Navigator in the back parking lot of the hotel.

"I asked Lindsey if she was absolutely sure that it was Gail's Navigator," she continued. "She said yes, and I grabbed the windshield wiper. It hurt my hand, but it was more painful in my heart. I started scratching the car with my fingernails, then Lindsey handed me a key."

Now Clara Harris was crying before the jury as she told how she couldn't find her husband's Suburban, then returned to the hotel lobby and paced, not knowing what to do. Some of the jurors watched her intently. Others looked away as she continued to speak and cry.

Davies broke for lunch. Before the trial resumed again, the defendant had a quiet moment to herself in the courtroom. Clara Harris sat alone at the witness table and prayed.

Again, Parnham began to question the woman gently, lobbing softball questions at her in preparation for the finale that was bound to come soon.

"How old are you, Clara?" he asked.

"I am forty-five," she answered.

"And you know that Lindsey just turned seventeen," he continued.

"Yes," she answered. "She was my daughter. She called me 'Mom.'"

"Were there many photos of Lindsey in your home?" Parnham asked.

"Yes," Clara answered, attempting to blunt the girl's prior testimony that there was only one photo of her in the mansion, but that it was filled with photos of the twins.

"She also went on vacation trips with us," she continued.

"You became very close to her now, didn't you?" Parnham asked.

"Yes," Clara answered. "I asked her, 'What should I do?' She wasn't the best person to give me advice. She was sixteen. She had never been married. The only thing we had in common was that we loved David. We wanted him to come home."

"And when Lindsey called David?" Parnham probed.

"She was right next to me," Clara answered. "I hoped he was not in the room with her [Gail Bridges]."

Now Clara told how she'd called her husband shortly after the call from her stepdaughter.

"I was happy to hear his voice," she said. "I asked him where he was and I told him that Bradley was getting sick again and. 'We need to take him to the hospital. Where are you?'"

"I am at Pappadeaux," he'd answered.

"Which one?" she asked him.

"Bay Area," he answered her.

"I couldn't hear restaurant sounds but I thought that since David's car was not at the Hilton, maybe he was telling the truth. We went back outside because I thought I could see him drop her off at her Navigator."

"What happened next?" Parnham asked.

"The elevator opened and people walked out," she began. "Lindsey was holding my arm. There were people in the lobby. I saw my husband getting off the elevator to my right and walking at a very fast pace. Gail was holding his hand, up in the air, like we used to do. He had a kind of Mona Lisa smile on his face. I walked across the lobby and I grabbed her hair, and I called her an S.O.B.

"I was still holding her by the hair. Within a second, we were both on the floor," Clara continued, telling the jury that she did not recall hitting the woman.

"I grabbed her sweater with my right hand and somehow I saw that she was slipping out of her sweater," she said. "I wanted to embarrass him. I shouted, 'This is David Harris, an orthodontist from Clear Lake. He is having an affair with this woman!' "

Next, Clara Harris told how her husband had used his jujitsu training to throw her to the floor after she got back up. "I remember I was facing the floor."

Outside, she described getting into the Mercedes, but doesn't remember getting the keys from Lindsey.

"And what happened next?" Parnham probed.

"I sat back and laughed," she said. "I was in so much pain that I wasn't thinking. Suddenly I thought about smashing my car against her car."

Now, Clara Harris closed her eyes as she continued to relate the horror of what had happened next.

"I remember coming around the wall," she said. "I intended to hit the Navigator. I didn't see David or Gail."

"Did you intend to hit Gail with your car?" Parnham asked.

"I didn't know where she was," Clara answered.

"Did you intend to hit David with your car?"

"No," she answered

"Did you consider someone might be injured?" Parnham continued.

"No," she answered. "I saw three people by the driver's door. I saw two people running toward it. He looked so close. I think I closed my eyes. I didn't know it was David."

"What was Lindsey doing?" Parnham asked.

"She was screaming, 'stop, stop, stop!' " Clara Harris answered.

"And after the car came to a stop, what did you do?" the lawyer probed.

"I got out of the car," his client answered. "I saw David and I couldn't understand what he was doing there. I had just seen him running. I said 'David, please talk to me.' His eyes were halfway open. His mouth was halfway open. I thought he was coming in and out of consciousness. He had blood running from his ear. I thought he had a head injury. I felt his heart on his chest, and it was very fast. I took his pulse, and it was very fast. He was breathing. I saw a man behind me. Everything was in slow motion."

Throughout the trial, Clara Harris was an emotional wreck, yet as she related the immediate aftermath, she was totally composed, as if she had rehearsed the testimony again and again, determined not to allow her emotions to fail her.

"I saw a woman shaking Lindsey," she continued. "I saw Gail by the Navigator, and she was acting like she was throwing up. At long last, an ambulance came and took David. I know everybody was standing and not doing anything for him."

"And at the police station, after you were taken there, what happened?" Parnham asked.

"I remember the police questioning me for hours, I think," she answered.

Clara Harris had told her story with amazing discipline. Now she had finished. Her performance complete, she believed, she collapsed in sobs as she sat on the witness stand.

At a bench conference, Parnham attempted to get an audiotape of her interview by police entered into evidence but was overruled. The state contended that the recording did not contain an adequate Miranda warning and was not admissible. The contention was strange because a defendant always has the right to waive the statutory warning.

Parnham contended that playing the tape would show the jury the state of mind of Clara Harris—that she had been largely incoherent as she gave her statement to police.

Clara Harris had turned in a bravura performance in her moment before the jury. It was her last good moment of the trial.

TWENTY-TWO

No matter how good, no matter how stout the reputation, no matter how innocent the defendant, the deck is stacked against criminal trial lawyers in the Harris County Courthouse. The people of Texas like it that way. They don't like criminals, and they want them to do hard time.

A one-time candidate for Texas governor once campaigned on the theme that if he were elected, criminals in the state would find themselves, "bustin' rocks." He was serious. Texas justice is harsh, and in Harris County, it is at its most harsh. Now, Mia Magness, a product of the toughest district attorney's office in a state famed for its grit, would face down Clara Harris. If Magness was as good as she had been in the past, the woman known in the tabloids as the "Mercedes Dentist" and the "Killer Driller" would go to prison for the rest of her life.

"He was handsome, wasn't he?" she began quietly.

"Yes," Clara answered.

"He was witty, intelligent?" the prosecutor continued.

"Yes," the dentist answered.

"After meeting him, you wanted him for your own," Magness said.

"Yes," Clara answered, a slight smile creasing her face. "But it didn't just happen. We were working toward it. We were both good at what we did."

"How many offices did you have?" Magness asked.

"Six," came back the answer.

"And what was the income?" the prosecutor asked.

"Six-hundred-fifty-thousand," came the answer.

"What was your monthly income, and David's?" Magness asked.

"Mine was twenty-thousand per month, and his was thirty-thousand to forty-thousand dollars per month," she answered.

"We brought in fifty to seventy-thousand dollars per month, and we had forty-thousand cash on hand," Clara said.

Now Magness broke new ground, getting the witness to reveal that the marriage was further along toward a break-up than had previously been revealed by the prosecution, defense, or press.

"Did you discuss a property settlement?" she asked.

"Yes," Clara answered. "I was to get the house and the cars. I asked him, 'How am I going to support the house and these cars?' "

"It was his choice not to be with you?" Magness asked, her questioning now becoming more pointed. "Wasn't that a choice he had a right to make?"

"To be with me? Yes," she answered.

"You were the last to know. You felt foolish. That humiliation turned to anger, didn't it?" Magness pressed.

"I wouldn't call it anger," Clara answered.

"You went at him, didn't you?"

"I guess I did," Clara Harris answered, shaking her head, frustration now evident as she fielded questions as they became more hostile.

"You grabbed his hairpiece," Magness continued, now pushing the witness to incriminate herself in the murder.

"Yes," Clara answered.

"You made the decision that Gail had to be fired," she continued.

"Yes," Clara answered.

Mia Magness continued questioning Clara Harris, getting her to tell about the meeting at Gerald and Millie's home, getting her to say that David had told her that he missed Gail Bridges terribly. Fatigue and stress now began to show on the face of Clara Harris as she answered question after question from the tiny woman before her, who sometimes spoke in such a soft voice, but who could be so caustic. Finally, at 3:05 p.m., she began to cry.

"Mrs. Harris, any time you want to take a break, please let me know," Magness now told the woman coldly.

"Yes," Clara answered as she reached for a tissue.

When Clara recovered her composure, the prosecutor directed her questions to meeting with her husband at the sports bar in the Marriott Hotel near Hobby Airport. Instead of the humiliation Parnham intimated that David had heaped upon his wife during the meeting, Magness now wanted to show a side of David that the jury had not seen before.

"Was he not pouring his heart out to you? How he felt about Gail?" she asked.

"We were making a list of what I should improve on," she answered, staying with the theme her handlers had coached her so carefully to deliver. "[We talked about], What was good or bad about me and her."

Magness now produced the napkins with Clara's handwriting on them.

"He was pouring his heart out, right?" She asked.

"Yes," Clara finally admitted.

"While some on the list had to do with physical attributes, the real important ones had to do with communicating?" Magness pressed.

"Yes," Clara answered.

"You turned it into breast size," Magness now said, cold contempt evident in her questioning.

"Yes," the woman admitted.

"You wrote down 'reasonably pretty,' " Mia pointed out.

"Yes," Clara answered.

"You were comparing yourself to the other woman," Magness continued.

"I was looking at things that were in the book," Clara answered.

"By the way, where is that in the books? That's not there, is it? These books are about reconnecting."

"Objection," Parnham shouted.

"Sustained," Davies said, then sighed.

"You had doubts that despite all the extraordinary steps you had been through, she was going to win. You were frustrated, tanning, working out, a personal trainer, even plastic surgery."

"I wasn't aware of how disturbed I was," Clara answered. "I was doing everything I could to save my marriage."

"You had talked about divorce before, hadn't you?"

"Yes," came back the answer.

"Two weeks before?" Magness probed, making sure that the jury knew that the troubles in their marriage didn't begin with Clara's talk with Diana Sherrill on July 16. "You had even talked about custody of the children," she continued.

"He said that he wanted to be happy," Clara answered. "I was going a hundred miles an hour, doing everything I could to try to save my marriage. I felt betrayed." Holding back tears, she continued. "I was not frustrated, I was not giving up," she told the jury.

"You went up and looked at a room and you saw where, ten years before, you and your husband got married," Magness continued.

"Yes," Clara answered.

"You asked Diana Sherrill and Susan Hanson to watch him," Magness continued.

"Yes, I did," Clara answered.

"Those doubts and distrust came because you thought that you might not be the winner and that he might not be coming back to you," Magness pressed.

"Yes," she answered.

"You weren't sure that Gail Bridges was out of his life," Magness said.

"Yes," she answered.

"That is when you hired a private investigator," she continued.

"Yes," Clara answered.

"You wanted them to listen to the conversation because you wanted to make sure that David was ending his relationship with Gail," Magness said.

"Yes," the woman answered.

"Susan Hanson called as she followed David," Magness continued. "Susan Hanson told you to get to Gail's."

Now Magness produced a slip of paper with the address of Gail Bridges written on it, forcing Clara to admit that it was hers. The prosecutor now walked Clara Harris through the litany of spots where she and Lindsey had gone looking for David on July 24.

"Then Blue Moon calls back and says that they are at the Hilton on either the fourth or sixth floor and that they have been there for two hours," Magness said.

"Yes," Clara answered.

Now Magness put three photographs of the Navigator

on the large screen and walked Clara through the vandalism she had inflicted upon the SUV.

"At that time, you were angry," Magness said.

"Yes I was," came back the answer.

"Lindsey was telling the truth when she said that you were angry," Magness probed.

"She always tells the truth," Clara said. It was a devastating answer for her cause. It was an answer that would almost assure that she would be convicted of murder, or at least manslaughter.

"You devised a plan to flush him out," Magness continued.

"Yes," Clara answered.

"Were you mad?" the prosecutor asked.

"No," the dentist said.

"You vandalized her car. You weren't mad?" Magness asked incredulously.

"No," she said.

"Lindsey always tells the truth, right?" Magness now asked.

"Yes," Clara answered.

"Then came confirmation of your worst fears," Magness continued, now even more aggressively. "He couldn't be there, but he was there. You saw him step off the elevator."

"Yes," Clara answered.

"They were happy, she was happy," the prosecutor said.

"He had his Mona Lisa smile," Clara Harris answered. "That didn't mean he was happy."

"You told the police that he was holding her hand the way he had held your hand for so many years," Magness said.

"That is not correct," the dentist answered. "I was really hurt. That broke my heart."

"Were you mad?" Magness asked again.

"No," came back the answer as Clara Harris rolled her eyes, frustrated that she was unable to expound with an answer to her liking, frustrated that courtroom rules prevented her from telling her story her way, frustrated that Mia Magness was besting her.

"When they got off that elevator, it was a pretty clean indication that he had not broken things off," Magness continued.

"Yes," Clara answered.

"He said, 'this is it, it's over,'" the prosecutor continued.

"Yes," the woman answered, her soft, accented voice showing more frustration. "But that's what he always says when he gets mad. I didn't want the relationship to be over."

Clara Harris told the jury that she could not recall details of the fight and had no recollection of seeing David and Gail outside the hotel.

"How is it that you remember some details at some point, and don't remember others?" Magness pressed as Clara Harris began to sob again.

"I'm trying to do my best," she cried.

"I was so hurt!" she now shouted to the court. "I was so hurt."

Now Davies shouted back.

"Will you try to compose yourself?"

"I was not angry, I was so hurt, Miss Mia," the woman continued, disregarding the judge.

Magness had Clara Harris where she wanted her.

"You got in your car and you drove around fast. You came around and you see him, right?"

"I was going to hit that car, but it was so big. I was going to avoid a collision," Clara sobbed.

"You saw him," Magness shouted.

"I didn't see him," Clara answered, crying, her proper

English now failing her. "I never saw hitting him. I never saw running over him. I swear. I didn't feel or see running over him."

Now it was the turn of Clara's friends and fellow church members from Shadycrest to cry as they heard their friend's testimony withering under Magness' relentless cross-examination. Tears welled in their eyes as they saw the prosecutor's relentless destruction of their friend and fellow congregant. Some watched, while others simply stared at the floor and listened and cried quietly.

"You said that you saw three people," Magness continued. "I assume that one of those people was David?"

"I don't have that recollection in my mind," Clara now said, frustrated. "I guess I'm going to have to tell what I don't remember."

"Are you telling me that you did not run over his body?"

"Yes," Clara answered.

"Do you remember Lindsey saying, 'Stop, you are killing my Daddy?'" came back the answer.

"I remember her saying, 'Stop'," Clara said.

Now Clara became evasive as the prosecutor continued to probe.

"Driving a car takes a certain presence of mind," Magness pressed.

"My car, that space, that time," she answered nonsensically.

"You were angry," Magness pushed.

"I was really hurt," she said.

"You were angry," Magness pressed again.

"No," Clara answered.

"You said, 'I'm going to hit him.' Remember, Lindsey always tells the truth," Magness said, moving in for the kill.

"Yes," Clara answered.

"Do you remember Lindsey saying that as you accelerated?"

"Yes, I recall Lindsey saying that," Clara answered crying, knowing that there was now little chance of recovery from the damage her testimony had inflicted upon herself.

"You would be able to see a five-nine man in front of you?"

"Yes," Clara answered.

"In fact, in your mind, you thought, 'I'm going to separate him from her,' " Magness said.

"That is what I had been working on all that week," she said, her answer catastrophic for her defense.

By now, Clara Harris had lost all credibility with the jury as ten of the fourteen looked away from her while Magness continued her devastating cross-examination. Parnham and his defense team sat helplessly at the counsel table, watching their client's self-destruction.

"As you hit him, Lindsey was screaming 'No,' was she not?" Magness probed.

"She was screaming, 'Stop, stop, stop,' " Clara answered.

"She was screaming, 'No,' " Magness asked again.

"Maybe," Clara now answered.

"You wanted to separate him, you made that statement to the police, didn't you?" Magness said. "Do you deny that you made that statement?"

"I probably said that."

"You had changed your hair," Magness said, returning to Clara's plans for a makeover. "You planned surgery. None of these things had worked. He was there with her. He wasn't with you, was he?"

"Yes, it hadn't worked," Clara answered. "I didn't have time to reflect. I wish I had."

"You used what would work," Magness pressed. "You used what you had available. Didn't you say to the police that you pushed him away with your car? You saw the look on his face and you just wanted to get him apart from her."

Clara was now sobbing on the stand as the jury was taken out of the courtroom until she could get control of her emotions. When they returned, Magness continued, relentless in her cross-examination.

" 'I tried to separate him from her,' did you say that to the police?" Magness pressed, showing no mercy to the woman who had already hopelessly incriminated herself.

"Yes," came back the answer.

"You said you would hurt him, didn't you?" Magness said.

"Yes," Clara answered.

"At that moment you were hitting him, it was clear that you had not broken off his relationship," Magness said.

"Yes," Clara answered.

"You wanted to separate them?" Magness asked again.

"Yes," Clara answered.

"At that moment, you were furious," the prosecutor said.

"Yes," Clara Harris finally admitted, broken.

A devastated Clara Harris now left the stand, her face puffy, her nose and cheeks red, her will broken. She had not heeded her lawyer's warning of what could happen to her on the witness stand, defenseless under the questioning of Mia Magness.

The defense had a few more witnesses to present to the jury, but Parnham knew that his case was lost no matter what he did. The dignified figure of Gerald Harris, Sr. entered the room, still filled with his fellow Baptists from

Shadycrest. His snow-white hair gleaming in the court-room light, the retired school principal looked down from the witness stand and smiled at the woman who had killed his son.

"During that meeting at your house with David and Clara, how were they doing?" Parnham asked.

"They were doing well early on, but we discovered they were having some difficulties, but we felt that we were making progress, quite a bit," he said.

"Did you confront your son about that?" Parnham asked.

"Somewhat," the elderly man answered. "We discussed what should be done and how it should be proceeding."

"How did you first learn of the affair?" Parnham asked.

"Lindsey told me about David's behavior at the office," Harris answered.

"You and your wife did not approve of that?" Parnham said.

"Of course not, we did not think it was proper," the father answered.

Parnham now passed the witness without having accomplished anything other than to take the jury's attention away from the glaring spectacle that had been the self-destruction of Clara Harris.

Magness asked the man about his son.

"He was a very good husband because he showed a great deal of respect for Clara," Gerald Harris began. "He maintained a good house, he took part in raising the children. He was attentive and kind, a hard worker. He included us in almost everything he did, and I guess a parent couldn't be more pleased than that. He liked playing Santa Claus, and he was very generous with our family and her family."

It was now Magness' turn to pass the witness without accomplishing anything before the jury.

"What about his relationship with Clara?" Parnham asked as his client smiled at her father-in-law.

"She is a lovely person," he responded as Clara again began to weep. "She is a loving wife and a good mother. She had a close relationship with Lindsey. She cared for her, took her shopping. They were together a great deal."

Clara continued to cry, and then smiled when the man on the stand described her as truthful.

Next, Parnham brought Gerald Harris Jr. to the stand. David's brother largely echoed what his father had told the jury about the relationship between his brother and the woman who had killed him. Finally, Parnham made a point to the jury as he concluded his brief questioning of the character witness.

"You realize that you were called as a witness for Clara?" he asked the brother of the victim.

"Yes," Gerald Jr. answered.

It was now time for Millie to take the stand in defense of her daughter-in-law. Smiling and pretty, she named all of her grandchildren for the jury as she looked fondly at Clara seated with her lawyers at the table.

"I thought they had a marriage made in heaven," she told the jury. "They thought that God had been good to them and they thought that they had to share with other people."

Clara again began to weep through her smiles as Millie testified that "He never had a negative thing to say about Clara. At times, I thought she loved him too much."

When Parnham passed the witness, he passed Millie Harris into the hands of a prosecutor who would attempt to answer a question that had been on everybody's mind since Gerald Harris had first come to Davies' courtroom back in July: Why were the parents of David Harris so adamant in their support of his killer?

"If she is convicted, and she says that you don't get to see them [the twins], the bottom line is that you love the boys and you want to see them, isn't it?" Magness said.

"I don't know what you are trying to get me to say," Mildred Harris said curtly, cutting off the prosecutor.

Magness knew that she was likely to get little from Millie Harris. She knew that she would never get the woman to admit that she and her husband had given Clara Harris their unyielding support because they were fearful that the twins would be taken to Colombia to live with their Latin American relatives.

There was no trump card that Magness could play against this small, attractive grandmother. She had no further questions.

After Mildred Harris left the stand, Parnham made one last attempt to get Davies to change a ruling that he believed was extremely damaging to the defense. He asked the judge to permit the defense to go into the relationship between Gail Bridges and Julie Knight. Parnham asked that phone records of calls between the two on July 24 be allowed into evidence. Parnham asked that he be able to document the alleged lesbian relationship between the two women.

"Those two individuals were in a conspiracy to defraud the Harrises of money," he told the judge, now desperate to interject the allegations about Julie and Gail that had persistently circulated around the small communities of Clear Lake. Parnham knew that time was running out for his defense. Any ploy was worth trying, even the legal equivalent of football's Hail Mary pass.

"My rulings aren't changing," Davies said from the bench.

"The defense rests," Parnham said. The time was 11:44 a.m.

Not content with letting the defense have the last word, Magness now finished with three more eyewitnesses who had seen the Mercedes making its deadly circles in the parking lot. Each witness would have nothing new to say, but would reinforce what those who came before had said. The witnesses, tennis players who had been attracted to the commotion in the hotel parking lot from across the street, again described the horror of what they had seen. She got what she'd wanted when Seabrook resident Chris Junco told the jury that he had seen the car go over the body three times.

"I thought it was a low rider because it was bouncing so high," he said.

At a break between the witnesses, a friend from church was overheard asking Clara Harris if she needed anything.

"Oh, I need a miracle," she was overheard to say.

Yet it was only talk. Clara had still convinced herself that an acquittal was possible. Her faith in her lawyers and the team they had assembled was still great. Parnham knew better. He had pleaded, using his strongest arguments, that his client not testify before this jury in this court. Clara had insisted upon taking the stand anyway.

Parnham expected the worst as both the state and defense rested their case.

Davies told the jurors that they would be sequestered for the remainder of the trial. Deliberations could possibly begin the next day.

TWENTY-THREE

Deputy Constable B. C. Pope took her accustomed position in the corridor outside the courtroom of Judge Carol Davies one last time as Clara Harris came to court to hear her fate. Pope watched reporters and witnesses, lawyers and spectators, ready to pounce as she had so often if there was conversation between participants in the trial, no matter how minor.

The court's bailiff had acquired a reputation throughout the trial for exerting her considerable power when a simple word of caution would have done the trick. Worse still, Pope was loud when she opened her mouth, which was often. The woman took her job seriously, and liked it. Perhaps her stern discipline would be needed this day. After all, the courtroom would be full for the final arguments of George Parnham and Mia Magness.

February 12, 2003, was a beautiful but windy day in Houston, where spring comes earlier than in most other parts of the country. The city's lush forest was budding out, a pale shade of green covering the bare branches of the trees. Just south of town, Clara Harris had slept in her bed in the mansion, after doting on her twins the night before. She dressed herself in an olive green suit, her hair pulled back for court.

As the room began to fill, familiar faces took their places. Gerald and Millie Harris were now permitted to sit with his brother Lowell, who had been in the room throughout the trial. In the third row, Reverend Steve Daily, the beloved pastor of Shadycrest Baptist Church sat with his flock. Short and stocky, the man looked more like a football player than a Baptist preacher. He got up from his seat and took a place in the front row between the two elderly Harris brothers.

Across the room, Lindsey Harris sat in the section reserved for guests of the prosecution. Her parents and her lawyers would join her in seeing justice done on behalf of her father.

"Please rise," the constable intoned, the first indication that the court was coming to order as Judge Davies made her way to the bench. It was not a happy woman who stared out at the news media.

"It has been reported to me that there have been at least two attempts by the media to talk to the jury in this case. I can't emphasize how offended by this I am," the judge said, skewing her syntax. "There will be serious consequences. Anyone who attempts to get to this jury, including alternates, will be held in contempt of court."

The judge then barred the media from the hallways outside the courtroom and reiterated her prohibition against interviews being conducted anywhere in the building, saying that journalists could sit quietly in the courtroom during deliberations, or stay outside on the sidewalk. They were not even allowed to do their work inside the courthouse.

Davies was disturbed because a rookie field producer from the Fox News network had attempted to contact a juror for an appearance on a talk show when the trial was completed. No harm had been done, and the novice was severely chastised by the judge. No journalist was involved in the incident.

Now, Davies released the two alternates, one black, one white, telling them they would be free to go after hearing the lawyers' final arguments to the jury.

At 9:23 a.m., Davies began reading from the document that explained the options to the jury on finding Clara Harris either guilty or innocent. They could find her guilty of the charge of murder, manslaughter, or criminally negligent homicide. As she read, the defendant watched the judge. Finally, Davies got to the part Clara most wanted to hear her say. The jury must acquit her if it could not find her guilty of any of the options they were presented.

Next, Davies read that the jury could also find Clara Harris guilty under what is called a "special issue" under Texas law. In that case, the woman would face a much lighter sentence than if she were found guilty of the crime of murder.

After the judge had finished reading, the time had come for the lawyers on both sides to have their last chance to speak to the twelve jurors now seated before them. Mia Magness turned the podium to the left, directly facing the jury, her back to Clara Harris and George Parnham, her colleague Dan Rizzo seated to her left.

She began to speak slowly, telling the jurors what evidence they could ask for. She reminded them that under the law, there are four ways to cause murder, admonishing them that the determination would be based upon the individual's own belief.

Magness explained the issue of lesser included offenses, but she cautioned, "You never get to these lesser offenses until you unanimously agree that she is not guilty of murder."

Magness' speech was brief. She sat down after going over the matter of the special issue one more time. She would again get to speak, the state getting the final word to the jury before they were sent to deliberate. It was time for George Parnham to speak.

Parnham walked to the podium looking better than he had looked in days. He smiled at the jury, and then began to speak to them like the grandfather that he is.

"I don't know about you," he began, "But the last two-and-one-half weeks have been the longest two-and-one-half years of my life.

"When you go back to the sanctity of the jury room, take the facts, apply the charge, you determine whether the prosecution has made its case, established in the mind of each juror that Clara Harris took the life of David Harris, you can determine the condition of the mind of Clara Harris. How many times the automobile hits David Harris? That is the issue of intent."

Clara watched the jury as her lawyer spoke to them on her behalf. The people who held her fate in their hands were watching the defense lawyer intently as he faced them, standing beside the courtroom podium as he spoke.

He talked about the doctrine in American courts of reasonable doubt. "It is the highest standard of the law that we have in this country," he told them.

Parnham moved to familiar ground with the jury, speaking about the life of Clara and David Harris from their beginning together. "She was married on February fourteenth, 1992, at Windemere yacht club," he said. "Clara put David on his feet for three years. They struggled to establish themselves in their profession."

He spoke of the prosecution's most devastating witness to his client, Lindsey Harris, careful not to make the jury believe that he was trying to beat her up verbally.

"She is a sweet girl, no question about it. Make no mistake; this is the one great tragedy of the whole case. I pray that one day, healing will occur." Parnham made no attempt to refute the testimony of David Harris' daughter, the state's closest eyewitness.

He spoke of Clara and David's struggle to have children, which had resulted in the birth of the couple's twin boys. Clara lowered her eyes at the mention of her two sons, and then looked up again, her attention riveted upon her lawyer and the jury as Parnham continued to invoke family.

"We've heard David Harris' own mother and father tell what a beautiful marriage it was, a marriage made in heaven, until somebody knocks on the door of that home—Gail Thompson Bridges, a home wrecker.

"She was after David. She seduced him into a relationship that never should have happened."

While hammering the other woman in the case, Parnham had to be careful in what he said about its victim. Now he moved cautiously to David Harris. "I'm not here to vilify David Harris. There is no question that she still loves him. He made some bad choices, folks," Parnham said as the pastor, Steve Daily, looked on. The lawyer returned to the other woman.

"The man was happy with Clara Harris until Gail Bridges came along. Somehow he falls prey. While Clara Harris takes one of the boys to Colombia, David Harris is at the Westin Galleria with his lover. His attentions were elsewhere."

Parnham moved on to the friends of Clara Harris.

"Diana Sherrill was concerned on July sixteenth." But he quickly returned to Clara, his summation becoming slightly disjointed. "In one week, this woman spirals down from a place of dignity," he told the jury. "She was foolish at a minimum."

But he had to return to David. He had to carefully plant the seed one final time that the person at fault for David's death was not his wife, but David himself.

"Why was David in the bedroom all the time on the cell phone? Why was he always playing drums? Because he was mentally somewhere else with another woman.

"Gail Bridges is out in the reception area [of the office]. I've got to do something to put myself between the man I love and Gail Bridges," he continued, voicing what Clara Harris must have thought.

Parnham appealed to every woman on the jury who believed that her physical attributes were inadequate as he reminded them that Clara had planned to surgically enhance the size of her breasts, get a personal trainer, color her hair, and read a book by Dr. Phil in an attempt to hang on to her husband.

"You realize that you are in competition and you are not winning," he told the jury. "Gail Bridges should have been disqualified. She shouldn't have even gotten to the starting line."

Clara Harris' eyes were lowered as Parnham spoke to the jury with all of the passion he could muster. He moved to the two cocktail napkins that had occupied so much of the court's time, reminding the jury of the outrageous things David had said to his wife about his lover.

"We fit so well together when we are sleeping together," he said, contemptuously, repeating the words that David Harris had said to his wife about his lover.

He reminded them that while her hopes for saving the marriage were high, Clara didn't trust her husband. "She's concerned because of a pattern of deception. He goes to the lake house with Gail Thompson Bridges. She's down here with the kids—deception beyond deception.

"David was a good man. David was a victim. David

was in a trap that was put together by Gail Thompson Bridges and her friend. She told this to the investigator."

Parnham now returned to Lindsey.

"She absolutely regrets the involvement of her stepdaughter," he continued. "Do you believe for one moment that if Clara Harris intended to kill her husband, she would have his daughter with her?"

Clara Harris' eyes continued to be closed as Parnham pleaded with the jury on her behalf, now verbally walking through the events at the Hilton.

The lawyer moved to the one expert witness whom he and Clara Harris believed could have saved her, still relying upon his work. "I thank my lucky stars every day in this case that we got a video—that tells you the rest of the story. She couldn't see Gail Bridges and David Harris until she rounded the Navigator. And Lindsey, God bless her, she doesn't even remember the collision . . . When you go back to that jury room, look at that video. Use common sense."

He reminded the jury of Clara's tears at the scene as David lay dying.

"Do you think that is rehearsed?" he asked the jury.

Parnham's argument was now becoming more disjointed as he spoke, the words flowing in a stream of consciousness, jumping from subject to subject, player to player. He returned to the Blue Moon video.

"Look at the video and the turns become tighter and tighter, then she parks next to the body," he says, arguing the defense theory again that Clara Harris could have only run over her husband once.

Now, the bearded lawyer became emotional.

"Gerald Harris, his father, and his wife, his brother tell you that Clara Harris is a good, loving, caring wife, mother, and sister-in-law. They tell you what a good person David Harris was and what a good person Clara Harris is. I can't tell you how deep the love goes. These parents came up here to tell you of the woman they love."

Finally, going over the time allotted by Davies for the final argument, Parnham looked at the jury.

"You told me in voir dire that you would have the courage to acquit."

At 10:57 a.m., George Parnham had had his final say on behalf of his client and it had been disjointed and rambling. He sat down, his work done.

Davies called a recess.

After the jury filed from the courtroom, Clara Harris got up from her seat and walked to her father, and mother-in-law and spoke quietly. She then looked at Steve Daily and the two began to pray together as the people of Shady-crest gathered around in support.

At 11:10 a.m., Mia Magness moved to the podium to attempt to seal the fate of Clara Harris by sending her to prison for the rest of her life, or at least the 40-year minimum a life sentence in Texas carries with it.

She began again by returning to the theme of what is required to find a person guilty of murder.

"You know David suffered serious bodily injury, David suffered death," she said. "You know that the car is a deadly weapon.

"For the hours and hours she spent on the stand, she talked about the affair, she talked about her marriage. She spent less than five minutes talking about her conduct."

Magness had come out blazing. Now she began to talk about what the witnesses had told the jury, beginning with her favorite, the man who had called her throughout the trial with words of support. "What is my definition of a good Samaritan?" she asked. "Robert Williams came in here and told you what he saw and did. They tried to show he was some kind of drunk. Not one person out there had a reason to mislead you."

She spoke of the civil suit filed by Lindsey Harris. Throughout the trial the defense had made allusion to the fact that the girl was suing her stepmother in an attempt to attach a financial motive to the young woman's testimony against their client.

"It doesn't seem all that unreasonable that a lawsuit is filed and her college money is protected," Magness said. Parnham objected, and Davies sustained the objection, a rare event for the lawyer.

"The bottom line was, Lindsey tells the truth. Lindsey always tells the truth," as Magness reminded the jury of Clara Harris' own words.

"Evangelos Smiros heard David telling her that it was over. He told you he saw the look on her face, saw her run over the body three times," He told you he heard Lindsey screaming, 'You're killing my Daddy!'

"Every one of them told you, 'I saw her run over the body,' some two times, some three times, but the most three times," Magness continued. She now named witnesses who had seen the car pass over the body of David Harris—Jose Miranda, Garrett Clark.

"Clark saw her run over him," she continued, her argument devastating. "Lindsey always tells the truth."

She named witness after witness who had testified that they had seen Clara Harris run over her husband's body multiple times despite the testimony of the handsomely paid defense expert, Steve Irwin.

"Every single thing Lindsey told you has been corroborated by an eyewitness or a piece of evidence," Magness said, sealing the fate of Clara Harris with her own words. "Remember, Lindsey always tells the truth."

Clara sat at the witness table, her eyes squinted closed

as she listened to Mia Magness bring home her arguments to the jury.

Clara had gone to the witness stand to speak to the jury herself. She had been at her most charming and she knew it. Surely the jury would see through what Mia Magness had said about her. Surely she would walk away from this dreadful courthouse with its television cameras relentlessly taking her picture. Surely these good people on the jury would vote to acquit her, or at least probate her sentence so that she would not have to spend time in jail. Surely the professional appearance she had presented to these people counted for something. She had dressed to perfection, never wearing the same thing twice.

Clara had told her friends that if she had to go to prison, she would commit suicide. Certainly nothing like that would happen. George Parnham and his team were good lawyers who had spared no expense in the experts that they had hired. Surely, surely she would walk away from this place and return to her beloved twins and her beautiful home.

Clara's jaw was clenched, her eyes were closed as Mia Magness droned on, citing the testimony of Julie Creger, the woman who had first reached the body of David Harris from the hotel's pool area.

" 'See what you made me do?' " Magness now reminded the jury that Clara was heard to say. "That is so important. She said, 'when I tried to open an airway, the jaw was clenched and his teeth were loose, and I saw a tooth on the ground.'

"Dr. Wolf told you that his body was run over two times, his face up and his face down," Magness now said as Clara sat in the courtroom with her eyes closed.

"She was aware and unimpaired and she knew what

she was doing. She said calmly and deliberately, 'I am going to hit him,' and then she accelerated.

"You heard the testimony that 'I could see he was scared and he put his hand out.' He touched the car and you got the fingerprint and you knew what happened."

The prosecutor invoked the name of Houston Police Officer Rolando Seinz, who had provided expert accident investigation testimony for the state to refute what Irwin had told the jury.

"We thought it was important that you hear from someone who has investigated accidents for twenty-two years and who has investigated 10,000 accidents. If you are going to come in here and tell a jury, you have a responsibility to do it right, there is no legal defense that it is an accident."

Now Magness contemptuously spoke directly to the testimony of Irwin, the defense accident reconstructionist.

"You should seriously question what he is trying to get you to believe. He ignored physical evidence. He told you no matter how many eyewitnesses came forward, nothing could change his mind. There is something extremely arrogant about that. The witnesses saw her running over him multiple times. Lindsey felt her running over him multiple times."

Next, Magness attacked the credibility of defense pathologist Dr. Paul Radelat, saying, "He hasn't been a medical examiner in over thirty-five years."

Magness moved toward her conclusion, the words that would climax her argument, and, she hoped, put the murderer Clara Harris in prison for the rest of her life.

"There has been an underlying theme throughout this entire trial that he deserved it," she began. "Maybe you want to conclude that David is a jerk, that he had an affair and that is wrong. David's bad choices shouldn't result in his death. If a man is cheating on you, you take him to the cleaners. You take his house, you take his car. But you don't kill him."

Clara Harris' eyes were tightly closed as Magness continued. She didn't see the tears welling up in the prosecutors eyes as she sealed her fate verbally. Clara's belief in herself and her lawyer was still unshaken as the prosecutor concluded. Clara Harris truly believed that the outcome would be good for her. After all, she had testified so well, she remembered, now putting Mia Magness' devastating cross-examination out of her mind.

"She just lost it," she heard Mia say. "That is what murder is. It is the momentary loss of the respect for the sanctity of human life. I'm not suggesting to you that she went to that hotel to kill her husband. I'm not suggesting that at that moment, she formed intent. She acted out of anger."

Now, the twelve jurors hung on every word as Magness concluded her argument with devastating efficiency. Across the room, Clara Harris' face clenched, the muscles in her jaw tightened, for the first time making the attractive dentist ugly. Her cheeks were more hollow than before and she looked older than she had appeared during the entire trial. A transformation was taking place in her as the stress of the moment became almost too much to bear. Finally, she took a deep breath and looked up.

"We are talking about a woman who is accustomed to getting what she wants," Magness continued. "She comes to the hotel and it becomes obvious that she is not getting what she wants. She says, 'I wanted to hurt him. I could kill him and get away with it. I wanted to separate him from her. I'm going to hit him.'

"She used what she had, and that was her car," Magness continued. "Lindsey Harris said, 'I felt myself go back in the seat.' Then she runs over him three times. When you run over a person multiple times, the intent is to kill."

Magness was now openly crying as she spoke to the jury. Davies ignored the theatrics as the prosecutor concluded her argument.

"There is no doubt that she was sorry when she was done," Magness said. "She's holding herself up and saying, 'Excuse me for murder.' The bottom line is this: She got mad. She engaged in intentional and knowing conduct. At this point it is time to call her what she is, and that is a murderer."

Magness sat down at the prosecution table exhausted and emotionally drained. It was 12:03 p.m.

The jury deliberated for a little more than seven hours before they reached a verdict in *State of Texas vs. Clara L. Harris*. During that time, the people of Shadycrest passed treats among themselves. Lindsey had lunch in the courthouse cafeteria with her parents, Deb and Jim Shank. She nibbled at a chicken sandwich, but she had no appetite.

As the jury deliberated, Davies decided to deal with the television team who had attempted to contact a juror. She called three Fox News employees covering the trial from across the street at the small city of satellite trucks that had sprung up for the event of the trial. Three women stood before the judge, more embarrassed than anything, as Davies listened to their story. In the end, she barred one of them from the trial, a tough lesson in media ethics for the rookie, saying, "Let me suggest to you and your employer that you are not adequately trained." The 21-year-old novice later cried her eyes out in the women's restroom across the hallway of the courthouse. Adrienne Wheeler, a producer with the CBS Early Show, compassionately consoled her.

Clara Harris and Mary Parnham sat quietly at the counsel table. As the hours droned on, Clara occasionally got up to speak with members of her church.

At 5:50 p.m., the jury sent a note to the judge asking that portions of the court transcript be read back to them. The portion they were asking for was testimony in which Clara Harris admitted that she wanted to "separate" David from his lover. The note was an indication that deliberations were not moving in Clara's favor.

Parnham objected that the transcript be given to the jury, but Davies denied the objection. The judge now had the transcript read to her.

"And did you say, the night of the arrest, 'I want to hurt him'?" the court reporter read.

" 'If it is written in there, I probably said that,' " Clara had answered.

The following morning, Pope told the press to take their seats. She had a message for them from the judge.

"She said that you are to treat the courtroom as if she is on the bench and in the courtroom. I will personally take your pass and escort you from the floor and from the building. The media can't even read a newspaper." The deputy appeared to relish delivering the message. The reporters were stunned at the outburst. They had been sitting quietly in the courtroom waiting for the verdict since deliberations began.

Yet the urge to interview got the best of them as they sat completely silent in the courtroom under Davies' new order, not even allowed to read a book or newspaper. Yet the BlackBerrys continued their constant communication with news desks across the country.

The room was filled with many of the members of

Shadycrest. Finally, when Pope left the courtroom, one of the reporters asked an obese woman about her church in defiance of Davies order to remain silent. The parishioner had been in attendance throughout the trial in support of Clara Harris.

"We are the conservative Southern Baptists. We are the ones who don't approve of homosexuals," she said. "My son was going on a foreign mission and David Harris offered to front the money, but the Lord provided.

"Clara and David and the older Harrises attended the 11 a.m. service," the woman gushed, happy to tell about the couple. "The parents were more active in the church than Clara and David."

The conversation was suddenly interrupted when, at 9:18 a.m., Janet Warner, the court system's media relations coordinator, entered the room and told press and lawyers, "There is a verdict."

Five minutes later, Clara Harris walked into court with George Parnham and took her seat.

The room again began to fill as the same players who had sat through closing arguments now prepared to hear the verdict.

Clara Harris sat with her back to the audience, speaking to the bailiff. Pope explained to her that if she were found guilty, she would immediately be taken into custody and would not be allowed to go home. She would also have to surrender all of her personal possessions.

As the reality that she could soon go to jail was explained to Clara, George Parnham talked quietly with his wife. Both knew what was likely coming. His face twitched involuntarily as he left Mary's side and began to pace the courtroom, lost in his thoughts.

Things suddenly changed as the state prepared for the

verdict. From a side door, leading to a tunnel that connects the courthouse to the county jail, two burly deputies took their places. The court had brought in muscle to control the defendant if she became unruly. At the back of the room, other deputies, large men all, took their places on either side of the aisle leading to the doors and the corridor.

Time dragged on and still the judge and jury didn't enter the courtroom. Finally, at 9:45 a.m., Judge Carol Davies entered the room wearing her black robe with the trademark expensive silk scarf draped around her neck.

Veteran courtroom observers knew the verdict the instant the jury entered. Two of the women were crying. The foreman handed the verdict to the bailiff, who in turn handed it to Davies.

Clara Harris had been found guilty of murder, Davies read.

The defendant sat at the table, her eyes cast down in the pose she had struck so many times during testimony. She then looked at the people who had found her guilty. She closed her eyes as her friends behind her again sat weeping.

Across the room, Lindsey Harris was crying as deputies moved to stand directly near Clara Harris. The woman who had slept in a mansion the night before would sleep in the Harris County Jail this night wearing an orange prison jump suit.

The court took a brief recess as reporters raced for the corridor and turned on their cell phones. Those with BlackBerrys had notified their desks instantly when Davies read the verdict.

Outside, a publicist for George Parnham who had helped Mary handle requests for interviews took a call from the *Dr. Phil* program asking for a booking. She hung up on them, angrily saying that "Clara desperately wanted to talk to Dr. Phil, and he trashed her on Leno last night."

Three husky deputies now stood behind Clara Harris as she sat writing thank-you letters with a Montblanc pen at the counsel table, her face red and puffy from crying.

When the brief recess ended, the punishment phase of the trial began as Lindsey Harris took the stand to describe her life since the murder of her father David. The jury was told that the girl had attempted suicide, given up music and cheerleading, and had little interest in her schoolwork.

Now emotional, Lindsey told the twelve jurors her thoughts as she watched her father dying, "I knew that he wasn't going to be okay, that I was only given 16-and-a-half years to spend with him," she told the jury. "I had planned to stay with Dad so long.

"It was a terrible way for a person to go," she continued.

Now contemptuously, she described her stepmother's words immediately after running over her father.

"She went over to him, calling him 'baby,' like nothing had happened," the girl cried. Lindsey Harris told how she had been informed that her father had died while she was at the police station.

But her next words were the most poignant.

"When I got home, his clothes were in the garbage can in the garage," she said. "I brought them upstairs and moved all of his stuff to my room. I felt like he was there with me."

As the girl described her suicide attempts, how she had attempted to slice her wrists more than once, Clara Harris again began to sob, the quaking emotional outburst that had so angered the judge so many times during the trial.

From the bench, a stern Davies looked down at the convicted murderess.

"Be quiet! Be quiet!" she shouted. "You are disrupting the proceeding."

Next to Clara Harris, Emily Munoz Detoto rolled her eyes at the insensitivity of the woman sitting on the bench.

"There are only two available options," Davies continued. "Remove her from the courtroom, or keep her emotions in check."

For the first time in the long trial, Magness' co-counsel, Dan Rizzo, rose to speak to the court, asking that Clara Harris be removed from the courtroom.

"We have a child on the stand who is a victim herself," he told the judge.

"I'll correct that," Davies told the convicted murderess. "I understand the young lady has suffered a lot of emotional trauma since the events. I am going to give you one more chance, despite the state's request. Don't blow it or you will be out of the courtroom."

Finally, Lindsey Harris testified that she had not seen her brothers since Christmas and that she was estranged from her grandparents.

"There is a lot of money involved," she said. "They are leaving me out of everything and they don't seem to even care anymore. I feel hurt. Somebody took my dad away from me."

On cross-examination, Parnham asked the girl if she had contact with her grandparents. Lindsey said yes, but that the contact had been extremely limited since the murder.

"Do you believe that your grandpa is going to gain financially by this?" he asked.

"Yes, partially," she answered.

It was now Parnham's turn to speak one last time to the jury, to plead with them that they show mercy on his client. He quietly gave a brief opening statement begging the jury to let his client go free to raise her twin boys.

"She has never committed a felony," he told the jury. "We will be asking the jury for a term of less than ten years."

Parnham could ask for that because in the guilt or innocence phase of the trial the jury had found that the killing of David Harris was a crime of passion, thereby enabling them to assess a lesser punishment, which included probation.

He began another parade of character witnesses, desperately hoping that they would save his client from prison.

The reality of her situation had now hit Clara Harris as she sat at the table, her face red and puffy as she listened to Gerald Harris plead for her freedom.

After a series of questions, Parnham passed the witness to Mia Magness.

"How has this impacted your life?" Magness asked the old man.

"It has had a great deal of impact on my life and the life of my family. It is very painful, sorrowful. It's disrupted my life tremendously."

"But you have forgiven," Magness now asked the deeply religious man.

"Forgiveness does not have to do with religion, but with a way of life," Gerald Harris answered.

Shouts of "Amen" came from the members of Shadycrest now filling the audience.

"Does it mean that God's forgiveness can break, and does it mean that there aren't certain consequences for actions?" Magness asked.

"That is correct," the father of the murdered man answered.

The friends, family, and pastor of Clara Harris took the stand to declare to the jury what a good woman they had known. Increasingly, almost all of them began to cry as witness after witness testified. Finally, Davies had had enough.

"It is distracting to see the sobbing that is going on. This is a courtroom. You sit there quietly or leave the courtroom."

Two members of the Shadycrest congregation got up and left, unable to contain their sadness for their friend Clara.

At 4:53 p.m., both the defense and the state rested and three deputies surrounded Clara Harris at the witness table as they prepared to take the convicted murderess to jail for the first of many nights of her incarceration. She was handed a plastic bag. In it, she placed her Montblanc pen, her watch, and her earrings. She got up from the table and walked to the rail, handing her notes to a neighbor, Anna Jones, as both cried.

The woman took a seat in the back of the courtroom and began to sob as she read what Clara had written. The parishioners of Shadycrest watched as their friend was handcuffed and taken to the county jail. She would spend the night on a hard cot behind bars.

Clara had only five minutes' sleep during her first night in the jail. The following morning she entered the courtroom on Valentine's Day, 2003, a different woman from the one who had married David Harris in the shadow of the hotel where she killed him ten years later. She wore no makeup, her hair wasn't perfect, and it was pulled back over her ears in a ponytail. Her face was puffy from lack of sleep. Moreover, she could no longer come and go from the courtroom as she pleased. She was an inmate, and the jury who had convicted her was about to pronounce sentence.

She wore a brown suit with a white blouse, but no jewelry. That had been taken from her the day before.

As she spoke to the jurors, Magness went directly to the option of possible probation for the woman, saying that it would be no punishment at all for killing her husband.

As the two lawyers jousted, the defendant sat with her head in her hands. Across the courtroom, David Harris' former wife, Debra Shank, looked at the wife who had killed him. None of the jurors looked at Clara.

Gerald and Millie Harris watched the jury. Others in the courtroom took different postures. Susan Hanson looked down at the floor as she listened, while her colleague, Diana Sherrill, fixed her eyes upon George Parnham. In the back of the courtroom, Robert Williams had come to court to see the trial play out. Wearing his black frock coat, he sat quietly watching and listening.

Clara began to sob again as Magness described her David as a decent human being and a faithful and good husband for years.

It was now Parnham's turn to have a final say.

He looked at the jury as he spoke earnestly saying that "Gerald and Mildred don't want those boys ripped away from the last parent they have on earth. A mother's love is still intact."

Parnham now talked about consequences, suggesting that what Clara Harris had already endured was punishment enough. "She lost everything, you betcha," he said. "Those are major consequences."

Finally, Parnham's argument was not for Clara, but for the two boys she would leave behind if she was sent to prison.

"It is absolutely critical; not only for Clara Harris, but for those kids. Probation should be granted to Clara Harris."

It was now Magness' turn to speak again, her words aimed at placing Clara Harris in a state prison. As she spoke, the prosecutor began to cry as she evoked the life Lindsey Harris would have had with her father.

"She cut her own flesh because she was so overwhelmed with the pain of the loss of her father. She deserved to have him there when she graduated from high school. She deserved to have him there when she walked down the aisle."

Behind her, in the spectator section, Lindsey Harris began to cry as the powerful words came thundering out through the prosecutor's tears.

Finally, still crying, Magness spoke of the pain David Harris must have felt.

"Remember those scared eyes? He knew what was taking place. Suffering is lying on the asphalt like a wounded animal drowning in your own blood. We all have the right to die with dignity, and she took that away from him. To add insult to injury, he is brought into this room in pictures where he is dissected like some lab experiment. It is not about her."

Magness asked the jurors to give Clara Harris the maximum amount of prison time allowed by law.

"It's not going to be easy. It's going to be hard."

Five hours later, the jury came back to the courtroom with its sentence.

Parnham had been pacing for hours. Now he took his seat at the table next to Clara and bit his nails. Clara's face was red from crying. She looked at her family and friends who again filled the large room to overflowing. At 4:58 p.m., the jury entered the room to hand Judge Carol Davies their Valentine's Day gift to Clara Harris.

Parnham stood with Clara between his body and that of Emily Munoz Detoto. The defense lawyer's arm was around his client's waist as he bowed his head. Clara stared straight ahead at the judge, then closed her eyes, as Davies said that the jury had assessed a sentence of 20 years in prison and a $10,000 fine.

Parnham's face twitched as he shook his head in disbelief. Now, the body of Clara Harris gave way, falling. She was caught and brought to the chair by her two lawyers. She continued to collapse into the arms of Munoz.

She sat there immobile, her head cradled by the pregnant lawyer. Minutes passed as she was consoled. Yet the state has no patience with convicted murderers. It was time for her to go. The big deputies again moved to positions directly behind her, and Clara Harris rose as the cuffs were placed on her wrists. She looked at the courtroom filled with sobbing friends, family, and press as she was led away. Clara Harris raised her hands, now held together by cold steel. She waved meekly at them as the doors closed behind her.

EPILOGUE

One month to the day after a jury sentenced Clara Harris to 20 years in a Texas prison, George Parnham, the former Roman Catholic seminarian, went to the Vatican for the first time in his life. He was drained by the illness that had consumed his body during the trial. He was also depressed, suffering from the same feelings of inadequacy that he had felt after Andrea Yates was found guilty of capital murder a year before. Standing before Michelangelo's *Pietà*, the lawyer found the moment of peace some religious pilgrims to Rome long for as he stared at the masterpiece. The trip was fun as George and his wife Mary jostled around Italy seeing the sights.

There was no such break for Mia Magness. A week after her triumph in the courtroom the petite prosecutor was assigned to try a man accused of strangling his estranged wife and three children and dumping the bodies in Houston's scenic Greens' Bayou. Magness' silent partner and boss, Dan Rizzo, was reassigned to another trial division with his own high-profile case to try. It was his job to gain convictions of three young black men accused of killing the clerk and a city cop at a Bayou City check-cashing establishment, a routine Texas cut-and-shoot.

Clara Harris was almost immediately transferred from the Harris County Jail to orientation at the Texas prison system's Skyview unit in Rusk, where mental health professionals would evaluate her. She also underwent freshman orientation, an effort made by the system to prepare her for her life behind bars. While she was there, she met Parnham's other former famous client, Andrea Yates, whose prison assignment is mopping floors. Yates reported to friends in Parnham's office that she was delighted to be treated so kindly by the prison's new superstar. After a few weeks, Clara Harris was again transferred, this time to the maximum-security Mountain View Prison at Gatesville, Texas. She would be trained to repair computers and work in the institution's electronics shop. Later, she got a better job in the system as a graphics designer.

Shortly after arriving at Gatesville, Clara Harris drafted a brief letter to fill in the gaps of her early life for this book. After providing routine biographical information on her parents, she wrote of her current situation in her broken English. "I fell in love with Texas. I identify myself with the state and his [sic] people open, friendly, generous, hardworking and proud. I can't believe now that I have been discriminated [against] and punished for having achieved the American Dream. I am not that cold-blooded manipulative and selfish woman that Mia Magness depicted. I am a very caring honest, hardworking, woman who loved her husband immensely and adores my twin boys. I would have never intentionally destroy [sic] the care of our family. My husband was a good man, he just made one mistake but he didn't deserve to die for it."

For Bobbi Bacha and her Blue Moon Investigations, there was a distressing addition to Lindsey Harris' wrongful death suit against Clara. Not only was the Nassau Bay Hilton added as a defendant, but the investigator and her firm became targets as well. In the wake of the case, Bacha signed a contract with the William Morris Agency to represent her based on the fame brought to her by Clara Harris. She sold the rights to her life story—for under $20,000, she claims—even though she never actually met Clara face-to-face. Bacha e-mailed the news to all of her media contacts. Reports of a CBS movie based on her life and the Harris case hit the newspapers and airwaves. However, four days after the trial ended, Lindsey Harris filed suit, saying "Defendant Blue Moon and the Bachas now seek to profit from their involvement in the death of David L. Harris by selling their story rights to CBS . . . Defendant Bobbi Bacha even has the gall to propose the actors/actresses that should play the roles in the movie." Attorney John Davis even added an unflattering footnote to the passage, saying, "Bobbi Bacha, the president of Defendant Blue Moon, suggests that her role be played by Kim Cattrall, Meg Ryan, or Debbie Harry. In case CBS is looking for unsolicited casting advice, Plaintiff's counsel suggests that Roseanne Barr would be more appropriate for the role."

Texas Monthly's Skip Hollandsworth also signed a movie deal with the producers, Storyline Entertainment, for a CBS Movie of the Week based upon his early article about the case in the magazine.

Lindsey returned to high school in Ohio after her testimony. The evening that Clara Harris was sentenced to prison, the girl went to her grandparents' home for a brief reunion with them and her twin brothers. The estrangement was over.

By all accounts, Gail Bridges and Julie Knight remain friends. Their lawyer, Valorie Davenport, was hospitalized shortly after the trial with a life-threatening illness.

Charles Knight and Laurie Wells wed. The couple now have a child of their own. The epic case of *Knight vs.*

Knight continues to make its way through the Texas court system. Financially devastated by the war, at least one of the Knights has filed for bankruptcy protection. Steve Wells is quietly raising his and Laurie's children in Dickinson, while Steve Bridges has custody of one of his and Gail's children and his wife continues to raise the other two.

Investigator Lindsey Dubec returned to Blue Moon and had her first surveillance assignment two months after her testimony.

Judge Carol Davies, under criticism for not releasing basic biographical information during the trial, permitted *Texas Lawyer*, a regional legal publication, to print a profile. For the story, only defense attorneys who practice in her court were quoted. The quotes were complimentary.

The group, Friends of Clara Harris, was formed after the trial to raise funds for the dentist's appeal. Their first goal, which the group achieved quickly, was to raise $21,000 to buy the trial transcript for the appeal filed by new attorney Mac Secrest.

A friendly judge briefly allowed Clara Harris to be housed in the Brazoria County Jail, as custody of her children was determined while she was to be incarcerated. Shortly after the trial ended, Clara had sued to remove custody of the twins from their grandparents, who had stood by her throughout the ordeal. The jail is a few miles from her former dental office in Lake Jackson. The judge ruled that Gerald, 73, and Mildred Harris, 70, will be allowed visitation with the kids while former neighbors of David and Clara raise the children.

On September 16, 2003, Clara Harris was transferred to the Mountain View Unit of the Texas Department of Corrections in Gatesville, Texas.

The dental empire built by David and Clara Harris is being sold. And Daimler Chrysler filed a suit that was settled for the remaining balance owed on a slightly dented S-Class Mercedes.

ABOUT THE AUTHOR

Steven Long literally wrote the book on catastrophic failure in a nursing home. His award-winning non-fiction work *Death Without Dignity* prompted the *Austin American-Statesman* to call the book the "literary equivalent of the movie *Platoon*." Frances Humphreys, the national director of the Gray Panthers, wrote, "Steven Long presents a horrifying account of conditions that can exist when the profit motive takes precedence over healing and compassionate care." The book won the State Bar of Texas Gavel Award for distinguished journalism. The work is found in the libraries of most medical and nursing schools. However, it is not a dry factual tome. Instead, it is true-crime writing at its best, reminiscent of the style of the late Tommy Thompson.

For most of 11 years, Steven Long served as editor and publisher of Galveston's *In Between* magazine, an award-winning alternative weekly. Later, he carved out a significant career as a feature writer with the *Houston Chronicle*, producing more than 700 stories in six years. One highlight was his investigative work, which resulted in the indictment, conviction and disbarment of the late Houston adoption lawyer Leslie Thacker, for buying and selling crack babies in the Harris County Jail. Another series of investigative stories ultimately resulted in the indictment and conviction of the head librarian of the oldest medical school west of the Mississippi, for stealing rare and historic medical texts, some dating to the sixteenth century.

Steven Long covered the Andrea Yates murder case for the *New York Post* from the scene to conviction. He covered the lengthy and complex trial of the Arthur Andersen accounting firm for Agence France-Presse, as well as *Crain's Chicago Business*. He has recently appeared on *Inside Edition*, the CBS *Early Show*, and *Catherine Crier Live* on Court TV.

An avid horseman, Long is a contributor to *Western Horseman* magazine. He also serves as editor of *Texas Horse Talk*. His work has appeared frequently in the *Houston Press*.

Besides his writing career, Steven Long holds a certification in corporate community relations from the Center for Corporate Responsibility at Boston College.

He is a co-founder of the National Alliance of Urban Literacy Coalitions, and recently completed three terms on the national board of CASA, the Court Appointed Special Advocates Association, based in Seattle, WA.

Steven Long lives in Houston, Texas, with his wife Vicki.